ROY HUDD'S
CAVALCADE OF
VARIETY ACTS

Also by Roy Hudd and published by Robson Books
Roy Hudd's Book of Music-Hall, Variety and Showbiz Ancedotes

ROY HUDD'S CAVALCADE OF VARIETY ACTS

A Who Was Who of Light Entertainment 1945–60

ROY HUDD
with Philip Hindin

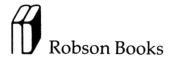

Robson Books

First published in Great Britain in 1997 by Robson Books Ltd,
Bolsover House, 5–6 Clipstone Street, London W1P 8LE

British Library Cataloguing in Publication Data
A catalogue record for this title is available from the British Library

ISBN 1 86105 115 8

Book design by Harold King

Photographs from the authors' collection

Printed by Butler & Tanner Ltd., London and Frome

For my wife Debbie –
who makes me laugh more than anyone in the following pages

ACKNOWLEDGEMENTS

My thanks to the ever-enthusiastic Lew Lane for the photographs from his collection and to everyone who supplied me with details for my labour of love especially: Bill Abbott, Nigel M. Anderson, Morris Aza; Gordon Irving; Len Lowe; Mike Martin; Patrick Newley; Michael Pointon; Michael Thornton; Max Tyler; also Guy R. Bullar and Len Evans (the compilers of *The Performer Who's Who in Variety 1950*) and all the anonymous contributors to the British Music Hall Society Journal *The Call Boy*.

INTRODUCTION

It was 1959 and I stood in the wings of the Finsbury Park Empire with Max Miller. We were both watching G.H. Elliott, at eighty plus, on-stage, struggling his way through 'I Used To Sigh for the Silvery Moon'. There were about thirty punters in the stalls and, in the circle, as the old comics used to say 'two lesbians and an Airedale'.

'Isn't he brilliant?' said Max.

'Magic,' I replied, and he was. 'What a shame there's nobody in,' I commented.

'It's all over,' said Max. I chuckled to myself, remembering that he always said in his act, 'When I'm dead and gone the game's finished.' Within four years he *had* gone and 'the game' had gone with him.

As a paid performer I just caught the last knockings of Variety. I was so glad I did. My apprenticeship was spent in the company of some of the giant top-of-the-bills – Max, Ted Ray, Jimmy James, Jimmy Edwards, Donald Peers and Max Wall. From the golden days of the music hall, I stood and marvelled at Hetty King, Randolph Sutton, George Elliott and 'Wee' Georgie Wood. I compared notes with other newcomers like Dave Allen, Tom Jones and Gerry Dorsey (we all thought he was out of his head when he changed is name to Englebert Humperdinck).

Of course, I'd been a fan of Variety for as long as I could remember. My Gran, who brought me up, insisted we climbed up to the gallery of the Croydon Empire every Tuesday first house. There, just after the Second World War, we saw not only the people who became my heroes but lots of new, young, mould-breaking, just-out-of-the-forces performers too: Harry Secombe, Peter Sellers, Spike Milligan, Max Bygraves and Norman Wisdom.

My very first Variety date was at the famous Metropolitan Music Hall, Edgware Road, the Met. I was half of a double act and we only got the week because the act Billy Whitaker and Mimi Law were indisposed. My agent persuaded the bloke who booked the acts to use us in their place. We got to the Monday morning rehearsal with the band and who was top of the bill? A young man who, only a few weeks before, had been working with us at Butlin's Holiday Camp Clacton – Cliff Richard. And the man who was conned into taking our raw but enthusiastic act was Philip Hindin.

When the idea of this book was mooted I insisted it should cover the Variety years I knew 1945–60. I think these are the years most people remember. It was a golden period. The mix of reliable old, brilliant new, up and comers, down and outers, has beens, never was-ers and some of the most eccentric acts ever seen provided the weekly entertainment in nearly every city and town in the British Isles. Just after the war was boom time and Philip Hindin was at the heart of it. He booked over three thousand different acts during those eventful fifteen years. As a Brother Water Rat I have revelled in his company. I've laughed at his stories, wondered at his wisdom and, occasionally, wiped away a tear at his colourful reminiscences.

For this book, I provided Philip with an alphabetical list of the hundreds of performers who were the stuff of Variety and left it to him. He provided, not only concise, accurate and witty pen portraits of the turns, but lots of wickedly acerbic personal stories too, some of which I've been able to include. The book is really to fill a long-felt need. So many people have said to me, 'Where can I find out about the acts I used to enjoy?' Here's where they can. Well, almost.

At a rough guess, there were more than ten thousand performers working throughout our period. To include them all would have meant Robson giving away a truss with every copy of the book so, inevitably, there are omissions. I apologise to those I have left out. I'm afraid, sometimes neither I or any of my gang of spies have been able to find out the things we really wanted to know. I hope that this volume will prompt someone, somewhere, to fill in the gaps. Then we can have volume two.

Roy Hudd

___A___

The Three Aberdonians

Acrobats. Tom and Charlie Barr born Fife, Scotland, and Roza Louise Thompson. They had my very favourite bill matter: 'Too mean to tell you what they do.' They were originally a duo, Tom and Charlie, ex-miners who trained as acrobats with Duffy's Circus in Ireland and who toured the UK in the 1920s as THE BARR BROTHERS. In 1930 Roza Louise joined the act and they changed their name to THE THREE ABERDONIANS. They soon graduated to the number one, appeared in The Royal Variety Performance in 1938 and were soon a featured act all over the world. Roza left the act in the late 1940s but the Barr brothers worked on in panto, variety and summer season, incredibly, into the 1960s. Tom died in 1964 and Charlie in 1978.

Stan Aces

Card manipulator and magical comedian. In the late Forties he was presenting a mental telepathy act, ZAHLA 'The Blindfold Intuitionist', but his specialty was card manipulation. He would spin playing cards into the audience and, when they were returned to the stage, catch them in his teeth.

Joe Adami

The Human Billiard Table

He was a ball juggler whose gimmick was catching the missiles in various pockets. The idea, and the bill matter, originally belonged to the music hall star PAUL CINQUEVALLI. Those were the days when a juggler could still top the bill.

Charles Adey and Dawn

Dance humorists and trapeze artistes. Born Charles Gray, London, 1910. Charles and Dawn were brother and sister who, after being trained in straight acting and dancing, promptly went into Variety as trapeze artistes with a famous American act, KAFKA STANLEY AND MAE FOUR. They toured in the UK, including seasons at the London Palladium, and all over Europe. The siblings parted company in 1937. Dawn went to the States as half of DION AND DAWN while Charles stayed here and formed the act DOROTHY GRAY AND BROTHERS. During the war Charles, in the RAF, produced shows and after demob joined Dawn again to become CHARLES ADEY AND DAWN.

Jules Adrian and Grace Spero

The Musical Act Superb

Musical duo. Jules, born Leeds, 1900 and Grace, his wife. Jules, a conductor arranger, was the solo violinist in the act while Grace was the pianist and accordionist. Philip describes them as 'a classy musical act'. They were certainly classy enough to be asked to entertain royalty, both in private and in the 1945 Royal Variety Performance. On this special night the sophisticated ambience their turn was supposed to engender was rather marred by a 'Demon King' – type of green spotlight being turned on them during their most romantic piece. This show was the first of twenty-five RVPs directed by ROBERT NESBITT. I bet Nesbitt, whose obsession with 'moody' lighting earned him the title, bestowed by ERIC MORECAMBE, of 'The Prince of Darkness' was very pleased.

Jean Adrienne and Eddie Leslie

Comedy double act. Jean was born in India in

1905 and trained as a dancer. Indeed she worked with ANNA PAVLOVA in the UK, and in America and Canada. She attained leading lady status with BOBBY HOWES in the West End and was principal boy in panto from the mid Thirties through to the Fifties. She teamed up with Eddie as an act in Variety and they also did panto together, feeding the comics. He worked with NORMAN WISDOM and is in several of Norman's early films. In effect he was the forerunner of JERRY DESMONDE. Jean died, in Brinsworth House, in 1994. (See Brinsworth House entry.)

Afrique

Impressionist. Born Alexander Witkin, Johannesburg, 1907. He was originally trained as an opera singer; indeed, in the Thirties, he was a member of the Old Vic Wells Opera Company. He discovered a talent for impersonation, got a single act together, and rapidly became a headliner both in the UK and abroad, famed for his impression of the then Prince of Wales. He was a much-in-demand Abanazer in panto and constantly employed in West End revue and Variety. Philip says: 'He was a heavy gambler. It was his Achilles heel and he died, in 1961, broke.'

Shek Ben Ali

Nothing inside – nothing outside

Magician. Born Mohari Ali, Bengal, 1912. 'Nothing inside – nothing outside' was the famous catchphrase of this genuine Bengali cod magician. In 1936 he produced and appeared in all-Indian show at Yarmouth and took the revue all over the world,

SHEK BEN ALI
INDIAN MAGICIAN.

but is best remembered as a solo act, playing all the leading venues in the UK. He featured many tricks with coins and his catchphrase came from one with an empty paper bag. ERIC MORECAMBE, that treasurer of off-beat Variety acts, used it on stage and on television. He died in 1978.

Ali Bongo

The Shriek of Araby

Magician. Born in Bangalore, India, 1929. Not his real name! Ali's parents were Scottish and Irish Though not well known as a performer during our period he makes this book for his contribution to magic as an adviser and adapter of tricks. He was the magic man, along with BILLY MCCOMB, behind the DAVID NIXON TV shows. Prior to that, he was the manager of Hamley's magic department – nobody knows how many magicians he helped into the business. Starting in the mid Fifties he has made props, written and illustrated books, won every possible award from magic societies all over the world, advised on countless films and stage shows, invented new

effects and been programme associate on all the top TV magic shows.

His own act was, and is, a combination of brilliantly mimed, zany comedy and quite breathtaking magic.

Ray Alan

Ventriloquist. For my money, technically the best 'vent' working today – and one of the funniest. His creation, the tipsy, upper-class 'throwback' 'Lord Charles' (made by the famous doll maker LEN INSULL) is a living, totally believable real character. (I used his voice whenever I had to play Denis Thatcher on radio.) Ray is steeped in Variety. At thirteen he was a callboy at the Lewisham Hippodrome and at fourteen had his own single act, doing impressions and magic. Then came ventriloquism and songs on the ukulele!

He became a pro and played Variety everywhere. The highspot was a tour of the number ones on the bill with LAUREL AND HARDY. They even asked *him* for *his* autograph.

Television was food and drink to Ray. He invented 'Lord Charles' especially for the new medium, created the children's series, *Tich and Quackers*, hosted panel games and did guest spots. He wrote, and presented, the definitive documentary on his art, *A Gottle of Gear* (later published as a book) and was the host of Radio Two's *The Impressionists*.

Today it is, mostly, the lucky passengers on the world's luxury cruise ships who have the pleasure of enjoying this master of his craft.

Jerry Allen

Organist. Born Deryck Neil Allen, Hemel Hempstead, 1925. Jerry began, at fourteen, as one of that vanished breed, the cinema organist. TOMMY TRINDER encouraged him and featured the lad in his road show. His well-known JERRY ALLEN TRIO was formed for the SID FIELD revue, at The Prince of Wales, *Strike A New Note*. He worked as a single act in Variety but it was good old steam radio that made him a 'name'. His swing style of organ playing featured in many top shows. I often saw his trio in the big Sunday concerts that were so popular in the Fifties.

Carl Ames

Harpist. Born Mill Hill, London, 1902. Variety welcomed unusual acts like Carl's. His spot, a mixture of classical and popular pieces, plus his simultaneous harp and piano playing was a winner on the halls. His height and good looks helped too.

His mother – wait for this – was the Countess Von Poelzig and he began as accompanist to her violin playing. After gaining an ARCM from the Royal College of Music for his solo harp work, and aware of the limited demand for serious harpists, he took to the Variety stage. He was a constant on the bills here and all over the Continent. He died in 1967.

Ted and Barbara Andrews

Tenor and pianist double act. Ted born Toronto, 1907 and Barbara Morris born Walton-on-Thames. Barbara began as a concert pianist in England and Ted as musical arranger in Canada. They met, in England in the Thirties, and formed

a top-rated double act. They married and had three children. Barbara's daughter from a previous marriage – JULIE ANDREWS – did pretty well. They featured her in their act long before she hit the jackpot. Sadly they separated but not before they had passed on the expertise that helped Julie to international stardom.

Bob Andrews

Comedian. Born Grahame Roy Cowardine Andrews, Stockwell, London, 1916. A CARROLL LEVIS 'discovery' who did make it. Bob was a first-class compere whom I saw on many of the big Sunday night band shows at the Davis Theatre Croydon, a great storyteller whose tales would be peppered with every dialect and accent imaginable. He always had good, clean, original, *funny* stories. I'd love to get my hands on his gag book!

He first appeared with Carroll Levis as 'Gunner' Andrews and later toured as his compere before joining the *Fol-de-Rols*, and then hosting PETE COLLINS' touring show *Would You, Believe It?* He did lots of radio in shows like *Variety Bandbox* and was kept busy on the circuit with SANDY POWELL and RALPH READER shows. When Variety finished Bob moved easily into cabaret and after-dinner speaking. He died in 1995.

Avril Angers

Comedienne. Born Liverpool 1922. Avril's long and highly successful career in the theatre began, almost, in Variety. Her dad was the music-hall comedian, HARRY ANGERS, and her mum was a member of the original *Fol-de-Rols*, LILIAN ERROLL. She was fourteen when she made her debut in concert party in Brighton and the same age when she played Cinderella with GEORGIE WOOD and CLARKSON ROSE in Birmingham.

She followed in her mother's footsteps and became a *Fol-de-Rol*. During the war she toured with ENSA. She began her touring with the concert party that I started in, *Out of the Blue*. The immediate post-war years really established Avril as that rare bird, at the time, the solo comedienne. She had a great personality, could sing and timed jokes like a man. Apart from her cabaret, radio and Variety appearances she started to work in the 'legit'. Her success in acting led to her being one of the first ladies to have a TV series with a proper story line, *Dear Dotty*, in 1954. Since then she has featured in countless TVs and is rarely out of the West End in either straight plays or musicals.

A cliché I know, but Avril is a real old-fashioned trouper who scores, and gives a hundred per cent value for money, in everything she tackles. Her early experience of getting out there in front of an audience on her own makes her invincible.

Anna and her Pals

Performing animal trainer and presenter. Born Jessie Gavillet, Bury, 1903. 'A very talented lady,' says Philip, 'whose act included borzois, pekes, miniature dogs and monkeys. Her dressing room was bedlam. If you popped in to see her and her husband, Jules, you didn't get a drink you got a Bob Martin's.' The act played successfully all over the world.

Jack Anthony

Comedian. Born John Anthony Herbertson, Glasgow, 1900. A hugely popular comedian in Scotland who played pantomime, every Christmas, at the Glasgow Pavilion for over twenty years.

I never saw him but Philip says: 'He did a very funny drunk and was a keen business man with interests in hotels. Somehow he never quite made the name that so many of his contemporaries did.' He died in 1962.

The Armour Boys

A comedy knockabout boxing act who played mostly the small halls.

Ernest Arnley and Gloria

The funny chap with the talkative hands

Comedy double act. Ernest born in Brighton.

After an apprenticeship that began in 1918 in musical comedy Ernie progressed to a dancing act, THE SYMONDSON FOUR, and a double act with his brother to comedian with CLARKSON ROSE's show *Twinkle* and principal comedian with the *Fol-de-Rols*. He played a single act in Variety till 1944 when he teamed up with his wife GLORIA DAY ('the soubrette with a voice'). Yet again GEORGE BLACK didn't forget those who had served him well in wartime and he featured Ernie and Gloria in *Strike It Again* at the Prince of Wales, when Ernie deputised for SID FIELD and appeared for him at various matinees. The double act played all through our period.

I worked with Ernie in my second pantomime. Gloria had retired then, and he was the perfect comic for this. He was a good eccentric dancer and a funny man who did indeed have hand movements that told a story. The double act played all through our period. Gloria died in 1993 and Ernie in 1988.

Don Arrol

Comedian. Born Donald Angus Campbell, Glasgow, 1929. Don's tragically short career began in his native Scotland, in the late Forties, at the Gaiety Theatre, Leith. He started as a double act but soon reverted to a single turn and rapidly established himself as a stand-up comic with great potential. He had good looks, a 'universal' accent and high-speed delivery. He made his mark on the Variety stage down south, successfully touring everywhere. I remember him living in certainly the biggest caravan I'd ever seen. Perfect digs in the motorway-free land we had in the Fifties.

He spent two years with *The Black And White Minstrel Show* and, when new faces were being sought for TV, he had a stint as compere of *Sunday Night at the Palladium*. He was married twice, his first wife being killed in a car accident in 1961. Don himself never had the chance to realise his potential. He died, in his sleep, of a heart attack in 1967. He was just thirty-eight.

Artemus and his Gang

Knockabout slapstick magic act. Artemus born Arthur Hayes, Dublin, 1890. An Irishman who was first inspired to go into the biz by watching the 'cod' conjuring of WALTON AND LESTER, 'The World's Worst Wizards', in Clapham, South London. He learned his magic from MAGICAL OVETTE in New York and made his first appearance in Chicago – all before he was twenty-one.

His mob-handed act (originally ARTEMUS AND HIS INCOMPETENT ASSISTANTS) featured himself and a gang of boys. Some of his gags are still well remembered: the scruffy boy holding a block of ice throughout the act, the lady sleepwalking across the stage and the boy in the audience sitting on a needle. I wish I'd seen them.

Dougie Ascot

Comedian and dancer. Born Douglas Frederick Hayes, Australia, 1892. Comedian and dancer and lots more besides. He started at the age of six and, throughout a long career, not only danced and comicked, but sang, juggled, acted and did acrobatics. He also devised and choreographed THE FOUR ASCOTS, a dancing act that played all over the world.

The Seven Ashtons

Tumbling acrobats. Australia's most famous circus family who were touring their act there back in the 1840s. The act I saw so often in Variety involved the sixth generation of Ashtons. As with almost every circus family they could do the lot: they were acrobats, musicians, horsemen and horsewomen. They came to the UK just after the war and their beautifully dressed, exuberant, high-speed combination of fast Arab-style tumbling and Risley (foot juggling with people rather than objects) caused a sensation. They played the London Palladium, the Royal Variety Performance and every number one date.

Arthur Askey

Hello Playmates!

Comedian. 'Big Hearted Arthur', born Arthur Bowden Askey, Liverpool, 1900. A tiny, bespectacled, trilby hatted, genuinely funny man whose career (covering concert party, radio, television, films, plays and musicals) has been well covered elsewhere, particularly in his autobiography (written in longhand), *Before Your Very Eyes*.

Seeing him, as a lad, he was, to me, just what a comedian should be: small, full of bonhomie, silly and very friendly. I worked with Arthur in the Seventies and spent many a lunch hour in his sparkling and witty company.

Despite his success in Variety he never really enjoyed it. He said the theatres were too big, he was too far away from his audience, they weren't intimate enough, and subtlety had to be sacrificed to get across. In his heart of hearts he was still a concert party and Masonic, after-dinner, act. It was his intimate approach that made him such a terrific television performer: one of the few who took to the new medium like a duck to water. Arthur died in 1982.

The Three Astaires

Baton twirling and dancing act. Earle Astaire, who founded the act, was born Frederick E. Gillespie, Hull, 1905. Earle, from an old theatre family, worked with many different acts: THE MILTON TRIO, THE THREE OLIVERS and, of course, THE THREE and THE FOUR ASTAIRES. He was even a stilt walker with THE GULLIVER TROUPE.

Joe Astor and Renee

Jugglers. Joe, originally Eddie, and Renee (the daughter of the circus clown LITTLE NIP) were a couple of good old 'pros' who played anywhere and everywhere. They met, married and worked as a double act, firstly as ASTOR AND ASTORIA and then as JOE ASTOR AND RENEE. In their last years the act was a single, JOE RUGGLES. Renee, however, was always at the side of the stage, shouting instructions!

Rita Atkins' International Nudes

Say no more! Did they kill Variety? I'm not sure but, once those 'naughty revues' began to replace proper Variety bills it certainly became terminally ill. Families stayed away from the theatres and so did I.

Philip remembers these ladies and says: 'They featured in the number two revues when nudes were thought to be daring. They were eight girls who would pose, stationary of course, draped with chiffon and the odd prop. International? Well, if you consider Wigan, Warrington, Bolton, etc. international – yes.'

Winifred Atwell

Pianist. Born Trinidad, 1919. The lady whom we all remember from her hit records, especially the ones she recorded on her 'other piano' (a battered, specially strung job that made a great honky tonk sound). Originally, in Trinidad, a child prodigy (she was playing Chopin Preludes at six), she studied classical piano in New York and London.

Like so many other unknown concert artistes, she found engagements hard to come by till she discovered she could play jazz and boogie-

woogie. She started playing clubs and KEITH DEVON, the agent, signed her. She never looked back. Hit record followed hit record and her effervescent personality made her a natural Variety headliner. In the late Forties she met, and married, former comic LEW LEVISOHN. It was Lew who added the 'other piano' to her act.

When Variety finished in the UK Winifred and Lew emigrated to Australia where she continued to pack 'em in. Here she dispensed with the honky tonk piano and had great success as a soloist with the various State Symphony Orchestras. Lew died in 1978, the year she retired. His death affected her greatly and she died, in solitude, in 1983.

Gus Aubrey

Dame comedian. Born Edward Brown, Salford, 1909. Poor Gus, after beginning as a boy soprano, dressed as a girl, in a juvenile act, JACK AND ROSE HULMES MERRY MITES and a promising career in revue and pantomime, fell in with the notorious FRANK RANDLE. He made films and toured everywhere with him. How he stuck with the mad genius we'll never know. Randle gave him a hell of a life. Because Gus was homosexual he was the perfect target for Frank, who would send him up on-stage and regularly sack him, sometimes several times in the same week! He even persuaded the gentle Gus to have all his teeth taken out 'or you'll never be a true artiste'. Then he sacked him!

Oddly enough, despite all their battles, the last words Frank Randle ever said were: 'I'm worried about Gus. I don't think he's happy.'

Mr GUS AUBREY

By GEORGE AUGUSTE
The well known Variety and Circus Artist.

He wrote a little book on keeping fit and counsels, 'Erotic novels – my advice is control your actions and not become a slave to them.'

B

George Auguste

Comedy on a bar

Trapeze artiste. Born George Edward Read, London, 1911. During our period George was a solo trapeze act but he'd been with *everyone* before then. In the Thirties he was half of CARO AND PARTNER, part of THE FIVE CANADIAN WONDERS, THE TWO ZORROS and THE FIVE ADREMARIOS. In 1946 he played the Empire Pool, Wembley in DON ROSS's circus as GEO. AUGUSTE. His last trick was a real belter. He would swing out over the heads of the audience then, seemingly, fall. He was held in place by just two straps attached to the trapeze.

Babette and Raoul

Adagio dancers. Babette, Elizabeth H. McLaughlan, born Glasgow, 1925 and Raoul, born Hugh Duff McLaughlan, Hamilton, 1920. There were lots of adagio acts in our period and Babette and Raoul (wonderful names for a Scots pair!) were a husband and wife team who played everywhere. Babette was a child prodigy and was principal dancer with G.H. ELLIOTT and JACK ANTHONY at sixteen. Raoul began with an acrobatic act THE THREE BRIGHTONS. They worked on the act before the war but didn't get it off the ground till Raoul was demobbed, in 1947.

Max Bacon

The Heavyweight Champion of Humour

Jewish comedian/drummer. Born London, 1904. Originally, in the late Twenties, a drummer with AMBROSE and his Band, he became a comedian by accident. He was given a spot with the band singing a parody in Jewish style. This took off and, via radio shows with SAM BROWNE, EVELYN DALL, VERA LYNN and MAUDIE EDWARDS, he devised a single comedy act. He did films and television as well as being featured in Variety. After his patter and parodies, a speciality was telling mixed up versions of nursery rhymes and fairy stories in an East End Jewish accent, he always finished his spot with some spectacular drumming. He died in 1970.

Harry Bailey

Missus woman

Comedian. Born Harry Daniels, Limerick, 1910. He was really the Irish version of TED RAY and JIMMY WHEELER, expertly playing a calabash-shaped violin, while firing out one-liners all through the piece. You know what I mean – a few bars of music then:

'Twenty eight children has Mrs O'Brien, she feels fine but the stork is dyin'' – then back to the music.

Harry – though those who saw him will find this hard to believe, was originally, an acrobat, foot juggler, strong man *and* trapeze artiste. His family were part of the fabric of Irish show biz and he too became a leading light with his residencies as principal comedian in Dublin and with his own touring Variety productions. His popularity on radio made him well known in England and he was prominently featured, though never a big star, at all our leading venues. He died in 1989.

Hylda Baker

She knows ya know!

Comedienne. Born Bolton, 1908. In my book, one of the Variety greats: the tiny, forceful figure, spewing malapropisms like machine-gun fire: 'Ooh, you don't know what I'm talking about do you? You have no contraception!' This dumpy know-all, with the bit of rabbit fur round her neck and the tall thin stooge, CYNTHIA (always a man in drag), by her side, was a glorious comedienne.

Hylda started in the game when she was ten. She knocked it out around the halls in her own revues (Philip remembers her giving him, and SID ELGAR, a fiver between them for thinking up the title of her best-known touring show, *Bearskins and Blushes)*, had written comedy sketches and songs, designed scenery and kept companies on the road. She left the business several times, for something safer, but always came back and in the mid Fifties she got her reward. BARNEY COLEHAN gave her a spot on TV's *The Good Old Days* and she was, overnight, a star. And how she deserved it.

One of her 'retirements' led, indirectly, to her later fame. She worked in a dressmaking factory, where the noise from the machines made it impossible to hold any sort of conversation, so the girls had devised a way of mouthing words to one another. She did it, in the act, with Cynthia, and it was a keystone of her style.

Everything came from her success on *The Good Old Days*. She topped the bill at the London Palladium, did *Nearest and Dearest* on the telly and showed what a tremendous straight actress she was in films.

Alas, she was, to put it nicely, a 'leetle' difficult. Poor JIMMY JEWELL, a consummate pro, says they hardly exchanged two words off the screen during their four years together on television. NOEL COWARD said of her: 'I'd wring her neck, if I could find it!' She drove everyone mad in the theatre by insisting her pet monkeys went everywhere with her. So, OK, she wasn't the easiest, (I did a television sketch with her and, believe me, I know!) but she had always had to fight for everything. In the male-dominated world of Variety Hylda hadn't even got looks going for her. Most top Variety turns were fiercely protective of what they had achieved, their positions on the bill, the number of their dressing rooms – everything – and she was no different. It was, I'm sure, because she was a woman that she just *seemed* more aggressive than most. She was a one-off, adored by the public, and a very funny lady. At her funeral, in 1986, there were just five of us there.

Joe Baker and Olga

Double comedy team. Alas I never saw them. According to Philip, 'They were the mother and father of Joe Baker jnr. (See JACK DOUGLAS). They were a standard man and woman cross patter act based on domestic problems. Joe played the henpecked husband and Olga the hard-done-by wife.'

The Balcombes

Comedy ladder act. The leader was John Wislang, born in Australia, 1921. He was a member of the famous Australian circus family, THE ASHTONS. He began, with his father and brother, as a *Chinese* comedy tumbling act. All his early experience was in circus clowning, tumbling and riding in Oz and South Africa. There he met his wife, a contortionist and rider – a clever trick if you can do it – and the two of them, plus his uncle AUBREY BALCOMBE (one half of the trapeze act THE TWO LACONAS), brought their unusual act to the UK where they featured both in Variety and, of course, circus.

The Three Barbour Brothers

Comedians and dancers. The three sons of the well-known comedian and producer ROY BARBOUR. They danced and did acrobatics on stilts. PETER BARBOUR is still very much in show business and only recently was working in America at one of the Disney parks.

KEN BARNES and JEANNE

Ken Barnes

Comedian. Born Islington, London. It was natural for Ken, whose dad was half of a club act, BARNES AND ELLIOT, to go into the biz as a young comedy magician. ENSA brought a meeting with his wife Jeanne and their double act KEN BARNES AND JEANNE was born. After the war, in response to the demand for Variety artistes to do two different spots, Jeanne and Ken obliged with a comedy roller skating act.

My great memories of Ken are seeing him as Dame in panto. He did forty-two consecutive seasons in skirts, and even played in drag in Variety. With the tolling of vaudeville's death knell, in 1958, Ken took on a pub in Dalston, London where he put on entertainment. The pub didn't stop his activities on-stage. He continued as Dame and Old time Music Hall Chairman. One memorable season at the City Varieties, Leeds (home of *The Good Old Days*) ran fifty weeks. Well into the 1980s he continued to play dame, do TV, produce and – his forte – direct pantomime. Ken and Jeanne now live in retirement in Norfolk.

Bunny Baron

Comedian and producer. Born Bruce Baron, London, 1910. I knew Bunny as a producer of summer shows and pantomimes, yet, unlike so many of that ilk, he'd had a thorough grounding as a performer. His début, as an actor, was at the age of eleven in the famous children's play *Bluebell in Fairyland* with SEYMOUR HICKS and ELLALINE TERRISS. He played all the well-known boy parts before, as a young man, becoming part of the Birmingham Repertory Company. He took on comicking during the war and was a popular, and always working, principal comedian in his own summer shows and pantos. His wife, LISA GAYE, co-produced and did the choreography. His Variety act filled in the time between seasons. Despite his legit roots he always came across as a Cockney. Philip says: 'He eventually gave up performing to concentrate on producing. He was much better at this.' He died in 1978 and Lisa carried on his work.

Billy Barr

Comedy speciality. Born Walter Shufflebottom, Manchester, 1897. One of the very best Charlie Chaplin impersonators. I saw him in the popular revue, *Hollywood Doubles* (A sort of early Variety version of television's *Stars in Their Eyes*). He began, just after the First World War, as half of a double act with his brother FRED SHUFF. They called themselves FRED AND WAL ELLIS. His Chaplin impression was devised for his later double act, BILLY BAR AND LADY. Then came *Hollywood Doubles*. He was a member of the company for many years.

Bartlett and Ross

Double drag act. Terry Bartlett and Colin Ross. One of the best known drag acts of the post-war years. They were great Ugly Sisters in panto: Terry was the witty comedian, always dressed in 'over the top' grotesque costumes and broad make-up, while Colin was the elegant, pretty foil. Their Variety spots were varied, not the usual smutty patter so often associated with drag. They had a mother and daughter patter act, a routine as two mermaids and a ballet routine, on pointe! They always went down well with the female members of the audience because, as with DANNY LA RUE, the ladies loved their dresses. Philip remembers the opening of their act: 'Much copied but never bettered. Terry would come down the aisle as an ice-cream girl calling out, "Chocolates!, ices!, me!" The act ended when Colin died but Terry worked on with a new partner, CHRIS SHAW, until his own death in 1976.

Shirley Bassey

Singer. Born Tiger Bay, Cardiff, 1937. A true international star who started in Variety in the early Fifties. She had a West Indian father and an English mother. At sixteen, after singing in local clubs, she joined, as soubrette, a touring show, *Memories of Jolson.* From this she joined another revue, *Hot from Harlem.* It was while she was doing cabaret at The Astor Club in London, in 1955, that JACK HYLTON spotted her and gave her her big break. After going into the Adelphi Theatre as a supporting act in the AL READ vehicle, *Such Is Life*, her career took off like a rocket. The show finished and she went to America for five months. On her return she topped the bill in TV's *Sunday Night at the Palladium.* The rest is history.

She is one of the few recording artistes who is even better 'live'. Her stunning looks, insistence on perfect musical accompaniment, sensational dresses and, best of all, her way of selling a lyric have all added up to a truly unique performer. She remains top of the bill all over the world.

Trio Bassi

Antipodists, foot jugglers. The Bassi family were of French origin and they would, while lying on their backs, juggle, with their feet, tables, chairs, lamps, etc. Their leader was LEO BASSI.

Robert Bemand's Pigeons

Patter comedian – with pigeons! Born Worcester. Bob was a fanatical golfer whose unusual mixture of gags and tricks with the birds made him a constantly working turn on all the leading circuits. He was originally a double act with his brother, Oswald, but he presented his single act (with the pigeons of course) from the early Twenties.

Ivy Benson

Bandleader. Born Leeds, 1913. Ivy, and her All Girls Orchestra, were at their peak during the whole of our period. She managed to keep a band together when so many were forced, through economics, to pack it in. An excellent musician herself, her father was a trombonist in the pit band at the Leeds Empire and started her at three. When I worked on a bill with her band in the Seventies, if she liked an auditionee's style, she would even teach her to read music so she could join the band.

After being part of several girl groups she became a bandleader in her own right in a revue headed by HYLDA BAKER. She toured the Moss Empire circuit fronting an eighteen-piece all-girls orchestra in a show with BILLY SCOTT COOMBER and FORSYTH, SEAMON AND FARRELL. However it wasn't the novelty of an all-girl line up that brought her a residency with the BBC and so many successful tours both here and all over the Continent. It was her value-for-money, immaculately schooled band show that did the trick. All the lads loved being on the bill with Ivy's ladies – *nothing* to do with their musicianship! She was a real old trouper and when the sex discrimination loonies, in 1980, insisted she dropped the word 'Girls' from the title, she packed it in.

I always looked her up whenever I worked in Clacton where, even at eighty, she was to be found 'keeping her hand in' playing the organ in a local pub. She died in 1993.

Michael Bentine

Comedian. Michael James Bentin, the only Peruvian to be born in Watford in 1922. A founder member, and perhaps the most underrated, of THE GOONS. He began his career, in London, as an actor with ROBERT ATKINS's Open-Air Theatre Regent's Park Company.

He was an old Etonian who, after the war, teamed up with a pal and formed a double act, SHERWOOD AND FORREST – well, they had only just started. They played the Windmill Theatre and it was there, and at the Forces meeting place, The Nuffield Centre, that he met all the new wave comics and writers who changed the face of British comedy. HARRY SECOMBE, FRANKIE HOWERD, ALFRED MARKS, FRANK MUIR AND DENIS NORDEN, JIMMY EDWARDS, BENNY HILL, TOMMY COOPER and, memorably, SPIKE MILLIGAN. (Oh for a time machine.) He adopted a wild hair-style and beard and, as a mad professor, devised a single act based on props such as a broken chair back, a sink plunger, a shooting stick and an inflated car inner tube. (One gag I've never forgotten: he would fold the tyre and say, 'Tessie O'Shea in full retreat.') His off-beat comedy took him to the London Palladium and all the number one Variety halls. In the company of Spike, Harry, JIMMY GRAFTON and PETER SELLERS, *The Goon Show* was born, and the rest, as they say, is hysterical.

Michael himself scored with his own, always original, television shows, *It's a Square World* and *All Square*. He was an excellent writer and his biography, *The Long Banana Skin*, is a smashing read. He died in 1996.

A personal note. I started doing shows at a boys' club in Croydon. Every year we, the concert party section, opened the big annual charity show at the Streatham Hill Theatre. One year Michael followed us and, as we came off, he caught my arm and said: 'You should do that for a living.' Oh dear. I never forgot and that's why you're reading these words now.

Harold Berens

Wot a geezer!

Comedian. Born Ivan Harold Berens in Glasgow, 1902. The amazing Harold will be remembered by Variety fans for his membership of the team in the radio show *Ignorance Is Bliss*. The others were GLADYS HAY (WILL HAY's daughter) and MICHAEL MOORE. The show ran from the mid Forties to the early Fifties and Harold's exasperated, 'Wot a geezer!' became a national catchphrase. He even managed to get it into his last film role – the band leader in *Hear My Song*.

His long career began in the Thirties with concert parties and, by the end of the decade, his brilliant gift for dialects and a meeting with the BBC Producer ERNEST LONGSTAFFE (who put together his twelve-minute act) led him to supporting the likes of FATS WALLER and MAX WALL in Variety and TERRY-THOMAS in cabaret.

During the Forties, he did over a thousand broadcasts on radio. He was the ideal compere with a terrific fund of stories, particularly Jewish ones, and never stopped working. A superb player of character parts on television and in movies, his film career started in 1945 and lasted fifty years. He loved jazz and indeed spent three years in

Spain as a singer. He did four Royal Variety Performances and was as bright as a button and as sharp as a tack in his nineties. It was always a joyous occasion when he turned up at a Water Rats Lodge meeting. The stories he didn't have to be persuaded to tell were always the most contemporary and delivered with all the panache of a master raconteur. Couldn't he handle hecklers too. He died in 1995 and is greatly missed.

David Berglas

International Man of Mystery

Psychological magician. Although, happily, I know David very well (he too is a past King Rat of the Grand Order of Water Rats), to explain exactly what he did, and still does, would take the rest of this book.

Before settling in England he lived, and was educated, in six European countries. Naturally he speaks several languages fluently and he can play thirteen different instruments. Before he came into the business he spent two years in the American Army in a special intelligence unit.

He looks and sounds like a man of magic should look and sound and I'm still very wary when I'm in his company. He says he *can't* read minds but I take no chances. He constantly says he has no psychic powers – he could have fooled me. He has done some incredible things like driving through the streets of big cities, blindfolded. He has demonstrated the 'impossible' Indian rope trick – in India. He has caused geysers to spout on command and even made an ocean liner tilt – in still waters. His television series, on which not only his guests, but the viewers too, did exactly what he predicted, were a sensation. Hypnotism? I think not, since he constantly warns against the danger of this. Because David was able to duplicate many of the things URI GELLER has done, the press tried to build up a war between them. David, diplomatic as ever, said: 'Whichever way you look at it, Uri Geller is to be respected. If his powers are genuine, then he is to be admired – for he is the only person in the world who can demonstrate these phenomena consistently. On the other hand, if he is a magician and has been able to dupe everyone into believing in him, then he is also to be admired. I count him as a great friend.'

David now spends much time advising technically on films, and teaching businessmen how to remember, how to motivate and how to improve their communication skills. But not how to read minds or do sensational magic.

The Bernard Brothers

Off the record

Pantomimists. George Bernard, born Maryland, USA, 1912 and Bert Bernard, born Bert Maxwell, Boston, Mass. USA, 1918. Although they both started as dancers, THE BERNARD DANCERS, it was their miming to gramophone records that took them to top of the bill. They even introduced the man who put on the records at the end of their act. George told Philip that the whole thing started as a gag at a party. It was a totally original idea and, as is usual with good ideas, suddenly everyone was doing it. Every touring revue and every working man's club had their own record mimers. There were some good ones and plenty of duff ones but no one got near the Bernards. The whole business squealed to a halt when, I think, the record companies refused permission to use their records. A blessed relief. George died in 1968.

The Beverley Sisters

Sisters

Vocal trio. All three sisters, Joy, Teddie and Babs, were born in Bow, London, in the early 1930s. It seemed inevitable that Joy and her twin sisters would go into the biz, for Mum and Dad were the music-hall artistes CORAM AND MILLS.

Their first break was with radio's *The Ovaltineys* (a children's programme sponsored by the health drink Ovaltine) but GLENN MILLER, who heard them while recording one of his own shows, took them under his wing and encouraged the BBC to sign them up. The girls agree that it was BBC TV that made them stars. A seven-year series established them with the public, and countless Palladium seasons, from 1951 onwards, Variety tours, summer seasons and pantomimes all helped to consolidate their reputation.

They had a string of hit records: 'I Saw Mummy Kissing Santa Claus', 'Little Drummer Boy', and, of course, their signature tune, 'Sisters'. In 1956, way ahead of THE SPICE GIRLS, they made the top ten in America with 'Greensleeves'.

That same year Joy married one of England's greatest soccer heroes, Billy Wright, and their two children, plus one from Teddie's marriage, made them rethink their lives. At the very height of their popularity they gave it all up to look after the kids. That should have been the end of the Bevs but no. The three offspring formed a trio, THE FOXES, and one evening the two mums, plus Babs, sneaked in to watch their girls at Stringfellow's in London's West End. The boss, Peter Stringfellow, spotted the three retired ladies and persuaded them to do a spot at his club. Suddenly they were in demand again and still are to this day.

Many vocal groups have had their brief hours in the sun but the Bevs remain head and shoulders above all the others. It's not only the pleasant noise they make that keeps them at the top. They are three jolly aunties, albeit immaculately dressed and glamorous ones, with a down-to-earth approach, a joint camp sense of fun, impeccable choreography and, best of all, a sheer joy in performing that make them still the force they were during the golden period.

Ali Bey

Magician. Born David Charles Lemmy, Newark-on-Trent, 1905. I suppose Dave Lemmy wouldn't have been a good name for magician. He spent the Second World War as an amateur entertaining the troops, factory workers, etc but became a pro as soon as hostilities ceased. Philip says about him: 'He was a fine carpenter and built all his own illusions. His box tricks being a great feature. Not surprising, his first job was making coffins! His spectacular, fast moving, beautifully timed act with six girls was featured at all the number one halls. He was a very popular support to many of the big Americans stars who came here after the war.'

Les Biancas

Trapeze act. The boss was Jean Rene Robbeets, born in Belgium, 1915. Yet another Continental circus act who came here after the war and played with success at all the leading halls.

Joe Black

Joe Black and fan

Comedian. Born in Yeadon, nr Leeds, 1918. A very funny man, especially in sketches and panto. Joe's grandparents owned the Theatre Royal in Yeadon where the pub (there was one near the stage door of every Variety theatre) was run by the mother of the legendary drag act JIMMY SLATER. His mum and dad were both 'pros' and they taught him, from the age of four, to tap dance and juggle.

He left school at fourteen and, almost immediately, played Variety at The Empire, Ashton under Lyne. 'A short tour,' says Joe. 'My voice broke.' He toured in Variety and revue. One comic he

remembers well was LAURIE HOWE (DICK EMERY's father).

In 1939, war broke out and Joe, after finishing another tour and doing summer season in Redcar, joined The RAF *Gang Show*. He was the featured comic on a concert with the GLENN MILLER orchestra just a week before the great bandleader disappeared. On demob he worked Variety as a single act, supporting many of the big American stars who dominated the top of the bill spots in the Fifties, among them LENA HORNE, THE PLATTERS, THE DEEP RIVER BOYS and AL MARTINO.

I first worked with him in panto. He was a superb Ugly Sister with BERNARD BRESSLAW. Twenty-four seasons after his first panto in 1936, he introduced two new young comics to the medium, MORECAMBE AND WISE. Joe is a tiny chap with great physical dexterity and a voice that can shatter glass, a natural choice to play with The New Crazy Gang in *Underneath the Arches*. What an asset he was. He had the old comic's gift of making every line much funnier than it read and his natural humour and timing was joy for us lesser mortals to behold. Joe now lives in Eastbourne.

The Blair Brothers

Musical act. Richard Blair, born Hamilton, Scotland, 1925. I have no information on his 'brother'. Richard left school to tour with HUGHIE GREEN and later with CARROLL LEVIS. He teamed up with another Levis 'discovery' and together they did several tours with HAL MONTY, notably in his revue, *Eve Goes Gay*. Eventually they returned to Richard's native Scotland where they carried on as a popular turn.

Wally Boag

Speciality act. Born Portland, Oregon, USA, 1920. 'Novelty dancer and balloon designing speciality' was how he described himself in *The Performer*, handbook of 1950. Philip says he was one of the first acts to be seen here that used balloons, moulding them into fantastic shapes and animals at lightning speed. 'Many people copied the act, notably HAL MONTY, but,' says Philip, 'no one did it better than the original.'

George Bolton

Comedian. Born in Portsmouth, 1900. Another early starter, who began in the game as a boy singer. He won a talent contest at twelve, in his home town, and joined a juvenile troupe. At seventeen, he was principal comedian in revue. His career as a single turn in Variety began at the Met, Edgware Road, in 1936. He continued, with highly successful forays into summer shows and, as Dame, he played pantomime till 1980. George, the uncle of AUDREY JEANS, was a great encouragement to that special lady. He died in 1981 leaving a widow, the soubrette FREDA GARDNER, whom he had married in 1940. Freda now lives in Eastbourne where George's brother Water Rats keep a close eye.

Issy Bonn

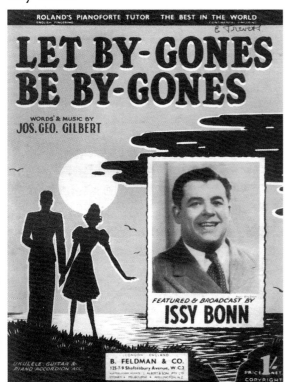

Born Benny Levin, London, 1903. Possessor of a belting voice which he used to great effect on-stage, and on record, with, 'over the top' ballads like 'My Yiddisher Momma', 'Shake Hands with a Millionaire' and 'You're Daddy's Little Boy'. He would intersperse the songs with Jewish jokes and sketches featuring the Finklefetter family. The xylophonist, SYD WRIGHT, played the son, Sammy.

Issy, even as a boy singer, had a great love of Variety, much so that his father sent him to Canada to keep him away from the halls! When his dad died he hurried back to England and joined THE THREE RASCALS, an anglicised version of the American team THE HEDGES BROTHERS AND JACOBSON.

It was JOHN SHARMAN, producer of a top radio show, *John Sharman's Music Hall*, who gave him his first break and changed his name to Bonn. He did over a thousand radio broadcasts and sang, he said, more than five hundred different songs. He topped the bill all over the country, eventually producing and starring in his own road show. Alas, his type of Jewish humour went out of fashion and things were looking decidedly dodgy till he persuaded a young trumpet player, EDDIE CALVERT, who'd had a big hit with his recording of 'Oh! Mein Papa,' to appear on his bills. Business soared. But when Eddie left to work alone, Issy discovered he was no longer the number one attraction. He became an agent and producer of Variety and summer shows.

In 1963 Issy was on the bill for the last night of The Metropolitan Music Hall Edgware Road. He never appeared as a performer again. He died on his 74th birthday, 21 April 1977.

Webster Booth

See ANNE ZIEGLER.

The Borstal Boys

Comedy acrobats. I never saw them but Philip says: 'The act was eight minutes of prolonged laughs. All they did was change clothes with each other, getting involved in all sorts of strange interlocking attitudes. The tragedy is no one knows how it was done.'

The Boswell Twins

Dancers and singers. Honor and Beryl, born Loughborough, 1920. They toured all the leading halls as a song and dance duo till 1939 when they

created the Tassel Dance. They then became 'exotic' dancers playing the Continent, the West End (theatre and cabaret) and touring in 'naughty' revues, notably *Eve Takes It Off*.

Eve Boswell

Singer. Born Hungary, 1924. A dainty, petite, vivacious, hit recording vocalist. She was a South African resident born on the Continent, a member of a famous family of jugglers. She came to Britain in 1949 under contract to the band-leader GERALDO. She left the band in 1952 and had several hit records with 'Transvaal' and other songs. The most famous was 'Sugarbush'. She sang in eleven different languages. Eve retired to South Africa.

The Four Botunds

Comedy acrobats. Alex Aldott, born Paty, 1923, Edith Aldott, born Czechoslovakia, 1922, Szilagyi Geza, born Felscut, 1924, and George Punkosdi, born Budapest, 1924. This was the line-up of the act in 1950 though Philip says it changed 'as time took its toll'. They were a four-handed acrobatic and head-to-head balancing act who first came to Britain, after success on the Continent, in 1948. They were a featured turn on the Moss Empire tours. They also toured with FRANK RANDLE, who, having been originally an acrobat, used to join in their act when he felt so inclined.

The British Music Hall Society

An organisation whose motto is 'Cherishing the Jewels of the Past and Actively Supporting the Interests of the Future'. The natural home for all fans of Light Entertainment, its members include pros, young and old, erudite experts and plain enthusiasts who simply love to laugh and remember (like yours truly). The Society publishes, four times a year, *The Call Boy*, the only magazine devoted to the art of entertainment. It is a treasure house of eye-witness accounts, carefully researched history, book and record reviews, and rare photographs which have been invaluable in the putting together of this book. If you're interested in the Society just drop me a line, and I'll send you the details.

Jack Bowers

Cowboy entertainer. Born Usk, Monmouthshire,

1917. After the war, in which he was a tank commander, won the Military Medal and was a prisoner-of-war until hostilities ceased, he joined *Stars in Battledress*. As a cowboy he sang, played the guitar, cracked gags and spun ropes: on radio, this born-and-bred Welshman played Americans.

Boy and Girl Dancing Acts

There were literally hundreds of dancing duos in Variety. They were usually used as 'ice breakers' directly after the overture or after the interval orchestral entracte. Names I'm sure aficionados will remember are MCANDREWS AND MILLS, MORGAN AND GRAY, RAY LAMARR AND STELLA CLARKE.

Brinsworth House

Brinsworth will be mentioned a lot in this book. It is the residential home, in Twickenham, of the Entertainment Artistes' Benevolent Fund (until the death of Variety, the Variety Artistes' Benevolent Fund).

The house was purchased in 1911 by a bunch of Water Rats and six hundred members of the profession, an event celebrated by a board in the house of the Noble Six Hundred.

A new wing was added in 1914, designed by the great theatre architect FRANK MATCHAM. Since then two further extensions have been added, including a nursing wing, both officially opened by the Queen Mother. Quite right. It is the annual Royal Variety Performance which has, since 1912, enabled the EABF to keep all its financial balls in the air.

The house is a *real* home for retired performers. A place where everyone speaks their language and the inevitable eccentricities that most pros have are sympathetically catered for. Its running is EABFs most high profile activity but the aid to those suffering outside is equally, if not more, important. The provision of pensions and the assistance with living costs to over three hundred ex pros every week means an enormous outlay. Help is always needed. The Fund's headquarters are at Brinsworth House, 72 Staines Road, Twickenham, Middlesex TW2 5AL.

Peter Brough

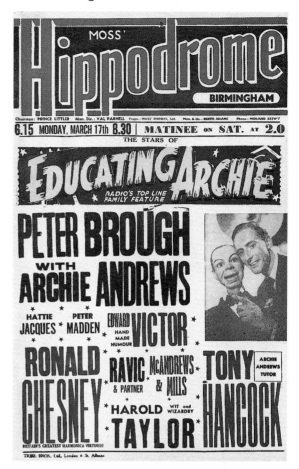

Ventriloquist. Born London, 1916. Yes, a ventriloquist on radio! Peter, with his dummy, ARCHIE ANDREWS, was Britain's answer to America's EDGAR BERGEN and CHARLIE MCCARTHY. Peter's radio show, *Educating Archie*, was immensely popular, not only because of Archie and 'Brough' (as the dummy called him) but equally for the supporting players. The list is a veritable 'Who's Who' of Light Entertainment: ROBERT MORETON, HATTIE JACQUES, MAX BYGRAVES, JULIE ANDREWS, TONY HANCOCK, ALFRED MARKS, HARRY SECOMBE, BERNARD MILES, RONALD SHINER, JAMES ROBERTSON JUSTICE, BERYL REID, KEN PLATT, GRAHAM STARK, DICK EMERY, JERRY DESMONDE, WARREN MITCHELL, PEARL CARR, GLADYS MORGAN, BERNARD BRESSLAW, BRUCE FORSYTH and SIDNEY JAMES. The name of the writers of the show, which ran right through the Fifties, are pretty impressive too: ERIC SYKES, SID COLIN, RONALD WOLFE (later to team with the harmonica player RONALD CHESNEY and write *The Rag Trade*) and MARTY FELDMAN.

Brough and Archie was a number one draw in theatres all over the UK. They were much more effective on radio (as their later television shows proved) but the Variety bills they headed were always packed with the very best. Peter, a very successful businessman, retired at just the right time and now lives in the actors' residential home, Denville Hall.

Janet Brown

Comedienne/impressioniste/actress. Born Glasgow, 1924, Everyone knows Janet through her impression of Margaret Thatcher but, as is always the case, a wealth of experience lies behind her. From the age of thirteen she has done well in everything she has tackled: hundreds of radio broadcasts (including three years playing all the ladies in *The News Huddlines*), Principal Girls and Boys in panto,

straight roles in theatre and on film, and her own television series.

She was married to the comedy actor and excellent pantomime dame, the late PETER BUTTERWORTH. Their son, TYLER BUTTERWORTH, is an acclaimed young actor. Janet is still as busy, and as popular as ever.

Albert Burdon

Albert Burdon (right) *with his son Bryan*

Comedian. Born South Shields, 1900. Albert's son, BRYAN BURDON, is a pal of mine, and he could fill this book with tales of his dad. I saw Bryan do the classic sketch 'The World's Worst Wizard' with his father. The tiny Albert, wearing the biggest turban in the world, would desperately try to demonstrate his Magic Cabinet, assisted by a lunatic 'volunteer' from the audience, Bryan. Albert was a master of physical comedy, thanks to years of knocking it out around the halls in twice nightly revue and Variety. He played the West End (first with JESSIE MATTHEWS and SONNIE HALE in *Evergreen*), made films and was perfectly equipped for television and pantomime. In 1958 he and Bryan played Ugly Sisters at the Theatre Royal Newcastle. Philip knew him well and says: 'He was a star from day one. A very lovable, and very funny, man.' Nuff said. Albert died in his home town, in 1981.

Max Bygraves

Max Bygraves (left) *with Sid Millward and Chic Murray*

Comedian. Born Walter Bygraves, London, 1922. In my book one of our greatest entertainers who simply seems to get better as he gets older. To share an evening with him in the theatre is like spending time with an old friend. From the moment he walks on you relax and sit back: the mark of a real performer. His mix of easy-to-listen-to-songs and stories, delivered with that laid-back, let's have some fun, approach is sheer magic.

His career, which has been well documented in his books, began during the war. He entertained the troops while a serving airman and, on demob, took his act into Variety. I saw him as first spot comic at the Croydon Empire, when one of his two appearances that evening was a medley of Jolson songs, blacked up.

Radio was perfect for him and his success in that medium led to dozens of recordings, umpteen revues in the West End, summer seasons galore, television, films and loads of tours abroad wherever English is spoken. To say I'm a fan would be putting it mildly. He is a master entertainer.

Douglas Byng

Comedian/Actor. Born Nottinghamshire, 1893. The mere mention of his name conjures up visions of the London of the Thirties. This was when Dougie was at the height of his powers. He was the darling of peculiar West End cabaret and revue, inventing all sorts of peculiar ladies to the delight of his up-market audiences. A mere list of some of the songs and monologues he wrote makes me wish, oh so much, that I'd seen him in his heyday: 'Oriental Emma of the 'arem', 'Hot Handed Hetty', 'Millie, the Messy Old Mermaid', 'Naughty Nelly Gwynn', 'Black-Out Bella' and 'Doris, the Goddess of Wind.'

I saw him, at the end of his career, in a two-man show with BILLY MILTON. He just sat and told stories, and occasionally did a song. He was pure magic then, at the age of ninety. He was, according to one of my heroes, JACK TRIPP, a brilliant Dame in panto. It was Dougie who taught the mirror routine to Jack who, in turn, taught it to me. That's the way to keep pantomime alive.

He was a fine actor. He played everything from musicals to farce and was in the Sixties film, *Hotel Paradiso* with SIR ALEC GUINNESS.

He also wrote a fascinating autobiography, *As You Were*. He died in Denville Hall, in 1988.

___C___

The Cairolis

Clowns. Originally Charles Cairoli, born Milan, 1910 and his father Jean Cairoli, born France, 1879. Charlie was the UK's most loved and respected clown of recent years, a brilliant musician and a masterly slapstick comedian. He played no fewer than thirty-nine seasons at the Blackpool Tower Circus, originally appearing there with his father and another brother, FILIP the clown, in 1939. After the war his brother returned to France, his dad retired and PAUL FREEDMAN, who had been with the DEBROY SOMERS orchestra, took over the white-faced clown role. Charlie had three more partners after Freedman, PAUL KING, PAUL CONNOR (who began his career as a multi-instrumentalist with me in *Out of the Blue* at Babbacombe) and, finally CHARLIE CAIROLI junior.

My very first pantomime was at the Leeds Empire (BILL PERTWEE and I were the Broker's Men characters) and, from outside our dressing room in the flies, I would watch Charlie, Paul Freedman, and their brilliant stooge JIMMY BUCHANAN (who never laughed) go through the messiest kitchen scene in the history of panto-mime. It was a masterpiece of meticulous timing and exactly the same every night. Yet – the mark of greatness – it looked as if they were making it up as they went along.

Whether they dimmed the Blackpool lights when the great clown died, I don't know, but they should have done. He was as much a part of the resort as the Tower and the Pleasure Beach. He died in 1980.

Norman Caley

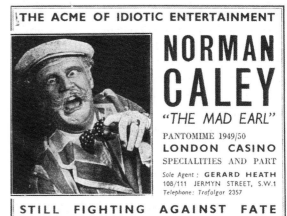

The Mad Earl

Comedian. Born Bridlington, 1920. I had the great joy of knowing Norman (I did a season in Margate and he was in the show next door). He was an unpredictable, very off-beat comic whose patter and visual gags were always interspersed with a wild maniacal, infectious laugh. I would watch him whenever I could sneak away between entrances in my own show, and have never forgotten how, whenever he got a laugh, he would throw his arms wide and, with a beautiful smile, say to his audience: 'Waves of love!' I tackled him about this and he said: 'At that moment in time there *are* waves of love from them to me and from me to them.' That's the best answer I've heard to the question 'Why do you do it?'

I first heard of Norman through an uncle who had served in Egypt during the war. He would tell me about this brilliant comic, who for four years, with his own concert party, entertained the troops all over the Middle East. 'We all called him,' said my uncle, ' "the Mad Earl of the Middle East".' Norman, when he returned home, kept the 'Mad Earl' bit.

He played lots of pantos for EMILE LITTLER, in a specially written part, Sir d'Arcy Decay, and was a favourite in summer season and Variety. He was ahead of his time. I heard from him quite recently.

He sent me a picture of himself pretending to be a dear old retired gentleman.

The Calores Sisters

Musical act. Three sisters born in London: Carole in 1912, Cammie 1914 and Marie 1923. The Calores sisters were of Italian parents. Carole was the first to go into the business, in the 1930s, playing the violin with GWEN ROGERS Ladies Band and in cabaret and concerts as a soloist.

The three sisters got together in 1940, playing variety and night clubs all through the war and into our period. Carole, of course was the violinist, Cammie played piano, accordion and sang, while Marie was the drummer and tap dancer. Philip says: 'They were always beautifully dressed and musically excellent. Their big feature was the STEPHANE GRAPPELLI type fiddle playing of Carole.'

When Variety faded away the sisters carried on with appearances on television and radio. They played in cabaret and for private parties until the late Eighties. Carole died in 1989 and Marie in 1993. Cammie is, happily, still very much with us and is the Permanent Musical Ratling of the Grand Order of Lady Ratlings.

Eddie Calvert

The Man with the Golden Trumpet

Trumpet player and band leader. Eddie found fame with his recording of 'Oh Mein Papa', the first UK chart entry to earn a Gold Disc. Philip remembers: 'As a boy he learnt to play the cornet in a local brass band. He eventually became lead trumpet with the BILLY TERNENT Orchestra. His recording success made him a number one draw at all the top venues here and abroad. He had to leave the UK permanently. The Inland Revenue wanted him to become a member! He went to South Africa. He was a most likeable man but, as a businessman, he was a problem.' Eddie Calvert died in 1978.

Wyn Calvin

The Welsh Prince of Laughter

Comedian. Wyn is one of my oldest friends and so I'm letting you read the potted biography he sent me for this book.

'I was born in Narberth, Pembrokeshire in the far West of Wales, as a result of a deep economic depression, in 1928. Straight from school, in 1945, I joined an ENSA revue. We were to play France, Belgium and newly liberated Holland so we all had to wear uniform. The day I got mine Hitler committed suicide!

'I was employed as juvenile lead but soon had to take over the comedy when the principal comedian was returned to London having helped to "liberate" large quantities of German wines and spirits.

'I followed this with several years learning the trade as a juvenile actor in weekly "rep". Unfortunately the more dramatic or romantic the parts I played the more laughs I seemed to get, so comedy prevailed. I went into Variety as second spot comic and did summer seasons. Seven at Llandudno, five at the Central Pier Blackpool, plus Weymouth, Worthing, Torquay and everywhere you can think of. I played Buttons, Idle Jack and Humpty Dumpty in pantomime till I was persuaded, much against my better judgement, to play the role of Dame. I've been at it ever since. My radio work includes dozens of *Workers' Playtime* broadcasts, *Music Hall, Saturday Starlight* and even Chaucer on the third programme. For seventeen years I have hosted my own chat shows on TV and radio for BBC Wales. I now do dozens of after-dinner speeches. It's one sure way an actor can ensure he sometimes eats.'

I must tell you that Wyn is a brilliant, in depth interviewer, one of our very best, traditional, 'butch' panto Dames and a superb after dinner speaker. He is a tireless worker for charity and, indeed, last year was awarded the MBE for just this. He's also wonderful company and owes me a drink for my tailpiece to his biog.

Big Bill Campbell

Mighty fine

Cowboy bandleader. Born Medicine Hat, Canada, 1893. Big Bill and his Rocky Mountain Rhythm were popular on radio and in their own touring Variety shows during the Forties. What he actually did, apart from introducing the turns and saying 'Mighty Fine!' when they'd finished, I really don't know. His radio shows were mostly music although I do remember some short dramatised sketches between the songs. The characters he introduced were all 'over the top' cowboy caricatures like BUCK DOUGLAS (a sort of GABBY HAYES), PEGGY BAILEY 'The Sweet Voice of the West', NORMAN HARPER 'The Yodelling Buckaroo' and JIMMY HAWTHORNE 'The Yodelling Buckaroo' – Mark Two.

Terry 'Toby Jug' Cantor

Comedian/Producer. Born K.E.Macnaghten Sheffield, 1912. A comedian who looked like everyone's idea of an old-fashioned funny man short, tubby, with a beaming, full of bonhomie face: indeed a living Toby jug. Originally a entertainer at the piano, then a straight man, he was a partner in three double acts – PAYNE and MACNAGHTON (with GILBERT PAYNE) and THE TWO PALS (with CHARLIE ELLIS). He married Adele (of the JEFF MANDEL TRIO) and they too worked as double act. He played Variety both solo and with Adele, then became a proprietor of shows, mostly resident in Dudley and Liverpool, at the Pavilion He produced the longest running pantomime in the country at the City Varieties, Leeds. He was

King Rat of the Grand Order of Water Rats in 1967 and a great worker for the Entertainment Artistes Benevolent Fund. Terry died at his holiday home in Majorca in 1979. His son, KENNY CANTOR, is a popular comedian and producer.

Roger Carne

Ventriloquist. Born 1912. I knew Roger from a summer season we did together, *The Ocean Revue* on Clacton Pier. He was a highly original vent with his two dummies, Canasta the Cat and Willie Heckle. He was also, very important for a resident summer show, excellent in sketches too.

The organisation that did the job of ENSA, post-war, was Combined Services Entertainment (CSE) and Roger probably did more overseas tours with them than anyone else. He died in 1997.

Terri Carol

Speciality act. Born Ivy Rosina Victoria Moore, Surrey, 1914. Another of those speciality acts that made Variety so special. Terri was, and still is, a paper tearer. She was taught the art by her father HARRY MOORE. To a musical accompaniment she tears paper into fantastic patterns, ending with an extending ladder that reaches to the top of the proscenium arch. Of late Terri has been discovered by the Comedy Clubs and her act, literally, tears up those tough, vociferous audiences.

Pearl Carr and Teddy Johnson

Singers. Teddy and Pearl were both successful solo artistes before they married in 1955 (they met while working as soloists with the bandleader STANLEY BLACK) and became one of the most popular husband and wife teams in Variety.

Pearl sang with all the best known bands on radio and was the lead singer with the vocal group, THE KEYNOTES. Teddy had a similar start, at seventeen, but he played the drums as well.

We all think that they won the Eurovision Song Contest in 1959 with 'Sing Little Birdie', but no. Their song, which became much better known than the winner, was second.*

The disappearance of the Variety theatres had little effect on their career. They carried on in radio, stage shows and on TV as singers and presenters. Teddy, especially, was the host of all sorts of record programmes.

I last saw them together in Stephen Sondheim's *Follies*. Their duet, 'Rain on the Roof', stopped the show.

*Teddy's brother, BRYAN, did have Eurovision winner with 'Looking High, High, High'.

Russ Carr

Ventriloquist. Born Frederick Russell Parnell, London, 1889. Son of one of the most famous figures in the history of music-hall and Variety, FRED RUSSELL (his brothers were the old Palladium boss VAL PARNELL and the agent ARCHIE PARNELL). He played a few years into our period as a vent assisted by his wife OLIVE GREY. In the early Fifties he left the halls to become a theatrical agent. His son is the drummer and bandleader JACK PARNELL. Russ died in 1973.

Ronnie Carroll

Singer. Born 1934. The velvet-voiced Ronnie, whom I first saw in a sound-a-like touring revue, *Hollywood Doubles*, as NAT 'KING' COLE. The manager of the show, EDDIE LEE, took Ronnie on as a single act and made him a top recording star and Variety headliner in the late Fifties and early Sixties.

He had eight chart hits, represented us twice in the Eurovision Song Contest and was married to MILLICENT MARTIN.

Ronnie has certainly had some rough times since those heady days but is now, happily, in charge of an entertainment complex in North London.

Peter Casson

THE
MOST PUBLICISED
LIVING HYPNOTIST

PETER CASSON

One of the Outstanding Attractions of 1949

THE FIRST ONE-MAN SHOW IN THE HISTORY OF TWICE NIGHTLY MUSIC HALL ENTERTAINMENT

★

Personal Management
JACK LISTER, 199 PICCADILLY, LONDON, W.1

Hypnotist. Born Bridlington, 1921. Certainly the first hypnotist to make an impact in Variety – and what an impact. He discovered his gift while in the Marines during the war. On demob he contacted an agent, JACK LISTER, and together they devised *An Evening With* one-man show for the halls. It was a sensation. Peter's original thought was to play Variety to make enough money to open his own clinic in Yorkshire. This he did with the re-settlement of shell-shocked servicemen as one of his priorities.

Peter was the first Variety performer to do a complete show on his own and broke box office records everywhere. He and Jack were masters of

pre-publicity and his arrival in a town or city was usually the cue for police-controlled crowds. He was the forerunner of so many others and did, seemingly, carry out minor medical miracles, lecturing all over the world, to the most august bodies, and constantly warning against the misuse of the gift.

In the Sixties he became a club proprietor and was at the forefront of the fight against provincial gaming laws. He died in 1995.

Roy Castle

Comedian/dancer/musician. Born 1932. One of our most loved, and missed, multi-talented Variety performers. The story of his brave, inspirational fight against cancer is too well known to repeat here. Roy was steeped in Variety, having begun as a child performer, been half of a musical double act with NORMAN TEAL and then joining the Company of JIMMY JAMES as one of his two stooges. With long coat and Guy Fawkes hat, 'Are you putting it around that I'm barmy,' was the catchphrase that no one who saw James's brilliant sketches will ever forget. His exceptional comedy timing rubbed off on Roy and it was this, and the hard work, that went into his dancing and playing of every musical instrument you can think of, that led to top of the bill status in Variety, revue, pantomime, cabaret and, of course, on television. He was the complete 'pro'. He died in 1994.

Peter Cavanagh
The voice of them all

Impressionist. Born Anerley, South London, 1914. In every decade there is always *the* impressionist and Peter was the top man during our period.

Radio was his forte and his vocal impressions were terrific. I remember he and ARTHUR ASKEY did alternate lines of 'The Bee Song' together and you really couldn't tell which one was the real Arthur. Visually he was not so impressive although his big finish in Variety was a stunner. He closed with Field Marshal Montgomery. The resemblance was amazing and the voice was perfect. To be fair, however, unlike MIKE YARWOOD and RORY BREMNER, he didn't have the benefit of the television make-up departments to work their magic on him. He was an old fashioned 'toff' who would never do an impression of anyone without their permission. I loved the closing of his radio spots where he would say: 'So it's goodbye from -' and then, at breakneck speed, give just a couple of words from each of the people he had done, finishing with: 'and this is the voice of them all, Peter Cavanagh, saying goodnight'. A guaranteed huge round of applause. He died in 1981.

Cave and Morgan

The Singing Dresdens

Singers. Kathleen Cave and Irene Morgan. Kathleen, operatically trained and Irene, a RADA graduate, both appeared individually in musical comedy and panto until they teamed up in 1940. From then on they presented their immaculate vocal duets, dressed as two Dresden figures, in Variety, and summer seasons. In pantomime they usually played Prince Charming and Cinderella.

Peggy Cavell

A lightning sketch artist. Philip says: 'An original and very effective speciality.'

Kay Cavendish

Kay on the keys

Pianist/singer. Born Kathleen Dorothy Cavendish Murray, Hong Kong. A Royal Academy trained pianist with Queen's Hall and Wigmore Hall concerts to her credit, as well as early classical recitals on radio. Just before our period she had arranged all the music, played piano and sung with several radio singing trios. In 1944 she became a solo turn and, within three years, claimed to have done more than 300 broadcasts of her show *Kay On The Keys*. The radio success, of course, made her a 'must' on the top Variety bills.

The Charlivels

Acrobatic musicians. John Andreu, born at sea, 1923, Charles Andreu, born London, 1925, and Valentino Andreu, born Brussels, 1926. What a pedigree these three brothers had. Their father was CHARLIE RIVELS, 'The Chaplin of the Trapeze', and their mother a well-known ballerina. They learned acrobatics and music (playing sixteen instruments between them) from their dad and dancing from their mum. A sensational blend of their many talents made them UK and worldwide favourites.

Chris Charlton

Comedy magician. Born Liverpool. A real cosmopolitan performer. He presents his act in three different languages and has appeared in more than forty different countries.

Charlie Chester (centre) *with his gang*

'Cheerful' Charlie Chester

Comedian/songwriter. Born Eastbourne, 1914.

'Down in the jungle living in a tent.
Better than a pre-fab, no rent!'

Not the greatest lyric Charlie ever wrote ('Down Forget-me-Not Lane', 'Primrose Hill' and 'The Old Bazaar in Cairo' were his) but those lines bring back everything Charlie was all about during the golden days of Variety. Although he started as a comic before the War it was his army radio show *Stand Easy* that made him a star. His 'Gang' was a good one. Comedians ARTHUR HAYNES, KEN MORRIS and LEN MARTEN plus singers RAMON ST CLAIR, FREDRICK FERRARI and later LOUISE GAINSBOROROUGH. He and him merry crew did series after series on radio, played the Palladium and toured the halls with various stage versions. In the early Fifties the Gang split up to pursue solo careers. They all did pretty well.

Charlie, like the amazingly adaptable chap he was, did everything: summer show, revue, pantomime, straight plays, farces, musicals and television (notably his give-away show, *Take Pot Luck* with ERIC 'JEEVES' GRIER). As theatres closed around him Charlie went back to radio and, for over twenty years was featured on Radio Two in his *Sunday Soapbox* show. After a lifetime's service to the business he loved, Charlie died in 1997.

Maurice Chester's Performing Poodles

Animal trainer. Born Fulham, London, 1898 Maurice, after creating his first act, MAURICE CHESTER'S SIXTEEN SPORTING DOGS in the Twenties put on dog acts for anyone who wanted them. He produced a miniature circus in Regent's Park in the Thirties and, during our period, presented the poodles in Variety, pantomime and circus, where he also trained ponies.

The Chevalier Brothers

Two-handed comedy acrobatic act. I know nothing about these two gents but Philip says: 'They were a standard act featured all over the world. At the end of their careers the 'bearer' was so old and frail you felt he was dicing with death to ever attempt carrying his partner. He could still do it though.'

Joe Church

Comedian. Born London, 1919. One of my very favourite front-cloth comics. I saw Joe so many times, at the Palladium and at my local, the

Croydon Empire. The perfect warm-up comic, his friendly, laid back, relaxed, off-beat style never failed. How many of us remember his routine with a plank of wood where he 'marked' us out of ten according to the laughs his gags got.

He holds the record for the most number of appearances at the London Palladium, having broken the ice for many an international star from FRANK SINATRA to TOMMY STEELE and deputising for everyone from LAUREL AND HARDY to GEORGE FORMBY. Joe started entertaining in the Forces, first with a show which toured the Middle East, *Nomads of the Nile* and later with the famous *Stars in Battledress*. By 1946 he was demobbed and one date at the Grand Clapham led to regular Variety weeks, summer seasons and pantos. In the mid Fifties he found the agent who changed his life: the legendary BILLY MARSH. Billy took VAL PARNELL and BERNARD DELFONT to see him and his first Palladium date followed – supporting DEAN MARTIN and JERRY LEWIS. Soon he was not only a regular at the Palladium, but also 'doubling' (playing two theatres in the same evening) at all the other London music-halls. He went as well in Australia and South Africa as he did at home.

His TV spots ranged from *Sunday Night at the Palladium* to *The Good Old Days* and all stations between. He was a regular on the 'live' lunchtime radio show (broadcast from factories all over the country) *Workers' Playtime*. The wise Billy Marsh, when Variety finished, got Joe booked as an entertainer on the American cruise ships and he adapted to this new challenge so perfectly that, with interruptions for UK work (notably his six months at the Palace Theatre with DANNY LA RUE) he stayed with the ships till the 1980s. These days Joe does what he feels like, encouraged by his missus – the witty and wicked comedienne and singer, PAT STARK. Quite right too.

Cingallee

Illusionist. Dressed as a Chinese Mandarin, he silently performed his spectacular illusions. He was a good first half closing act on the number one tours and a top of the bill on the number twos.

Cingallee

Charlie Clapham

Comedian. Born Birmingham, 1894. Although I have seen them on film, and heard them on record, I never saw the act that established Charlie Clapham, CLAPHAM AND DWYER. I did, and still do, enjoy their strange partnership. They always look as if they are nothing to do with each other: the straight man, Bill Dwyer, with his burly shape and confident delivery, and Charlie, with his angular figure, monocle, slightly 'off' top hat and evening dress and hesitant, unfinished burblings. The record I wish I still had was their 'Alphabet' which started: 'A is for 'orses. Beef for mutton'. The act sadly broke up in 1940 with Bill's illness (he died in 1943) but Charlie carried on as a single act till 1954. He lost his voice altogether and died in 1959.

Bobby Clanford

Singing accordionist. Born Fulham, London, 1920. A poacher turned gamekeeper. Originally he played the accordion and sang in several different voices: baritone, tenor and soprano. He was a band leader and, during the war, part of RALPH READER's *Gang Show*. After seasons for HARRY and MARJORIE RISTORI he crossed the floor and became an agent.

The Clarke Brothers

Dancers. Steve and Jimmy. Two of the great American dance stylists. A combination of synchronised tap, comedy and superlative jazz 'feel' made them a show-stopping act. They still are.

Clark and Murray

Mr and Mrs Glasgow

Comedy double act. Gracie Clark born Yoker, Clydeside, 1904, and Colin Murray born Glasgow, 1905. They married in 1931. Scotland's Burns and Allen. Well, they certainly were a highly successful husband and wife team but *their* relationship, on-stage, was quite different to the famous Americans. Colin played the henpecked husband and Gracie the hectoring wife. They were hugely popular in their native land, especially at the famous Gaiety Theatre, Ayr. They did make the occasional trip down south where they scored well but it was at home where they became a show biz legend.

They met in concert party at Dunbar in 1926. Gracie was the pianist and Colin the singer. They formed a double act quite different to the one that made them stars. They were a musical and light comedy duo for twenty-two years till, in 1948, a Glasgow theatre owner, ALEX FRUTIN, advised them to go for the broader type of sketch comedy. They did and from then on went from strength to strength. During their fifty years as performers they appeared with all the famous Scottish names and in the very first Scottish Royal Variety Performance. They were the first husband and

wife in Scotland to be honoured with the BEM for of course, services to entertainment.

As late as 1976 they were offered the summer season at Ayr but they decided a whole run would be too much for them. They relaxed by touring with DOUGIE CHAPMAN's music hall revival show! They did eventually retire, to Doodfoot Ayrshire, not far from the scene of their happy seasons at the Gaiety. Colin died in 1989 and Gracie in 1995.

Clarkson and Gail

Dancing duo. George Clarkson jnr, born Wishaw, Scotland, 1918 and Mrs Clarkson (Gail Leslie). The son of the Scottish comedian and producer, GEORGE CLARKSON snr. (George senior lived to a ripe old age, ninety-six, and recorded his memories on video. One of his dancers was MARGARET KELLY who later became MISS BLUEBELL of the world-famous BLUEBELL GIRLS.) George junior, after sterling service with the Balmoral Concert Party during the war, formed a double act with his missus. They travelled the world til George became DES O'CONNOR's manager and Gail part of the BBC wardrobe department. He died in 1970.

Jimmy Clitheroe

The Clitheroe Kid

Comedian. Born Clitheroe, Lancs, 1916. How many times have I eaten my roast beef and Yorkshire to the Kid's voice. I can't really remember a time when he, PETER SINCLAIR, DANNY

ROSS, DIANA DAY and MOLLIE SUGDEN weren't part of my family's Sundays.

That piping, precocious little voice came from a perfectly formed little body. Jimmy was, like 'WEE' GEORGIE WOOD, a midget, not a dwarf. Unlike George, Jimmy was perfectly at home in the rough and tumble of Variety. He loved his work which had begun in a juvenile troupe. He sang, danced, played the accordion and sax *and* did female impersonation. All for seven bob a week!

His comic gifts were developed by the impresarios JACK TAYLOR and TOM ARNOLD who featured him in their revues and pantomimes. (He did season after season with ALBERT BURDON. What a way to learn about comedy.) He did lots of British 'B' films alongside FRANK RANDLE, GEORGE FORMBY, LUCAN and MCSHANE, etc. In 1958 he renewed acquaintance with a chum from his juvenile show days, JAMES CASEY (son of the great JIMMY JAMES). Jim Casey was a producer for BBC Radio in Manchester and it was he who came up with 'The Clitheroe Kid'. Radio was the perfect medium for the 42-year-old little boy, and the show became the longest running comedy show in the history of radio (fifteen years) until, whisper it, *The News Huddlines* came along.

The following year, 1973, Jimmy died, on the very day of his mother's funeral.

Vera Cody

Horse trainer. Born, we think, in Germany. Vera, with GOLDIE the Wonder Horse, was a featured act on so many Variety bills that I had to find out something about the lady. I was lucky that MARTIN LACEY of Circus Harlequin put me in touch with one of her greatest friends, JULIE DARE.

Julie told me: 'I first met Vera in the mid Forties, when she was appearing with her husband (TEX MCLEOD) in his show, *Rhythm on the Range*. Vera did a spot with her horse Bracken and her Scotch collie dog, Corin. She had an amazing affinity with her animals especially the three high-school horses she featured on stage. They understood every word she said. When Bracken started to age she looked around for another horse. She found the brilliant Goldie pulling a milk float in Morecambe and immediately bought him. How did she know? Apart from doing the act with Vera, Goldie worked with stars like DICKIE VALENTINE, GUY MITCHELL, MAX BYGRAVES, TERRY-THOMAS and the clown, DON SAUNDERS. They did several stints at the London Palladium plus Variety for Moss Empires and summer seasons.

Goldie and Vera retired together to a small farm at Crowborough in Sussex. A troublesome filly called Sorrell was sent to Vera to sort out and, once again, a horse and her owner were one. Off she went on the road again with yet another Wonder Horse. She died in 1987.

Alma Cogan

The girl with the laughing voice

Singer. Born 1932. A pre rock and roll top of the bill singer whose bubbly personality came across perfectly on her many hit records. She became known to a wide public as the featured vocalist in *Take It from Here*, FRANK MUIR and DENIS NORDEN'S hit radio show, where her sense of comedy led to her taking part in the sketches as well. A greatly loved lady (by the public and her fellow artistes) she died, at the height of her fame, in 1966.

Maurice Colleano

Acrobat. Born Narrabri, Australia, 1908. A dancing acrobatic comedian who started in his father's (CORNELIUS COLLEANO) circus in Australia at the age of one! He toured his own show with his wife, his sister Joyce, his brother Lyn and his cousin George. His sailor routine, which he opened by hanging himself on a clothes rack, became a well-established Variety act. His brother was the world's greatest wire-walker, CON COLLEANO and his wife ELSIE BOWER a comedienne and pianist. Their son was BONAR COLLEANO. Maurice retired in the late Fifties and died in 1975.

Collinson and Breen

Comedy double act. Bill Collinson, a big, traditional, straight man had two partners. His first was the diminutive ALFIE DEAN, when the act was COLLINSON AND DEAN. Alfie later worked with SID FIELD in his hit Prince of Wales revues. He was the caddy in the famous golf sketch and the marker in the follow up snooker routine and heckled Sid when he played Slasher Green. Bill and Alfie did make records and their routines were rather like the schoolroom scene in panto. Questions and silly answers:

'If I've got two pounds in this pocket, two pounds in this pocket and two pounds in my back pocket – what have I got?'

'Someone else's trousers!'

Bill's later partner, Breen, was another tiny man and their routines did have more of a plot in that the straight man was trying to teach the comic something, rather like JERRY DESMONDE for Sid.

I wish I had more information on Bill and his two partners but I haven't. I just hope that, as with some of the other more sketchy biographies in the book, someone will write to me and fill in the details.

Collinson and Breen

Bobby Collins

Comedian. Born Bow, London, 1935. I never saw Bobby but Philip remembers: 'He began as a boy vocalist at the age of seven. When his voice broke he turned to comedy and scored a big success at the Prince of Wales London. Sensing he had little chance of becoming a star here he emigrated to Australia where he received the recognition he desired.'

Elizabeth and Collins

Knife thrower. Martin Collins, and his wife Elizabeth were both born in Budapest, he in 1914 and she in 1924. Quite the most sensational act of its kind I ever saw. Martin began as a child acrobat and had his own Western spot at the age of seventeen. He met Elizabeth when she was picked, at the age of fifteen, to be his partner. It took them six years to perfect their finishing trick. He would balance, on one foot, on a slack wire while she, fastened to a circular board, would be revolved at high speed. He would then throw knives at her, or rather all around her. They must have loved each other very much. Elizabeth retired in 1957 and let her daughter be the target. Martin died in 1967.

Connor and Drake

Male comedy double act. I remember their routine as two tramps. Vernon Drake was the typical 'toff' straight man. He was always known as 'The Duke' and was an excellent feed for Eddie Connor, the comic. In my early days I did lots of extra work for TV and Vernon was often with me. He was a delightful bloke. How I wish I remembered just half of the scandalous stories he told me.

Hamilton Conrad and His Pigeons

Pigeon act. Philip says: A standard pet pigeon act. Just as KARDOMA filled the stage with flags Conrad's pigeons filled the audience with fear!

Russ Conway

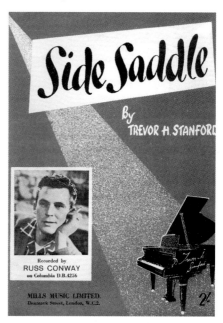

Pianist/composer. Born Terence Stanford, Bristol. WINIFRED ATWELL, MRS MILLS, JOE 'PIANO' HENDERSON and BOBBY CRUSH: we have always had a performer who plays the piano in an individual and 'join in' way. Russ is still the best of them all. He began as accompanist to top of the bill singers like DOROTHY SQUIRES but his composing talents soon led him to recording a string of Top Ten hits. His appearances in TV's *Billy Cotton Bandshow*, (where his self effacing, full-of-charm personality and great looks secured him a regular spot) made him the Variety headliner he remains to this day.

Jack and Joan Cooper

Stage Academy proprietors. Jack born Birmingham, 1913 and Joan born Birmingham, 1923. The Midlands have produced hundreds of good dancers and many of them have come through Birmingham's stage schools. Today BETTY FOX (the original Betty Fox's daughter) produces excellently trained boys and girls. Before the two Bettys there were Jack and Joan. Their pupils were lucky because their teachers had been highly experienced pros. The Coopers had toured here, there and everywhere as a dancing duo until, in 1938, they formed their school. They were responsible for so many youngsters coming into the business.

Tommy Cooper

Just like that!

Comedy magician. Born Caerphilly, South Wales, 1922. What can I add to what has already been said about the immortal Tommy? He was a genuine 'one-off', someone who made you laugh as soon as he walked on, sometimes even before he appeared. I saw him in a club where his act opened with just the sound of him trying to get out of his dressing room. The place was in an uproar before he even showed his face.

This sort of audience anticipation is reserved for the crowd's best loved favourites. Remember the stir in the audience as the band struck up, oh so slowly, 'Mary from the Dairy' heralding the entrance of MAX MILLER?

Tommy began as an amateur in the army and I'm sure it was this air of 'a fool having a go' that made him such a success. He drew us all into his lunatic world where anything could happen. The magic is proverbial but my favourite bits were the monologue with changing hats and (I only saw him do it once) a tune played on motor horns that he had secreted in his long overcoat.

I asked him once, damn fool that I was, how he achieved his off-beat timing of a tag line. 'Er, I'm just trying to, er, remember – what I'm, er, supposed to say next.'

His ridiculous token gesture to being a magician (the fez), maniacal laugh, enormous height, huge feet and somehow graceful movements, all added up to the 'from another planet' whole. No one could ever sit down and design a Tommy Cooper. He died in 1984, in the way every performer would want to go, paralysing an audience of millions topping the bill at peak time on television.

Leon Cortez

Wotcher cocks!

Comedian. Born Richard Alfred Chalkin, Greenwich, 1899. Suddenly everyone is interested in Leon again. Although he began in Variety as the leader of a comedy band, LEON CORTEZ AND HIS COSTER PALS, I remember him best for his Cockney explanations of Shakespeare's plays. He did publish some and I'm looking through his version of *Hamlet* right now. Like all good Variety comedians he did something different. His subject matter was original, even though burlesques on the Bard go way back to SAM COWELL and before. His BILLY BENNETT, JIMMY WHEELER type delivery was perfect for the job.

When Variety was no more he became a successful character actor on television in series such as *The Saint* and *Dixon of Dock Green*. He died in 1970.

Billy Cotton

Wakey! Wakey!

Band leader. Born Westminster, 1899. How we miss the sort of show Bill used to give us – good, middle of the road music and lots of fun. His band show in Variety with its well sung ballads from KATHY KAY, comedy from ALAN BREEZE and BILL HERBERT, amazing dancing from ELLIS ASHTON and big, spectacularly staged instrumental numbers such as 'The Dambusters March' plus the audience participation spots like 'I've Got a Lovely Bunch of Coconuts', made the avuncular Bill and his 'boys' (they all seemed older than God and most of them had been with him for years) a big attraction.

He began as a choirboy at St Margaret's, Westminster, led his own band from 1925 onwards, made a name for himself as a racing driver and amateur boxer, toured the halls with TESSIE O'SHEA and eventually hosted his own *Billy Cotton Bandshow* on televison.

He was a darling bloke, ever ready to give new-comers a word of encouragement and, more importantly, a break. One of my first 'tellys' was on his show with a singer called TOM JONES. Bill died, watching a BILLY WALKER fight at Wembley, in 1969.

Howard De Courcy

The Magic Man

Magician. Born Switzerland, 1914. Howard originally was bound for the hotel business but became interested in magic and, under the auspices of WILL GOLDSTON, became a pro. His first job was at the notorious home of the nude, the Windmill Theatre. Later he starred opposite the 'Queen of Striptease' PHYLLIS DIXEY in her revue *Peek-a-Boo*, not only doing his magic act but also giving demonstrations of table-tennis with the European champion BOROS. The trick that made

his name was 'Garbo the disappearing canary'. He appeared at all the number one dates here, on the Continent and in America. He retired in 1970 and died in 1990.

The Cox Twins

Double comedy act. Frank and Fred, twins born Cardiff, 1920. Fred and Frank's irresistible personalities and multi talents (they play four instruments, sing and dance, both tap and acrobatic) would be enough to guarantee their inclusion on any Variety bill but they have the bonus of being identical twins. They are an uncanny pair – one will start a sentence and the other will finish it: they think as one. They even married identical sisters, THE MILES TWINS.

They began, at twelve, with STEFFANI'S TWENTY-ONE SINGING SCHOLARS playing every major hall and working with the biggest names. After five years in the RAF with *The Gang Show* they went into Variety where their greatest fan was the inscrutable CISSIE WILLIAMS. Her support enable them to become regulars on her circuit (they supported JOHNNY RAY at the Palladium) and with HOWARD AND WYNDHAM for pantomime and TOM ARNOLD for summer season.

The ebullient pair, after more than sixty years, are still at it. Their enthusiasm is undimmed and they are regularly featured, not only in what

remains of Variety, but on TV in everything from *Barrymore* and *Candid Camera* to commercials and documentaries. Such is their love of performing that they recently visited a sick chum in hospital and ended the evening by doing their act to the entire ward!

Doctor Crock and His Crackpots

Comedy band. Dr Crock and Harry Hines, born Tottenham, London, 1903. Harry and his maniacal, merry band followed SID MILLWARD AND HIS NITWITS on to radio's *Ignorance Is Bliss* in 1947, providing the musical interludes on the show.

Harry, whom I met long after the demise of the comedy band on a TV film, *The Malajusted Busker* (written by JOHN LAW, and winner of the Press Prize in Montreux) was an excellent clarinet and sax player who had worked for names like AMBROSE, AL COLLINS, TEDDY BROWN and MAURICE WINNICK before the birth of The Crackpots. He was a fascinating, eccentric character who learned the clarinet while a bandboy in the Navy. In 1933 he became a full-time pro. He bought a saxophone, blacked up and toured in WYLIE WATSON's all-coloured revue. While in Edinburgh, as a member of a dance band, he met his wife. Of his spell with Teddy Brown's orchestra he wrote, in his 1950 biography: 'Happy with wife, happy with the band, happier with Savoy Hotel (more money) but not so happy when Germans dropped bombs on Piccadilly and put me out of the engagement.' It was his ability to write crazy arrangements that led to *Ignorance Is Bliss* and his own fourteen-piece band. They toured everywhere as bill toppers. Harry died in 1971.

Billy Crotchet

Crotchet – the Mad Musician

Comedy musician. Born William Davidson Crockett, Edinburgh, 1920. A legendary Scottish musical clown from a famous circus family (the great animal trainer GENE DETROY was a cousin). He began as a 'lime' boy in 1934 and was an apprentice wire-walker. Not for him. He joined the famous MUSICAL ELLIOTTS and later was a member of SYD SEYMOUR'S MAD HATTERS. He was one of Elstree's THREE STOOGES before he created his own musical clown single act which he toured all over the world. He is now back home, still at it, in Scotland.

___D___

Billy Dainty

Going mad – coming?

Comedian. Born Dudley, 1927. You must forgive me waxing eloquent in my summing up of Bill. He was one of my best friends. His history starts in a fairly normal way. Dancing school in the Midlands and as a pupil of the legendary BUDDY BRADLEY in London. Then, surprise, surprise, The Royal Academy of Dramatic Art. He was a

superlative Dame. He was in several Royal Variety Shows and was 'discovered' every time he did one.

We did a book show together, not long before he died and, in this, he not only did all that we knew him for, he acted as well. He was, quite simply, stunning. He could switch from comedy to pathos (never bathos) in the blink of an eye. I get very angry indeed when I think of just what we have all missed by his early death. He wasn't even sixty when he died, of cancer, in 1986. I miss him every day.

Dudley Dale

Dudley Dale and His Gang

Comedian and dancer. Born Liverpool. Dudley, after years as a single turn at all the number one venues, developed his 'Gang' – a collection of boy singers and dancers who were always a well-featured act on the halls. He was a popular, and evergreen, panto Dame.

Jim Dale

Comedian. Born James Smith in Kettering, Northants, 1935, Jim is one of the names I always quote when talking about Variety being a great training ground. It is difficult to believe but the man who has triumphed in plays and musicals both in the UK and especially in America has his roots in the halls.

His is also the name I quote, along with BARRY TOOK and the film star ANNE HEYWOOD, when asked: 'Who did CARROLL LEVIS actually discover?'

Jim learned to dance at the age of nine and, at seventeen, toured all over the UK as part of Carroll's stage show. He was billed as JIM SMITH, 'Britain's youngest comedian'. He reckons he played more than eighty of the old halls in the Fifties. In the Sixties, after National Service with the RAF and with the help of his record producer, the legendary GEORGE MARTIN (of BEATLES fame), he became a successful pop singer. He toured all the halls that were left again, only this time as top of the bill. Since then he has done the lot. Theatre, films, TV, smash hit musicals, you name it. He now lives in America but occasionally

scholarship student there for two years but, against all the rules, moonlighted. He was the rear half of 'Asbestos' the donkey (JOHN SHACKELLE was the front half) in a NORMAN EVANS panto at the London Casino. Along with ERIC MORECAMBE, ERNIE WISE and his sister BETTY DAINTY, he was in the SID FIELD revue *Strike a New Note* at the Prince of Wales. It was taking on this job that finally got him slung out of RADA.

From then on his was the comedians' well trodden path. Concert party, summer season, panto and Variety. His act was, during our period, basically, eccentric dancing with a few gags in between. I had the great joy of watching him, like a butterfly emerging from its chrysalis state, develop into a unique, other worldly, moving, dancing, epitome of all that is best in comedy. LEN LOWE, his long-time straight man and feed, has a great phrase that goes: 'A comedian says funny things, a *great* comedian says things funny.' Billy looked funny, moved funny and spoke funny. His burlesques on Nureyev ('Near enough'), *The Student Prince* and SHIRLEY BASSEY were cartoons of the highest class and, of course, his dancing style, both eccentric and straight, was just the best. He was a good panto comic and a

was as the Mate in *Dick Whittington* – with wait for this – DOROTHY WARD as Principal Boy, SHAUN GLENVILLE as Dame, RANDOLPH SUTTON as Alderman Fitzwarren and G.H. ELLIOTT as the Sultan of Morocco. He is now a rather special Dame and has played 'Mother' to KATE O'MARA, MAX BOYCE and even IAN BOTHAM.

As so often happens to performers with a Variety background, he has developed into a good straight actor and, after being 'discovered' by the powers that be, often pops up on the telly. Johnny lives and works from his home town, Leicester.

Johnny Dallas

brings his talents back home, for example as Fagin in the recent revival of *Oliver!* He remains a huge star and a great example of what a twice nightly Variety background can lead to.

Johnny Dallas

Comedian. Born Peter Ross, Leicester, 1929. Johnny began his long career under his real name, PETER ROSS, as a boy actor in Leicester. His first pro work was as an impressionist 'discovered' and featured in his touring revue, by BRIAN MICHIE. He was 'discovered' again by ALEC FYNE and DON ROSS. Indeed Don put him under contract for twenty-five years! What a start for a young comic, two years touring with the Don Ross revues. He graduated to Variety and was 'discovered' one more time by RALPH READER. Ralph gave him a spot in his *Bid for Fame* TV show. This, in 1955, led to his being part of one of the first TV comedy teams along with JUNE WHITFIELD, BRUCE FORSYTH and BILLY DAINTY. Television changed his name to JOHNNY DALLAS.

He developed in an excellent all-round performer able to cope with everything. He did twenty-four consecutive summer seasons in Rhyl, and still appears there at least once every year. He became a Variety regular and played pantomime – 'the finest Buttons of his generation'. His first panto, in 1956,

Claude Dampier

The Professional Idiot

Comedian. Born Claude Connelly Cowan, Clapham, London, 1879. Claude, like DAN LENO, had a friend he talked about whom we never saw, Leno's was 'Mrs Kelly' and Claude's was 'Mrs Gibson'. It seemed a very funny name when spoken through his protruding teeth in that 'silly arse' voice.

He became a big star in Australia and South Africa (he spent seventeen years between the two countries) in the early years of the century and didn't really crack it here until he met BILLIE CARLYLE, (born Doris Davy, Australia, 1902) in

1925. They teamed up as a double act, on and off stage, and came to the UK in 1927. They played Variety, and Claude became a popular character actor in films. Channel Four sometimes shows them: if you spot one, do watch, for he was a very funny man and would have been as big a star today, with television a great medium for his wonderful face and real acting ability. Even though he was an excellent visual comic and Billie was a beautiful and perfect foil, it was radio that helped to establish Claude, Billie and 'Mrs Gibson' as national institutions.

In 1978 Billie wrote a smashing little book, *Claude Dampier Mrs Gibson and Me* about their happy life together. In it she reveals that 'Mrs Gibson' happened through Claude forgetting part of a routine and simply saying the first name that came into his head. He died in 1955.

Claude Dampier

Bebe Daniels and Ben Lyon

Actress/actor comedy team. Bebe born Texas, USA, 1901 and Ben born Atlanta, USA, 1901. Britain's favourite American husband and wife team endeared themselves to audiences here by sticking with us all through the Blitz. It was then that their hugely successful radio show, with VIC OLIVER, *Hi Gang!* was born. A later radio series, *Life with the Lyons*, featured not only Bebe and Ben but, also their children, Richard and Barbara. Bebe, who was a highly creative comedy writer, wrote this sitcom along with BOB BLOCK.

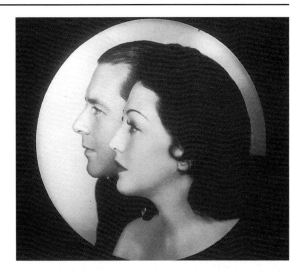

What a track record Bebe and Ben had. In Hollywood Bebe was a well-known film actress from the age of four. She played opposite RUDOLPH VALENTINO and HAROLD LLOYD and, fortuitously, Ben Lyon too. Ben himself became a film star when he played opposite JEAN HARLOW in *Hell's Angels* – the mention of this film was a running gag in their radio shows. He was later involved with film production and is credited with having discovered MARILYN MONROE.

They came to London in 1936 and remained here all their lives. As a team they played Variety and revue and Bebe starred in stage musicals, notably *Panama Hattie*, which she later filmed, likewise in England. Bebe died in 1971 and Ben in 1979.

Joe Daniels

And His Hot Shots

Drummer/bandleader. Born South Africa, 1909. Joe and his Hot Shots were among the longest surviving bands; they began in 1945 and were still at it, long after the demise of Variety, with seasons at holiday camps. Joe, the brother of Sirdani the magician, was part of HARRY ROY's Ragamuffins for seven years before he formed his own band. Their success in radio and with records – over a million sold – ensured their top of the bill status on the halls. Joe died in 1993.

Billy Danvers

Cheeky, cheery and chubby

Comedian. Born William Mikado Danvers, Liverpool. An old time music-hall comedian whose long career took him from the great days of music hall through to touring with veteran Variety shows in the 1960s. He not only scored in Variety, but was also a superlative Buttons in pantomime and a good comedy lead in musical comedy. In the Forties he began his final phase with DON ROSS's *Thanks for the Memory* and did a Royal Variety Performance with that show in 1948. His last week in Variety was at the Brixton Empress in March 1964. He died two weeks later.

The Dargie Quintette

Musical act. A very classy musical combination. Five violinists doing miniature-type MANTOVANI arrangements.

Albert Darnley

Comedian. Born Albert Dennis Darnley McCarthy, London, 1898. A prodigious talent, he was the son of a previous Albert Darnley of THE DARNLEY BROTHERS and EMILY DELEVANTI of DELEVANTI'S WIRE WALKERS. A principal comedian already at the age of eighteen, he did season after season in panto and claimed he had played every first class music hall in Great Britain.

Les Trios D'Artagnans

Adagio act. The Three d'Artagnans' act was inspired by the Dumas novel and featured 'a real live duel on-stage with genuine rapiers'. Philip says they were a most exciting and totally original turn with all sorts of filmic ideas included in their presentation. They were a huge success on the UK touring circuit.

Joe Davis

Snooker player. Born Whitewell, Derbyshire, 1901. One of the great joys of Variety was the inclusion of novelty acts and Joe Davis, the snooker champion, was certainly that. Years ahead of the fantastic popularity of snooker on the telly Joe appeared in Variety. He was the Stephen Hendry of his day, won every world championship from 1926 to 1940 (and in 1946) and achieved the first official maximum break in 1955.

As a speciality act he played the Palladium and all the number one halls in the country. A full-size snooker table would be levelled to compensate for the rake (the slope) of the stage and a huge mirror would be suspended at just the right angle above. This meant everyone in the audience could see the play and Joe's trick shots. He died in 1978.

Sonny Dawkes

Female impersonator. Born Richard Wilson Dawkes, Wolverhampton, 1921. Sonny was the feed, in drag, of the act DAWKES AND ROSE – Tommy Rose was the comic. Sonny took the well trodden path of most of the post-war female impersonators, beginning as a boy singer, then a light comedian in concert party and a juvenile lead in revue. During the war he played all over the world with RALPH READER's RAF *Gang Show*. On demob he joined, as leading 'lady', the famous touring show, *This Was the Army*. He and Tommy were natural Ugly Sisters and he played pantomime Dame till he retired. He now lives in Weston-super-Mare and is an enthusiastic and popular member of the Somerset and West Music Hall Society.

Jill Day

Singer. Born Yvonne Page in Brighton, 1930. A tiny, five-feet-two-inches singer and actress who became a Variety top liner in the mid Fifties.

Originally a singer with SID DEAN'S band in her home town, Brighton, she first hit the headlines when she sued another band leader for sexual harassment. He tweaked her bottom. She won the case and was awarded a farthing in damages.

Better still, the huge publicity she gained made her a household name. But, unlike so many she was household name who could deliver and, via TV, films and recording, she starred in the West End in plays and alongside JIMMY EDWARDS and TONY HANCOCK in revue. Blackpool and Yarmouth summer seasons followed and top billing at all the Moss Empire Variety halls. She always wanted everything right – something that is guaranteed to gain any performer a 'reputation' – and she certainly had one. Throughout the Sixties she stayed in demand in the clubs and on record but by the Seventies she had become a virtual recluse wrestling with a booze problem and ever-increasing weight. She died in 1990.

Jeanne De Casalis

Mrs Feather

Comedienne. Born South Africa, 1897. 'Mrs Feather' (a scatterbrained lady) was the character Jeanne invented for her one-way telephone calls that became a popular radio turn in the 1930s. As usual, audiences clamoured to see the faces behind the voices and she played 'Mrs Feather' in a Variety act. She was originally a pianist then a straight, and revue, actress before becoming a nationally known radio comedienne. She had first broadcast in 1931 with her husband COLIN CLIVE, an actor who, in 1932, was the first Dr Frankenstein, on film. She died in 1966.

The Marie De Vere Dancers

Along with the TILLER GIRLS, one of the most popular dance troupes in Variety. They had one very memorable spot, a cancan (the best outside Paris) under the name of THE BALLET MON-MARTRE.

Tommy Dee

Comedy magician. 'He was,' says Philip, 'a standard burlesque magic act. There were quite a few in the Variety days. Only TOMMY COOPER really made it. I remember Tommy Dee for his arriving at the theatre as the band started his 'play on' music. He would fly through the stage door and go straight on to the stage with his tray of goodies. He never, to my knowledge, ever missed an entrance but he did give many a stage manager a minor heart attack.'

The Deep River Boys

Vocal group. HARRY DOUGLASS, EDWARD WARE, VERNON GARDNER, GEORGE LAWSON and the musical director, CAMERON WILLIAMS. A five-handed black American singing group who made a big impact at the Palladium after the war, first appearing there in 1949 and subsequently playing all the number one halls as did most of he Palladium top liners. Originally, as students in America, they formed an amateur glee club and turned pro in

her unique voice on radio with a song called 'The Spinning Wheel' (adapted by herself, from an old Irish song):

'Merrily, cheerily, noisily, whirring,
Swings the wheel, spins the wheel, while the foot's stirring.'

She wrote another very popular song, the RONNIE RONALDE hit, 'If I Were a Blackbird.'

1936. They claimed to have a repertoire of more than 2000 songs, from spirituals to classics.

Dehaven and Page

Comedy double act. Billy De Haven and Dandy Page, born Odessa, Russia, 1896. A popular standard double act famous for being members of the original Crazy Gang in 1931, and the featured principals in the touring versions of the Gang's shows. I knew Dandy when he became a director of the theatrical agency and show production company, Reeves and Lamport. I did just one panto for him, and wish it had been more as he was an encyclopaedia of comedy gags and sketches. He was the first person I ever heard use the word, 'lardy' for a top of the bill performer: ('lardy dar' = star). Dandy died in 1981.

Delya

Singer. Delia Murphy. A multi-range Irish singer (from soprano to bass) who was a popular radio and Variety star. She played all the number one dates in the Forties and early Fifties. I remember

Desmond and Marks

Comedians. Frederick George Dawson born London, 1915 and John Henry Marks born Cardiff 1915. Fred trained to be a jockey, put on weight became a member of the famous LANCASHIRE LADS and had his own knockabout comedy act before the war. Jack (John) began dancing to strengthen a leg injured in a motor-cycle accident and got so good he eventually did it for a living. He danced with several bands, worked in ARCHIE PITT revues and also had a double Variety act JACK AND JILL.

Fred and Jack met in the RAF and, when it was all over, formed the act that was so well known here on the Continent and in Las Vegas. They were two burly blokes who did an old-fashioned music-hall routine packed with dangerous acrobatics and prat falls.

OH! WHAT A SURPRISE FOR THE DU-CE!

(HE CAN'T PUT IT OVER THE GREEKS)

English Lyrics by PHIL PARK
Music by NINO CASIROLI

CHAPPELL
PRINTED IN ENGLAND

RECORDED AND BROADCAST BY
FLORENCE DESMOND

1/- NET

Florence Desmond

A Hollywood Party

Impressioniste. Born London, 1905. Probably the most famous female impressionist we ever produced. Unlike today, when so many performers begin as impressionists and then develop into other things, Flo did it the other way round. After being a dancer, a Cochran young lady and a revue actress, in 1933 she hastily put together, for radio, a spot featuring her gift for mimicry. It was such a success that the very next day HMV recorded the act, which she called 'A Hollywood Party'. The record became the best selling one for that year. From then on her future was assured. She was a top of the bill turn till her retirement in 1954. On top of the act (which was featured for four weeks every year at the London Palladium) she played numerous parts in films, including a co-starring role with Max Miller in *Hoots Mon*, the only film in which he did his stage act.

She married twice. Her first husband was the aviator CAMPBELL BLACK who died in an aircraft accident and her second, another flier, CHARLES HUGHESDON. She came out of retirement in 1958 to co-star with BEATRICE LILLIE in *Auntie Mame* at the Adelphi Theatre. She died in 1993.

Jerry Desmonde

Actor. Born James Robert Sadler, Middlesbrough, 1908. The Straight Man Supreme. Straight man, foil, comics' labourer, stooge, feed – the one who makes the comedian funnier. Jerry is still remembered as the best of them all. To be a good straight man it is essential to have had experience of as many facets of the business as is possible. He certainly did. He began in his family's act, THE SADLER ELSIE FOUR, in the 1930s, was in the chorus of *This Year of Grace*, playing in the show all over America, and came back to the UK to join his brother in a dancing act. He did a double act with his wife, PEGGY AND JERRY DESMONDE. He joined SID FIELD for the Prince of Wales revues which catapulted Sid to stardom; their great sketches included 'Golf' and 'The Photographer'. Happily they are both on film, together with Jerry's encounters with 'Slasher Green'. (The film *London Town* was a real 'turkey' but it's worth seeing for these classic items.) He stayed with Sid until the latter did *Harvey* in 1948, then joined NAT JACKLEY as his straight man and, eventually, NORMAN WISDOM. I saw them together at the London Palladium and still cherish their partnership. Soon the world appreciated Jerry as the arch-enemy of Norman's 'Gump' character in films.

Sadly, Jerry's urbane, pompous, know-all, type of feed went out of favour. He tried other things. I remember him, on-stage, playing a heart-throb music-hall star in the WOLF MANKOWITZ/MONTY NORMAN musical of the Crippen case, *Belle*: a show destroyed by the press that well deserves a revival. Poor Jerry then fell on hard times and became a mini-cab driver. He died in 1967.

Gene Detroy and Marquis the Chimp

Animal trainer. Born Samuel Wood, Stockport, 1909. Best known for one of the most famous chimpanzee acts in the world. He introduced Marquis in 1947. Not only was he a brilliant animal trainer, he was a first-class wire walker too and presented lots of different acts including THE DETROY BROTHERS and JEAN. But Marquis was his ace in the hole and, in addition to his work in the UK, he played long seasons in Australia and Las

Vegas. When he and Marquis were scoring a huge success at London's Prince of Wales, a stage-hand said to him, about the chimp: 'He's clever but not as good as the ones in the Brooke Bond commercial. Why don't you teach him to talk?' Gene died in 1986.

Deveen and His New York Blondes

The Distinguished Deceiver

Magician. Born David Deveen, London, 1900. He tells us, after his first attempt at magic, that as a small boy he stepped off a boat and tried to walk on the sea at Eastbourne (only one person has ever done it successfully). He became a professional just after the First World War, and in the 1930s devised his silent magic act, assisted by six beautiful blonde girl assistants – I bet his toast always landed butter side up too! He was awarded the North Africa Star for his work during the Second World War and continued into our period with tours both here, on the Continent and to all corners of the globe.

Ernie Dillon

Trampolinist. Born New York, 1900. His mother and father's act THE BOUNCING DILLONS is the one I remember. That act carried on well into our period. Ernie started with the family but, as a solo turn, played in the UK and, regularly, in America.

Phyllis Dixey

The Girl the Lord Chamberlain Banned

Actress. Born Selina, Newport, Wales, 1914. 'Actress' is how Phyllis described herself in a trade directory in 1950 but we all knew her as the Queen of Striptease. Now Philip tells me: 'She wasn't a stripper in the true sense of the word. Her girls did the stripping while she did the talking and gave the audience the occasional "flash".' So there. I, alas, never saw the 'Peek-a-Boo Girl'. She was thought far too racy for even my jolly Gran to take me to. She certainly was the name old soldiers think of with lusting joy. She started as a ballet dancer and was producing her own shows and troupes of girls when she was seventeen. She was ERNIE LOTINGA's leading lady in straight plays and revue. She met and married JACK 'SNUFFY' TRACEY, touring in Variety with him as half of the act billed as 'The Sap and the Swell Dame'. In 1940 she took on the lease of the Whitehall Theatre in London and presented her own revue 'Peek-a-Boo'. In this show she presented her act based on GYPSY ROSE LEE. Throughout the war years the Whitehall became almost as famous

as the Windmill for this 'naughty' extravaganza. Again Philip remembers: 'She was a most ladylike lady who promised a sexual thrill that never really materialised.' Under Tracey's managership she headlined both here and on the Continent until the increasing tattiness of the nude shows forced her to quit. Bankruptcy hit the Traceys and 'The One and Only Phyllis Dixey' (the title of a 1978 two-hour Thames TV biopic of her life, which captured the flavour of our period beautifully) ended her days as a cook. She died in 1964.

Reg Dixon

Confidentially

Comedian. Born Coventry, 1915. At fifteen Reg ran away from home to join the circus: 'Alas,' he said, 'I never got into the ring but I did learn how to clean stables.' He eventually toured in revue as half of a double piano act SCOTT AND DIXON and ran his own 'fit up' show all over Scotland. After his wartime RAF service he got into radio and never looked back. He was an excellent comic whose gentle, daft, almost whispered confidences were a breath of fresh air. In a way he was a throwback to the lugubrious styles of ALFRED LESTER, JACK PLEASANTS and GEORGE FORMBY senior. During our period only he, KEN PLATT and GEORGE WILLIAMS were left of that school of comedy.

His perfect signature tune, which he wrote himself, was 'Confidentially' and his catchphrase was 'I've been proper poorly'. During the Forties and Fifties he was a constant in radio Variety and on the halls. He was a big dopey bloke who wore a little trilby and, boy, could he work an audience. He took over from GEORGE FORMBY junior at The Palace Shaftesbury Avenue in *Zip Goes Million* and handled the musical beautifully. He was a superb pantomime Dame too. When his star ceased to shine quiet as brightly he could still pack 'em in and it was only ill health, not lack of popularity, that caused him to retire. He died in 1984.

Reginald Dixon

I do like to be beside the seaside

Organist. Born Sheffield, 1906. In our period the strains of that famous music-hall song meant just one thing – Reginald Dixon was 'on the air'. I should think his was the longest residency of any musician. He was the organist at the Tower Ballroom, Blackpool, with minor wartime interruptions, from 1930 until he retired. Between summer seasons he would tour in Variety with a specially built portable instrument but as soon as the deckchairs were pulled out from under the pier he would be back in Lancashire. Generations of holiday-makers danced to his playing in that extraordinary Tower Ballroom and millions more, through his countless broadcasts, *imagined* they did. He died in 1985.

Ken Dodd

Comedian. Born Knotty Ash, Liverpool, 1929. In my book the greatest stand-up comic since MAX MILLER. Ken's machine-gun technique is totally different to the Max Miller I saw, yet there are similarities – notably the outrageous suits and sprinkling of sentimental ballads. Ken, like EDDIE IZZARD, is one of the few modern performers to achieve fame without the hype of television. His notoriety for giving the customers value for money, regularly overrunning his allotted time on stage, is legendary. I remember the famous theatre director, DICKIE HURRAN, being asked by a stage manager: 'We've got Ken Dodd next week. Can I have some time sheets?' (to note down the running order of the show and the time allocated to each act). The laid-back Hurran answered, 'You won't need a time sheet – a diary!'

Dog Acts

The many performing dog acts, mostly from circus, were ideal for Variety bills. Unlike some of the more spectacular animal acts, dogs did as they were told, were easy to accommodate in dressing rooms and didn't need much space to work in. Whatever your views on the subject of performing animals, I have to say I've never seen a dog act where their tails weren't wagging *all* the time. Here are just a few names you may remember: CAWALINI AND HIS CANINE PETS, ANNA AND HER PALS, MAURICE CHESTER'S PERFORMING POODLES, MADAM KITTY'S POODLE REVUE, MME TRUZZI AND HER DOGS, BETTY KAYE, IDA ROSAIRE AND HER POODLES and DARCY'S DOGS.

Dolinoffs and Raya Sisters

Dance Act. The two principals were Daniel Dolinoff and, his wife Raya, both refugees from Russia. Dancers, but dancers with a difference. Philip says: 'They were a sensational "black light" act. (Where ultra violet lighting is used to show only certain items on the stage). They played all over the world and the UK, whenever they wished.' They settled in America in the early Fifties. Daniel and Raya both died in 1966.

Lonnie Donegan

Singer. Born Anthony Donegan, Glasgow, 1931. Lonnie was the banjo player with the CHRIS BARBER traditional jazz band in the 1950s. A recording, with the band and Lonnie singing, of an old American song, 'The Rock Island Line', shot to the top of the hit parade and he later became a solo star. It was the birth of skiffle in the UK. I was a lad at the time and soon we were all learning the three essential guitar chords , playing a tea chest bass or pinching our mum's washboards and thimbles to supply rhythm. It was great time for making music and Lonnie led the pack with a string of chart hits, deservedly becoming a Variety top of the bill. I am a great fan of him and his attacking, punchy type of popular jazz. Via pantomime, concerts and musicals he continues to captivate audiences all over the world.

George Doonan

The life and soul of the party

Comedian. Born Sunderland, 1897. Although George was a Brother Water Rat (Indeed King Rat in 1944) I never met him, but Philip knew him well and tells me he was one of the first comedians to work in a smart lounge suit, as opposed to the funny 'over the top' music hall-type outfit. But I do remember him on the radio. He used to say, to himself: 'I don't much care for that very much, old man. You deserve a kick in the pants. Take that!' To a drum effect he would then kick *himself* in the pants. I wish I'd seen him 'live'! He came from a theatrical family and was at it from the age of eleven, initially with *Casey's Court* (the touring revue that nurtured the talents of CHARLIE CHAPLIN, JIMMY JAMES and lots of others). His signature tune was 'Make It a Party, Gay and Hearty' and, certainly on radio, he did create a very easy, jolly atmosphere. He died in 1973.

Val Doonican

Singer. Born Michael Valentine Doonican, Waterford, Eire, 1928. Our favourite Irish singer/guitarist. He began in Variety as part of the vocal act THE FOUR RAMBLERS. His folksy,

Val Doonican (right) *with the Ramblers*

relaxed approach to an audience in the theatre and, particularly, on television has endeared him to the British public. He still packs every venue, whenever he feels like working! Val has written a fascinating autobiography, *The Special Years*.

Jack Douglas

Alf Ippititimus

Actor/Comedian. Born 1927. Son of a famous theatrical producer, WILLIAM ROBERTON, he is a steeped-in-the-business memory man of gags and sketches, a 'comic's labourer' (straight man) with a difference. He gets laughs too. His double act with JOE BAKER, JNR BAKER AND DOUGLAS is well remembered. When Joe (the son of the husband and wife double patter act JOE BAKER AND OLGA) left for America Jack became straight man for DES O'CONNOR. The twitching, malaproping character 'Alf' based on a bandleader he and Joe met at Butlin's, became a national institution. He continues to be much in demand in TV, panto-mime and films.

Cyril Dowler

Comedian. Born Liverpool 1906. Another graduate of concert party, Cyril started in 1927. In 1932 he teamed up with KAY WHITE (later the wife of SANDY POWELL) and they worked the halls with a double act, DOWLER AND WHITE. They toured successfully and were together in panto (Kay as

Principal Boy and Cyril as Dame). They worked together all through the war presenting a series of successful revues. Peace saw the dissolving of the partnership and he carried on as a comic and show presenter. He met and married RHODA ROGERS and they too presented a double act and their own touring revues. Cyril died in 1986.

Bunny Doyle

The Minister for Idiotic Affairs

Comedian. Born Bernard Doyle, Hull 1898. A great favourite up north, particularly in his home town of Hull, where he played many times. He was yet another whose early days in the seaside concert party (he was a pierrot at twelve) stood him in good stead. When he graduated to the number one halls in revue, Variety and pantomime (FRANCIS LAIDLER, the doyen of northern panto producers called him 'one of the finest pantomime comedians ever to tread the boards') he was fully equipped for them all.

During the First World War Bunny won the Croix de Guerre for 'Conspicuous Gallantry'. Any performer who kept returning to Hull deserved it. He played with ENSA, made films and, in the Fifties, became a character actor. Sadly, as his work in this field was about to take off, in 1955, he died. Bunny is just one of fifty odd comics, well known and not so, written about with great affection and knowledge, by GEOFF MELLOR in a smashing book called *They Made Us Laugh*.

Charlie Drake

Hello my darlings!

Comedian. A, tiny droll comedian with a high-pitched voice, great tumbling ability and an off-beat approach. He achieved popularity through television. Originally half of MICK and MONTMORENCY (Charlie and JACK EDWARDS), a slapstick act that became famous through children's television. Charlie headed several series of his own, did pantomime and films and soon became a big draw in the theatre too. Of late he played in JIM DAVIDSON's 'blue' pantomime, *Sinderella*. I've always thought he is a highly underrated, genuine original.

Betty Driver

Comedienne. Born in Leicester 1920. Once again one of our most famous television faces had her roots in variety, She began in amateur shows at the age of four. Her mother, who Betty says was even more ambitious for her than she was for herself, took her to London and did the rounds of the agents and producers. In desperation, having achieved nothing through the usual channels they called at the stage door of the Prince of Wales theatre. There, the management, ARCHIE PITT and his brother BERT AZA, were so impressed by the eagerness of Mum and the confidence of

Betty that they introduced her to the audience and let her sing a couple of songs. She did and paralysed 'em.

Archie and Bert immediately booked Betty for their touring revue, *Mr Tower of London*. The tour established her and she graduated, in the Fifties, to top billing in Variety, numerous broadcasts, records, films, and her own TV series.

She married the entertainer WALLY PETERSON in 1952 and together they topped in Variety both here and abroad. The marriage ended in divorce and Betty returned from their South African home to take up her career again here, making her mark in plays and sitcoms. In 1968 came, what would have been to lesser pros, a disaster. An unsuccessful operation for nodules on the vocal cords meant she couldn't sing any more. The very next year she joined the cast of *Coronation Street* and the rest is history.

Benson Dulay and Company

Comedy illusionist. Born William Dooley, Northampton 1899. As Billy Dooley he was a comedy conjuror from 1919 until he joined a Tommy Trinder revue, *Why go to Paris?* Tommy said he didn't sound French enough and from then on he was Benson Dulay. Like so magicians who invent tricks, he was a first-class cabinet maker and manufactured magical items all through his career and long after Variety died. His last appearance in Variety was at the Palladium with GYPSY ROSE LEE. J.O. Blake, of the British Music Hall Society, remembered his comment on that bill: 'You'll know my act. I'm the one with the clothes on.' His son was the comedian PETER DULAY (who was one of the practical jokers in *Candid Camera*). Benson died in 1991.

Frances Duncan

Aerialist/acrobat. Born Australia 1927. A highly experienced circus performer in Australia (where she worked as LA FRANKIE), she came here in 1949 and did a trial turn for LEW and LESLIE GRADE. She scored heavily and from that week on was a featured act at all the number one halls and in top circuses.

Ted and George Durante

Direct from the 'Bal Tabre' Paris

Comedy acrobats. Ted Durante, actually Ted Aston, was the son of a pro. His dad was 'The World's Strongest Man', ASTON, who did an act with Ted's mother too, as ASTON AND ZENA. Their son developed his comic talents during the Second World War doing a tramp clown solo act. In 1946, he was one of an acrobatic troupe whose routines were livened up by the comedy bits he and GEORGE MOONEY put into the act. George and he became a double act, TED AND GEORGE DURANTE, an act that was silent because, as Ted says, 'All the best acrobats were supposed to be French.' The sound of Ted's fruity London accent would have killed the act stone dead.

They worked together well into the Fifties till Ted and his wife, whom he met while they were both in panto at the Camberwell Palace, became TED AND HILDA. Their daughter is the singer JAY ASTON. TED AND HILDA present one of the best, and funniest, burlesque acrobatic acts I've ever seen. I remember a panto we did together in which Hilda, who incidentally doubled as the Fairy Godmother, had a fall on stage and had to visit the doctor. I'd loved to have seen the look on his face when, in answer to the question, 'How did it happen?' she replied, 'I fell off my husband's head.'

Hilda and Ted Durante

Renee Dymott

Acrobatic dancer. Born Clapham, London, 1922. How lucky Renee was to be born into an old-established show biz family who taught her all they knew (she first appeared on stage at three). Renee described herself as 'an acrobatic, contortionistic toe, tap and ballet dancer'. In effect she could do the lot and Philip remembers: 'She was a versatile lady with a strong single act that played summer seasons and panto everywhere.'

___E___

Earle and Vaughan

Comedy duo. Kenneth Earle born Liverpool, 1930 and Malcolm Thomas, born Merthyr Tydfil, 1929. In my book a double act who should really have been big stars. They had the lot: a highly experienced, witty, inventive comic in Kenny and an excellent straight man and superb tenor in Mal.

Kenny is the son of a well-known Variety act, PERCY RICH AND EVA. He was practically born in a trunk and on the road with his mum and dad from the age of three. He began as an actor and played small parts in films till National Service with the RAF. On demob he resumed his acting career and in his own words, 'starved!'

He went into variety in the OLD MOTHER RILEY road show as half of the act MACEY AND MACEY. In this show he met miner's son Malcolm who was part of an act called THE STREET SINGERS. They decided to get together and Earle and Vaughan were born. Their first act was written by two school chums of Kenny's, BOB MONKHOUSE and DENNIS GOODWIN. They opened at Hull - and died - didn't we all! They rejigged the act until it worked. While playing the Chelsea Palace, the top of the bill, JACK JACKSON, arranged for a man from EMI to come and hear Malcolm's singing. It was the start of a recording career that led to ten Top Twenty hits. They stuck together as an act and Malcolm's popularity led to the lads taking out their own bills to all the number one dates, a London Palladium season, a Royal Variety Performance, TV specials and tours of Australia.

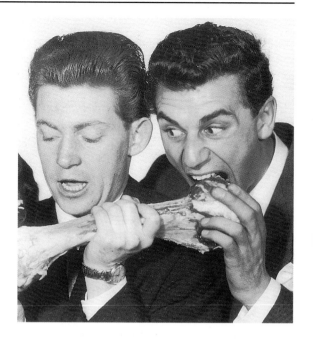

Rock and Roll, of course, bought an untimely end to the age of the real singer and, at the same time, Variety was squealing to a halt. The lads battled on but eventually, after seventeen years together, they decided to go their separate ways. Kenny was getting parts in films and Malcolm had had enough of being constantly on the road. In 1972 Kenny, with all his know-how of light entertainment, became, and still is, an agent. Malcolm retired a few years later. A CD of Malcolm's many hits has just been released by Magpie Direct Music Ltd.

Jimmy Edwards

Professor Jimmy Edwards

Comedian. Born James Keith O'Neill Edwards, Barnes, London, 1920. A big bluff, supposedly irascible, hugely moustached comedian who, with his radio catchphrases, 'Wake up at the back of there!', 'Clumsy clot!' and 'Black mark Bentley', and his inventing of 'Pa' in the sketches about 'The Glums' made him a national institution.

A university graduate, it was during the Second World War (where he won the DFC) that Jim first began to think of entertaining for a living. His professional début was at the Windmill Theatre in 1946, a baptism of fire. Billed as 'Professor Jimmy Edwards', with a mixture of university lecture,

RAF slang, the playing of various loud wind instruments and old-fashioned attack, he more than held his own in the comic's graveyard.

It was FRANK MUIR and DENIS NORDEN's *Take it From Here*, on radio that did the trick for Jim. He was teamed with the Australians DICK BENTLEY and JOY NICHOLS for the first series in 1948. Dick and Jim remained with the show throughout its run (it finished in 1959) and, after Joy returned to Australia, the ladies' parts were taken by JUNE WHITFIELD and ALMA COGAN. Jim led the West End revue and the spin-off Variety tours. He was the powerful driving force of the team and, with Dick semi-retired, he went from strength to strength, headlining everywhere in his own right. He had successful TV series, *Whacko!* and *The Seven Faces of Jim*, and one very unexpected hit. He and ERIC SYKES, faced inside out, ad-libbed, worked in their acts and transformed every performance into an adventure for them and the audience, It was called *Big Bad Mouse* and they did umpteen seasons in the West End and innumerable tours both here and all over the world – to the great joy of all concerned, especially the management.

Jim devised, and starred in, a long-running radio show, *Does the Team Think?* – a sort of Brains Trust for comics. With a team that included those other masters of the ad-lib, TED RAY and TOMMY TRINDER, every episode was a joyous mix of old gags, brilliant flashes of wit and lateral thinking.

I had the great pleasure of working with Jim for six months in *Oliver!* Against his image he was a most caring, gentle, old-fashioned gentleman and the best Mr Bumble the Beadle I ever saw. He died in 1988.

Percy Edwards

Animal and bird impersonator. Born Ipswich, 1908. 'I Travel the Road' was his signature tune. Percy was probably the most famous animal impersonator of all time. His uncanny 'voices' of birds (he could do, he said, 150 different ones) and animals led him to a highly successful career in Variety, radio and even on the soundtrack of films. He was made a Fellow of the Royal Zoological Society and honoured by ornithologists all over the world. His memorable role as Psyche the dog in radio's *Life of Bliss* demonstrated how useful it was to have an actor who could express canine emotions to order.

In Variety he introduced his sounds in an inimitable Suffolk burr which made his gentle observer of the natural world image seem totally authentic. Almost his last stage appearance was in the Grand Order of Water Rats 100th Anniversary show at the London Palladium in 1989. He died in 1996.

Ray Ellington

Ray Ellington (second right) *with his Quartet*

Musician. Born London 1916. Radio fans will remember Ray for his terrific musical interludes and deep-voiced characterisations in *The Goon Show*, but his adventures, before his quartet's involvement with Spike, Harry and Peter, deserve a book of their own.

He had a black American father and a Russian mother (the Goons would have loved that) and was originally trained as a cabinet maker. Alas, he spent most of his apprenticeship making the drumsticks that would lead him to his proper job. He played all the legendary Thirties nightclubs: The Bag of Nails, The Nest, and The Shim Sham, where he 'jammed' with names like COLEMAN HAWKINS, BENNY CARTER and FATS WALLER. He was the drummer/vocalist with HARRY ROY and, after the war (where he was a PT instructor) he freelanced with the great STEPHAN GRAPPELLI.

He formed his quartet, via radio broadcasts with TITO BURNS, for the express purpose of taking new and progressive jazz to the uninitiated. Their popularity on Variety bills proved they did. Their vocalist for five years was MARION RYAN. Ray died in 1985.

Chic Elliott

Comedienne. Born Violet Wooll, Sydney, Australia, 1900. An Australian comedienne who blacked up. I wonder if that's where the 'Elliott' bit of the name came from (see G.H. ELLIOTT). She first appeared, at the age of four, in her mother's act, graduated to Principal Boy, then dame, and finally in Australia, a black-faced act in vaudeville. She came to the UK in 1930 and played Variety both as a 'coon' singer and as herself – but in evening dress. She certainly was versatile having played in farce, drama, musical comedy and films. She entered our period in the operetta, *Merrie England*. She was featured in the ARTHUR ASKEY vehicle, *The Kid from Stratford* and, in the early Fifties, returned to her Variety roots.

G.H. Elliott

The Original Chocolate Coloured Coon

Singer/dancer. Born George Henry Elliott, Rochdale, 1884. The best known, because of his long, long career, of all the music-hall survivors. Surprisingly he was a Lancashire lad, but he, and his family, went to America when he was four. There he played juvenile parts in melodrama including the title role in *Little Lord Fauntleroy*. His adventures in the American 'legit' deserve a book to themselves. It was as a member of the PRIMROSE WEST MINSTRELS, at the age of nine, where he first blacked up.

The family returned to England in 1901 and from then on it was the familiar story of hard graft until George became a top of the bill. When exactly he started to use the chocolate colour make-up, as opposed to the black that everyone else sported, I don't know but it did make him that bit individual. Of course the number one 'Negro delineator' was EUGENE STRATTON but Elliott took over his mantle and, apart from his own songs (the most famous was 'I Used to Sigh for the Silvery Moon) he did feature Stratton's songs, particularly 'Lily of Laguna'. Being an old-fashioned 'toff', he always prefaced the Stratton songs by telling his audience that this was a

G.H. Elliott's marriage to June

tribute to the original singer. He did this even when no one in the audience knew who he was talking about.

I stood in the wings at the Finsbury Park Empire with MAX MILLER in the late Fifties where both of us enjoyed the, by then, extremely carefully executed soft-shoe dancing and unique half-yodelled singing of the great G.H. As with all class performers it didn't matter that he couldn't get some of the notes or that his movements were a bit laboured. The magic remained undimmed. He told the stories in the songs with total sincerity and the audience loved him. Off stage he was a sweet man who was always ready to sit you down and chat about the great days. I think it was the stories he told and the snatches of long forgotten songs he sang to me, that first turned me on to music hall.

He was married twice, first to EMILY HAYES, who died in 1940, and then to FLORENCE MAY STREET, whom we all knew as June. She had been an acrobat in acts as various as the MARTINEZ TROUPE/DUO and SERENO (HARRY SERENO) AND JUNE. When Florence (June) retired the act became SERENO AND JOY. George, along with GERTIE GITANA, was the main draw in the legendary *Thanks for the Memory* revue. The amazing success of this DON ROSS veteran's show led to George's second Royal Variety Performance (1948), his first having been in 1925.

When *Thanks for the Memory* finished G.H. embarked on his 'Farewell Tour'. This tour became a running gag in show business as it went so well it was only the first of many. He made over a hundred records (his first, on wax cylinder, in

1904 and his last in 1960). He lived through the golden days of the music hall and the best years of Variety, and died in 1962.

Peter Elliott

Dancer/straight man. Born Chatham, Kent, 1935. Peter is now The Executive Administrator of the Entertainment Artistes Benevolent Fund.* I've never worked out what an 'Executive Administrator' is but in Peter's case it means he runs the fund, is the link man between the governing body and the grass root beneficiaries. He was a performer for more than thirty years and so understands all the vagaries of a pro's life.

He began, as a hoofer, in the early Fifties, as half of a double act, THE ELLIOTTS. The other half was his wife, BILLY ANTHONY, who later became a well-known pop singer. As THE ELLIOTTS they played variety everywhere and, in 1952, did a long summer season in Leven in Scotland. Talk about learning the game the hard way. In Leven the show was changed twice, every week. Peter says: 'We arrived there with two spots and left with a hundred and forty-four!'

In 1958 Peter toured Italy as a single dancing act and, the following year, returned home to become the juvenile lead at the Windmill Theatre. It could only happen to Peter! There he met the comedian JIMMY EDMUNDSON and the highly successful double act EDMUNDSON AND ELLIOTT was formed.

Jimmy and Peter worked Variety, summer season, pantos and, as resident comedians on TV with BILLY COTTON and ROLF HARRIS. Jimmy packed it in in 1967 and Peter joined DICK EMERY as his straight man on stage, in cabaret and on television. In 1973 the poacher turned gamekeeper. He went into management via THE GRADE ORGANISATION.

He was one of our top pantomime producers till 1989 when he joined the EABF. They are lucky, and so are the pros, to have a man in charge who has done the lot.

*See Brinsworth House.

Emerson and Jayne

Magic speciality. Jack Emerson Skinner and his

wife Joy. They were one of our leading speciality acts, their most famous routine being 'The Flying Carpet'. This made a sensational effect and was in great demand, every Christmas, for *Aladdin*. The secret was kept until Jack died in 1995.

Dick Emery

Comedian. Born in London, 1930. Another dyed-in-the-wool pro from a show biz family. Indeed Dick was born while his dad was on stage at the Palladium. He originally trained as a singer and, after a beginning in good old concert parties, he joined the RAF and worked for one of the great nurturers of talent RALPH READER in his RAF *Gang Shows*.

After the Second World War, Dick was one of the performers, directly out of the services, who changed the whole face of Variety. Like so many of the new wave it was radio that gave him his big break. *Variety Bandbox* and memorable voice work in *Educating Archie* led to television and as one of the team in MICHAEL BENTINE's *It's a Square World*.

In 1963, he won his own TV series and *The Dick Emery Show*. With its collection of Dick's carefully crafted, monstrous characters, it became one of the BBC's top comedy shows. Dick, like so many great comedians, was a complicated man. He could be 'very difficult' – so the bosses used to say. He wasn't difficult, he just wanted everything perfect and he was right. I cherish a letter from him about a pantomime he had seen me in. It is a

masterpiece of constructive and helpful analysis. He died in 1993.

Arthur English

The Prince of the wide boys.

Comedian/actor. Born in Aldershot, 1919. A house painter who started his career as a comedian, at the age of thirty, at the legendary Windmill Theatre. He auditioned in the morning and was in the show the same afternoon! He appeared regularly on radio and his catchphrase, 'Open the cage!' became part of the language. As the archetype 'spiv' with padded shoulders and enormous 'kipper' ties, he was very popular in Variety, often playing in spin-offs of the CRAZY GANG revues with his idol, 'MONSEWER' EDDIE GRAY. Arthur's career took a completely different turn when Variety died. He became an excellent, and much in demand, character actor, enjoying great success on television in series such as *Are You Being Served?* and *In Sickness and In Health*. He died in 1995.

Eno and Lane

Comedy double act. Eno born Leon Enot, Guernsey, and Lane born George Max Korelin, Kingston, Surrey. An act I'd never heard of but Philip says: 'Eno was very like the character the cartoonist, Strube, drew to represent England (the little man with the tiny bowler and straggly

moustache).* The act was destined for great things but it never matured. If TV had arrived earlier they would have been a real tour de force, but failing theatre dates predetermined their leaving the profession. A great pity.'

*See GRACIE FIELDS illustration.

La Esterella

Singer. Born Esther Mathilda Lambrechts, Antwerp, 1916. Here's an act I wish I'd seen, or at least heard. She was an amazingly multi-voiced singer with a range from soprano to bass baritone. She came to Britain, to the London Casino (now the Prince Edward Theatre) in 1948. After her stint there she toured, successfully, all over the UK and the Continent.

Norman Evans

Over the garden wall

Comedian. Born Rochdale, Lancs, 1901. *The Performer* (the Variety artistes' weekly newspaper) reported, in 1934. 'GRACIE FIELDS has made what she considers is a great find. He is a man who is working all day as a salesman but amateur theatricals are his great hobby. A friend sent him to see Gracie and she insisted he did an audition for her in her dressing room. Gracie was so enthralled by his talent that on the Friday night of the following week she put him on her bill at the Chiswick Empire as she knew Sir Oswald Stoll paid his weekly visit to that hall on Friday evenings. He made such a big success that Stoll booked him into the Alhambra two weeks later. He was also booked for the forthcoming Chiswick Empire pantomime and ARCHIE PITT put him under contract for the 1935 tour of *Mr Tower of London*.

Gracie, a fellow Rochdalian, had actually seen Norman on-stage before this so he didn't have to audition for her but the rest is true. The tour of Archie Pitt's show, where he shared top billing with BETTY DRIVER, was his making. Within two years he was known throughout the country and had done the first of three Royal Variety Performances.

The memory of Norman's famous 'Over the Garden Wall' sketch is still cherished by all of us who had the joy of seeing it: the toothless, red-wigged, mob-capped Lancashire harridan, 'Fanny Fairbottom', resting her huge bosom on the top of the garden wall while she confides the street's gossip to her invisible neighbour. Her one-sided discussion embraced everything from her odorous tom cat – 'Oh it does whiff – I could smell it in the custard last Sunday' – to the amorous coalman: 'Don't tell me it takes thirty-five minutes to deliver two bags of nuts!' The classic reaction to the bashing of her bosom on the wall as she slipped 'That's the third time on the same brick!' was the line we all waited for. Happily this routine is preserved on video but, of course, you had to be there to really relish every beautifully observed, rich homily. Although this is the spot that everyone remembers he had lots of other equally effective routines. His brilliant MARCEL MARCEAU-type dentist's sketch, his routine with the panda glove puppet – a forerunner of Sooty – and the double act with BETTY JUMEL (Norman as a huge soprano and Betty as a tiny tenor).

He achieved everything a great comedian desires, top billing in Variety and revue, record breaking seasons in Blackpool, pantomime Dame at the Palladium and every number one theatre, huge success in America and, above all, the genuine love of the public and his fellow pros. He died in 1962.

___F___

Al and Vic Farrell

Gymnasts. Victor Farrell born Hertfordshire, 1915. Vic and his brother Al were comedy trampolinists. The medal winning gymnasts we now see on television and in the Olympics doubtless go far beyond the acts that played the halls but in our period, we haven't seen these rather scary machine-like child prodigies. The trampoline was a simple piece of equipment that could easily be accommodated on the sloping stages of the Variety theatres. Acts like those of Al and Vic were good, early-on-in-the-bill, ice-breakers. After a pre-war apprenticeship on the

Continent, Vic became, first with his sister, DOREEN AND VICTOR and, for most of our period, AL AND VIC FARRELL.

Tony Fayne and David Evans

Impressionists. Both born in Bristol. Tony was originally Anthony Senington. Theirs was a great idea – a way of presenting impressions differently. 'Imagine two radios side by side,' was the premise. Then, in perfect sync, they would comment, à la John Arlott, on imaginary sporting events, ending with an impression of a singing double act, FLANAGAN AND ALLEN, BOB AND ALF PEARSON, etc.

They came into Variety in 1949 on the back of their success in radio. When the two voices as one gimmick no longer proved effective, they split up. David died, in poor circumstances, in 1980, but Tony stayed in the game and became an excellent straight man and feed – a job he does to this day with NORMAN WISDOM.

Felovis

Juggler. Born George Felovis in Switzerland. Jugglers seem to come in two types: those who come from a circus background, whose talent is inherited, and those whose journey to technical excellence is totally unexpected. George's beginnings couldn't have been less show biz. He studied, and indeed won prizes for, architecture and geometry in Geneva. How, from that background, he became one of Europe's greatest jugglers we can only imagine. He was a constantly working act, specialising in the juggling of musical instruments, both in the UK and worldwide. He married an English girl, and made his home in Cheshire.

Lester Ferguson

The sunshine of your smile

Singer. Born Pennsylvania USA, 1917. A very popular tenor who won new audiences for opera and operetta with stints in Variety, radio shows and concerts. Following a distinguished wartime career, Canadian Lester, sponsored by SIR THOMAS BEECHAM, obtained a work permit and, in this country, never looked back. He toured with opera and musicals and, after a five-year run with *Your Song Parade* on radio became a favourite in Variety and summer season. Regular appearances in *Friday Night is Music Night* further enhanced his drawing power. Sadly, from the mid Sixties on, he suffered from cancer and this stopped him doing too much. He died in 1995.

Frederick Ferrari

Tenor. Born Manchester, 1912. Radio brought Fred to public acclaim. As he did with so many, it was CHARLIE CHESTER who 'discovered' him and made him part of the *Stand Easy* team. Fred, however, was no raw talent. He had studied singing for five years before joining up and then spent most of his time giving shows for the troops, factory workers, etc. He claimed to have given over 2500 performances during the war years. Fred was with Charlie and the Gang in Variety and, in 1948, the Royal Variety Performance. His many Parlophone recordings show what a true tenor voice he had. When the gang broke up he continued as a single act. He died in 1994.

Sid Field

What a performance!

Comedian. Born Sidney Arthur Field, on April

Fools' Day, Birmingham, 1904. Truly the comedian's comedian. A man whose name still draws gasps of awe from anyone who had the pleasure of seeing him 'live.'

It was in 1943 that Sid cracked it. He became a West End star 'overnight' – after years of comicking all over the UK in number two revues. His story is a real rags to riches, show biz, fairy tale. He began in juvenile troupes and even understudied 'WEE' GEORGIE WOOD. He progressed to straight man, his own act being a song and dance offering. One night the comic was the worse the wear for booze and Sid played his part in a sketch that explained golf to a beginner. Years later this sketch was to become, in his and JERRY DESMONDE's hands, a classic. Sid and Jerry were 'discovered' together in 1942.

It is my great regret that I never saw the man who is always reckoned to be a comic genius. Apparently, once he hit the big time, in his revues at the Prince of Wales, he never did a solo routine. All his appearances were as the characters he created. The spiv 'Slasher Green', the camp photographer, the cinema organist, the incompetent instrumentalist, the quick change artiste and the would-be snooker player.

It is impossible to tell you exactly what he did

even harder to tell you how, or why (although John Fisher does a great job in his definitive book on comedians, *A Funny Way to Be a Hero*). One of the duff films Sid did, *London Town*, still exists and thank goodness it does. Although the plot is daft and the dance routines frightening, it has six of Sid's best sketches intact. Of course they suffer from the lack of an audience but the timing, the characterisations and the sheer inspired baby-like behaviour is all still there.

My pal JACK TRIPP understudied Sid at the Prince of Wales. A great choice as Jack, too, is a master situation comedian. Probably the nearest I'll get to Sid is watching Jack demonstrate his gestures, his intonations, his walks and his indefinable funniness.

Sid Field's first three stage triumphs were in *Strike a New Note, Strike It Again* and *Piccadilly Hayride*, at the Prince of Wales. His 1949 success in the play *Harvey*, where he played the lovable drunk whose best friend is an invisible rabbit, was, so many said, typecasting. He did drink. It led to his early death in 1950. How rotten that, after thirty years of knocking it out round the halls, he had only six years at the top. What wouldn't he have done if he hadn't hurried away so quickly?

Gracie Fields

Our Gracie

Comedienne/singer/actress. Born Grace Stansfield, Rochdale, Lancashire, 1898. Quite simply the greatest female performer we have ever produced. The story of her rise to national institution and international stardom has been told so very many times* I shan't go into great detail here. Suffice it to say that her combination of stunning singing, down-to-earth chat, and highly underrated acting made her a superstar before the word had even been thought of.

Her early life was one of hard graft and then more hard graft. From juvenile troupes in her native Lancashire through touring revues to stardom in the West End. The show that did the trick for her was *Mr Tower of London*, presented by her first husband ARCHIE PITT. They toured the show for seven years until one season, in 1925, at the Alhambra, Leicester Square, led to her

"OUR GRACIE"

When Gracie was near to death in 1939 this cartoon appeared in the Daily Express

'discovery'. Then followed bill topping in Variety, at home and in the States, starring roles in films (she was, at one time, the highest paid female star in the world) and huge success on record. The marriage was dissolved in 1940. A second marriage, to the film comedian and director MONTY BANKS, was a happy one till his death, in her arms, in 1950.

It was this marriage (Monty was Italian) that led to all sorts of rumours that Gracie had deserted us in our hour of need at the outbreak of the Second World War. The truth was that a high-ranking member of the government had phoned her to say the war would be starting in just a few days and if she didn't get Monty out of the country, quickly, he would be interned for the duration. She took him to America. There she toured and collected more than a million and a half pounds for the war effort. She returned here pretty smartish and raised a further half million with concerts all over the UK, spending most of the war entertaining us and the troops, wherever they were.

Her agent, for many years, was my agent's dad, BERT AZA (after Bert's death his wife, LILIAN, took over). Lilian told me a great story of Gracie's return to the London Palladium at the end of the war. The allegation of deserting her homeland still stuck, like mud to a blanket and Bert and Lilian (not Gracie) were worried about her possible reception. Together they went through her act with a fine-tooth comb, to ensure that everything was just right. Beg her as they did,

57

she refused to tell them what her opening number would be. Cut to opening night: Bert and Lilian standing at the back of the stalls holding hands and offering up a silent prayer. Gracie's number comes up on the proscenium arch and the orchestra play 'Sally'. On she comes to polite applause. Segue into her first song. It is 'La Vie en Rose' the first line of which is: 'Take me to your heart again'. The house fell in. Lilian said: 'She was the greatest putter together of a programme of songs I've ever known.'

In 1952 she married her last husband, Boris Alperovici, whom she met in her adopted home, Capri. They were together for twenty-seven years.

I saw her whenever I could. Everything she did on-stage was simply the best. Her approach to an audience, her telling of just the right jokes and, most of all, her handling of every song from daft character ones to ballads and semi-operatic classics. She breathed life into the corniest of pop songs because she 'lived' the lyrics. Funny, sad, joyous or jingoistic, she made every one a complete little play. As with so many other fans, we corresponded regularly. I dropped her a line wishing her well after she'd had a fall. On the morning of 27 September 1979 I received a picture postcard of Capri with the message: 'Thanks for thinking of me. This old girl is doing fine – love Grace'. I switched on the radio to hear Dame Gracie Fields CBE had died.

*Notably in *Gracie Fields* by Muriel Burgess with Tommy Keen (W.H. Allen, 1980), *Our Gracie* by Joan Moules (Robert Hale, 1983) and *Gracie Fields – the authorised biography*, by David Bret (Robson Books, 1995).

Tommy Fields

London's Lancashire Comedian

Comedian. Born Thomas Stansfield, Rochdale, 1908. Tommy was the brother of GRACIE FIELDS and started his career with her revue *Mr Tower of London* in the 1920s. Before our period he toured South Africa as half of a musical act, FIELDS AND ROSSINI. By the late 1930s he was a single act and played all the top Variety dates, including the London Palladium and America with his sister. Not that Tommy needed Gracie, he was a good

comic and a good Dame in pantomime. I worked with him on Clacton Pier. Tall and good looking, with a charming, cheeky personality, some people said he spoiled himself by doing slightly 'blue' material but I never noticed it.

Philip says: 'He was very successful playing the leads in the number two tours of the West End musical comedies.' He died in 1988.

Alec Finlay

Comedian. Born Glasgow, 1906. Not too well known down south but a great favourite in Scotland – he played pantomime for sixteen successive seasons at the Alhambra, Glasgow and was a regular in the legendary *Five Past Eight* spectacular revues.

He was a little man ('Wee Alec') who, by accident – he'd forgotten his trousers – appeared in cabaret at a London golfing 'do' in top hat, white tie, tails and kilt! This got him noticed and he, and his wife RITA ANDRE, were very successful down south in the Thirties. He not only comicked, he danced and played the saxophone, clarinet, concertina and bagpipes.

During our period he toured all over the world taking, to ex-pats everywhere, his All Scots shows. In the Seventies, along with WILL STAR and RON COBURN, he has a television hit with a series for Grampian TV, *The Royal Clansmen*. Alec died in Glasgow in 1984.

Flack and Lucas

Tap and ballet dancers. Leslie Flack born London, 1921 and Alan Lucas, born London, 1921. Two classy boy dancers, beautifully dressed in tails or grey morning suits and toppers, with outstanding tap routines. They got together in the early Thirties and, immediately, were booked for all the number one halls. They must have been good as, unusually for two English dancers, during the Second World War, they supported all the top American performers when they entertained their troops. After the war they played the Palladium and all the top venues. Leslie's later partner was RAY LAMAR, the last husband of RUBY MURRAY.

Bud Flanagan

Underneath the arches

Comedian. Born Reuben Weintrop (Robert Winthrop) London, 1896. Oddly, Bud just about makes this book. Most of his big Variety successes happened in the theatres before 1945, the year the act, FLANAGAN AND ALLEN, finished. Chesney Allen (born William Ernest Chesney Allen in Brighton, 1894) retired from performing in 1946. Bud did do occasional stints in Variety but most of the years 1945–62 were taken up with The Crazy Gang revues*. The Gang, by then BUD, NAUGHTON AND GOLD, NERVO AND KNOX and, on and off, MONSEWER EDDIE GRAY held sway at the Victoria Palace for fifteen years. Their success led to Bud and his compatriots being practically resident at the annual Royal Variety Performance. The Royal Family loved them.

The shows at the VP were an anarchic, bawdy and brash mix of audience participation, innuendo-loaded sketches, colourful song and dance scenes, speciality acts and surprise items. They were glorious vehicles for a bunch of much-loved old comics who never tired of chasing chorus girls, sending each other up, getting into drag and forcing the audience to be part of the show.

Bud tells, in his autobiography, *My Crazy Life*, the fascinating story of his early years in the East End of London, his working his passage to New York, his show biz adventures all over America,

his pre- and First World War meetings with Ches, and their eventual teaming in the FLORRIE FORDE touring show.

I never saw the act Flanagan and Allen, but the speed with which they shot to the very top proves they must have been quite something. During our period their appearances together were usually 'surprise' guest spots when they would sing medleys of their many hits.

The memory of Bud, the great ad-libbing, fruity comic, will vanish when those of us who were part of his worshipping audiences have snuffed it. Happily, though, he and Ches will live on through that magic blending of voices. The swooping, lyrical cantor of Bud and the stabbing, half-spoken, punctuations of Ches will forever remind future generations of a national institution.

Bud's last solo recording was the signature tune for *Dad's Army*. He died in 1968.

Bud's wife, Curly, told me once he had said: 'If they ever do my life story I want Roy Hudd to play me.' Dreams do sometimes come true. I had the happiest time of my career playing him for two years in *Underneath the Arches* in Chichester and at the Prince of Wales Theatre.

*People tend to think, because Bud became the Master of the Revels in the Gang shows, that he was part of the team from the beginning. Not so. The original Crazy Gang was NAUGHTON AND GOLD, NERVO AND KNOX, CARRYL AND MUNDY and the MONSEWER.

Cyril Fletcher

Odd Ode Number One Coming Up!

Comedian. Born Cyril Trevellian Fletcher, Watford, 1913. Cyril's long career began in 1936. He became a member of the famous *Fol-de-Rols* concert party company. What a start: the show had been the cradle of so many popular comics from ARTHUR ASKEY to THE WESTERN BROTHERS. He'd only been in the business a couple of years when, short of material for a radio broadcast, he recited, 'in an extraordinary voice', a poem of Edgar Wallace's, 'Dreaming of Thee'. It was the start of his 'Odd Odes', the founding of his radio and Variety fortune.

Broadcasting made him a top of the bill and he

played the halls both as an act and in sketches in revue all over the country from the Palladium onwards. To me, he never seemed totally at home on the halls; like Arthur Askey, he was more effective in smaller, more intimate venues. Yet he loved Variety and, in his excellent autobiography, *Nice One Cyril*, he sums up the death of the medium in the most perceptive way: 'As a cradle for stardom it was unsurpassed: each artiste, given but a few minutes, frequently in a front cloth, had, with his own personality and his own material, to entertain an audience, take it by the scruff of the neck and insist that it enjoyed every precious minute that the act was on the stage. It was an exciting and exacting science, and the entertainment world is very much the poorer without its Variety theatres and artists.' And so say so many of us.

Cyril and his lovely wife, BETTY ASTELL (they married in 1942) sussed that the old format had run its course and went into management. They presented, and appeared in their own summer shows, for twenty-seven years. I saw many of their pantomimes in Croydon and I loved them. They were always strong on story line with perfect costumes, music and scenery. Cyril always played Dame and he was a good one. Betty, who devised the shows, was the most beautiful of Principal Girls.

Cyril's long career included television from the Thirties through to *What's My Line?*, *That's Life* and his gardening programmes. His thousands of radio appearances were equally successful.

Today he and Betty are retired in Guernsey but he still occasionally delights audiences with his one-man show, *After Dinner with Cyril Fletcher*.

I had the pleasure of working with Cyril and Betty's daughter JILL FLETCHER in *Oliver!* She has inherited all her mum and dad's capacity for hard work, attention to detail, and finger-on-the-pulse adaptability. Jill acts, does cabaret, after-dinner speaking, is 'Bolly the Clown' and a dyed-in-the-wool pro.

The Amazing Fogel

Mentalist. Born Maurice Fogel, London, 1911. According to the reference books, Maurice's big claim to fame was his ability to read minds and transmit thoughts. I never saw him do this, but remember him well as the man who caught bullets in his teeth. He came to the RAF camp where I was doing National Service and did that very thing. I was the volunteer who had to check that the bullet he spat out on to a plate was the same one that a pal of mine had to fire at him. It was an amazing trick.

He began as front man to the illusionist, RAMESES and later did a fascinating Variety act where he impersonated other magicians. His adventures in mind reading during the war led Captain GEORGE BLACK to suggest an act on these lines, and he did it all over the country. Philip says: 'He did not claim to be psychic but he certainly amazed the punters and all sorts of scientific experts. He claimed to simply play a hunch but the odds were too great to be offset by this statement.' He died in 1981.

Banner Forbutt

Trick cyclist. Born Branston James Forbutt, Australia, 1910. You will notice, throughout this book, how many speciality acts came here from the Antipodes: trick cyclists, jugglers and acrobats seem to have been their main export during Variety's heyday. Banner was originally a racing cyclist but it was bicycle polo that led him to his Variety act. He perfected his tricks between midnight and six am in a local Sydney public park. In 1950, he said: 'In 1937, on an ordinary bicycle, I stood still for a duration of two hours and thirty nine minutes.' Why?

Ford and Sheen

Drag act. Vic Ford, born George William Spinks, London, 1907 and Chris Sheen, born Christopher Shinfield, Derbyshire, 1908. No wonder they changed their names. Probably the longest running act on the drag scene. They were together for nearly forty years.

Vic began as a tramp comedian, WEE GEORGIE SPINKS, and graduated to his first double act, RAVEN AND FORD. Chris was originally a member of the knockabout act, JOE BOGANNY'S BOYS. In 1936 they both found themselves in a version of the legendary First World War drag show, *Splinters*

In this show their double act was formed. They were together, during the war, in *Stars in Battle-dress* and, on demob, played every Variety theatre in the country with all-male revues that seemed to be on nearly every week at my local. They all merged into one for me but Philip remembers the titles of the shows: *Showboat Express, Forces Showboat, Forces in Petticoats, Misleading Ladies* (in which DANNY LA RUE had his first speaking part) and, most famous of the lot, *Soldiers in Skirts*.

They were great Ugly Sisters in panto and, unlike most drag acts today, they always took their applause in male attire.

Frank and Lou Formby

Lou Formby

Tap dancers. Both born Wigan. Son and daughter of the music-hall star GEORGE FORMBY SNR and so, of course, the brother and sister of the famous George junior. Frank and Lou were excellent tap dancers and were seven years together on the halls. After the war Lou was the comedienne in an act with BOB HALL. Frank worked on as principal comedian in number two revues.

George Formby

The Lancashire Lad

Comedian. Born George Hoy Booth, Wigan,

1904. Surely one of the most recognisable voices on records. Those double entendre-laden lyrics, the 'daft' Northern accent, the infectious chuckle and masterly right-hand technique on the banjulele can only ever mean – the Lancashire lad himself. Amazingly his looks fitted the voice: the full moon face, the constantly grinning mouthful of teeth and the tiny eyes that were innocently honest with just a hint of nudge, nudge knowingness.

He was the son of a famous father, the music-hall star GEORGE FORMBY whose stage invention, the 'let loose on the town' Lancashire 'John Willie', was really what George junior himself eventually became. Like all good pros, George senior tried to steer his son away from the footlights and his first work was as a jockey. He grew too heavy for this and, after his father's death, went into the game. Originally, as George Hoy, he did pale impressions of George senior's routines and songs. By 1924 he had started to put in bits of his own and this was the year he first said 'Turned out nice again!' He was now GEORGE FORMBY.

There are all sorts of stories as to how he first started playing the banjulele (an American invention – a cross between a ukulele and a banjo) but he himself said he bought his first one from another turn. He paid fifty shillings for the instrument that was to make him a star and seven and sixpence for the licence that wed him to Beryl Ingham from Accrington, the lady who ensured he stayed a star.

Together they worked everywhere and anywhere in Variety and in their own revues, until records and then films turned him into a stellar attraction. His first recordings were of his father's songs but his own material soon took over. Between the early 1930s and 1945 he recorded well over a hundred titles.

His film career started with *Boots! Boots!* in 1934. It was made for three thousand pounds. His eleven years as a movie actor established him as one of the few Variety comedians to succeed in that very different medium. He became known world-wide and, in 1944, was voted the most popular man in Russia – after Stalin! I love his films. They are simple, slapstick comedies with a survivor as the hero and, best of all, without any

Beryl and George Formby

He started as 'Boy Bruce the Mighty Atom' in Variety at Bilston, as a dancing act. Years of playing all the number twos, threes (and fours!) in Variety, pantomime and summer shows, gave him the experience that has stood him in such good stead. Here he learned his most valuable asset – the art of ad-libbing and audience participation.

His London Palladium *Beat the Clock* was the high spot of the week's TV. He progressed from there to one-man shows, compering several Royal Variety Performances, etc.

A versatile performer, he plays piano, dances, sings and gets laughs. Things weren't looking too well for him when he was booked for BBC TV's *The Generation Game*. He controlled the games brilliantly, somehow managing to make the contestants the stars and himself the fall guy.

Happily he is still demonstrating his unique skills on the box but I wish we could see more of him demonstrating his other talents.

Forsythe, Seamon and Farrell

Singing, dancing comedy trio. Charles Forsythe born Canada, Addie Seamon born Newark, New Jersey, USA, and Elinore Farrell born in Providence, Rhode Island, USA. They formed their trio in 1931 and toured all over the world before becoming resident in the UK where they topped bills from the mid Thirties onwards. Charlie Forsythe was a baritone singer, his wife, Addie, danced and comicked while the large lady, Elinore, was the pianist and comedienne.

I haven't been able to find out what happened to

banal sentimental moments. He did always have a girl friend but Beryl's vetting of the scripts and her attendance during the shooting ensured there was no kissing or love stuff. One of the reasons, I'm sure, that kids today enjoy them so much.

I don't have to remind you of his records. They have become almost folk music and are still heard regularly today. Beryl Formby has, like other show biz wives, been given a bad press by so many but she did steer George to the top and, by taking on all the rotten jobs like arguing money, position on the bill, tax demands, etc she left him free to be Mr Nice Guy. They had been together for thirty-six years when she died at Christmas in 1960. George himself lasted less than three months more, dying in March 1961.

To learn so much more about our George, on and offstage, I recommend *George Formby*, a biography by Alan Randall and Ray Seaton, and a book in 'The Entertainers' series – *George Formby*, by John Fisher.

Bruce Forsyth

The Incredible Character

Bruce is yet another example of how Variety could produce entertainers who were versatile, adaptable, family favourites. I am an unashamed fan of our very best game show host so, rather than me going into paroxysms of hero worship, I'll leave a summing up of the man to Philip.

them. Someone did tell me they lived on their own farm in Hertfordshire but that, alas, is all I can tell you about a very popular broadcasting and Variety act.

Jack François

Comedian and acrobatic dancer. Born Edinburgh, 1911. A real, old-fashioned, dyed-in-the-wool, turn-his-hand-to-anything pro. From the famous François family Jack learned his trade, via Continental tours with his dad's act, MANUEL AND FRANÇOIS, concert party, Variety and revue.

I first encountered him, from my seat in the gods, as a player of small parts in the Palladium pantomimes. He seemed a permanent fixture there in the late Fifties and Sixties. Much later I did several pantos with Jack as company manager. Even in this administrative job it was hard to keep him off and, at the drop of a hat, he'd be on-stage 'feeding' whenever he got the chance. All the experience he'd gained as stooge to NAT JACKLEY and a host of others was there in his immaculate timing.

I was lucky that he said 'yes' when I asked him if he'd dress me during the run of *Underneath the Arches* at the Prince of Wales. His organising of thirty-odd changes inside two and a half hours was ace and his advice, when a gag wasn't quite working, was invaluable. Jack died, at Brinsworth House, in 1997.

François and Zandra

Entertainers. François Manny François, the brother of JACK FRANÇOIS, born London, 1918, and Zandra, Joy, born Birmingham, 1937. Two great variety stalwarts who are still at it, playing cabaret as MANNY AND JOY.

Manny started at twelve, in West End hotels and Variety. At sixteen he joined the act *Kay Kay and Kay* (BILLY KAY AND DICKIE BELL). For three years they topped Variety bills all over Europe and were featured in the UK as a number one supporting act. During the war he was a sergeant-major, so no theatrical activities for him. On demob, though, he was back in the biz – in an al-male revue, *Get In* (DANNY LA RUE was in the chorus). He was booked for a revue at the County Theatre, Bedford where he met Joy and the double act was formed. Joy began as a BETTY FOX BABE in panto. The great British invention, pantomime, played a big part in both their careers. Their best friend KEN DODD made his panto début with them. Together, and singly, they worked everywhere and with everyone.

They were signed by THE DEFONTS and played Variety at every number one hall in the country

and their numerous summer seasons included the legendary HAROLD FIELDING's *Music for the Millions.*

Manny and Joy are true, turn-their-hands-to-anything, pros. At one time Joy toured Scotland, with Manny compering, as the *Daily Express*'s Hula-Hoop Queen. During their Variety days they presented six different acts at the Finsbury Park Empire. When the halls closed they concentrated on cabaret and their hotel work included an eleven-year stint at the Royal Hotel in Whitby.

So now they take it easy? Don't you believe it. They still entertain at day centres and retirement clubs and never stop raising money for The Entertainment Artistes Benevolent Fund. They are the most stage-struck pair I know.

Ronald Frankau

Comedian. Born London, 1894. Originally a chorus boy, FRANK RONALDS, he reverted to his own name in the early 1920s. He was a concert party man through and through, appearing in, and presenting, his own shows, most notably *The Cabaret Kittens* – the nursery for performers like NAUGHTON WAYNE, NAN KENWAY and CARL FREDERICKS ('Ramsbottom' in radio's *Happidrome*, see HARRY KORRIS). One of the party's pianists was later Ronald's accompanist in Variety – MONTE CRICK (the first 'Dan' in radio's *The Archers*). He was a pioneer in radio: his concert party was broadcast from the Chiswick Empire in 1927. He got a guinea for the entire company!

Radio played an important part in making him a Variety headliner both as himself and with TOMMY HANDLEY as MURGATROYD AND WINTERBOTTOM. Philip says: He wrote all his own lyrics (he told me once he wrote them in the 'lav' – on 'lav' paper). His style was a cross between NOËL COWARD and MAX MILLER, with an 'educated' Cockney accent. The combination of Handley and Frankau's accents was an odd one. Liverpool and 'cod' Eton. He was a great talent. He died in 1951.

Morton Fraser

Harmonica player. Born Leeds. His first break came when he won a National All-American harmonica contest in Philadelphia! As a soloist he

played his way all round the world. In 1946 he produced the act we all remember, THE MORTON FRASER HARMONICA GANG. Based on the American act BORRAH MINEVITCH'S HARMONICA RASCALS they soon established themselves as headliners at all the number one theatres in the UK, continuing well into, and beyond, our period.

An old pal of mine, TONY VINCENT, ran the band for many years after Morton died and TINY ROSS, the midget butt of all their knockabout comedy, was with them till the lack of top venues forced them to disband.

Red Fred

Unicyclist. Born F.W. Lowes, Sunderland, 1903. Fred served his apprenticeship with a man called A.D. ROBBINS whose bill matter was 'The Canadian Cycle Tamer'. He worked all over Europe, South America and Australia as a single act but we knew him best as RED FRED AND ROSA. They both worked in cowboy gear, spinning ropes while still on the bike.

Adele French

Musician/singer/principal boy. Born Forest Gate, London, 1920. Adele is the perfect example

of the adaptability of the dyed-in-the-wool Variety artiste. She began, at fifteen, as 'The Singing Page Girl'. As the cinema organist, PHIL FINCH, rose into view, next to him would be Adele to sing between the films. One of the cine-variety stage shows featured GERALDO AND HIS GAUCHO ACCORDION BAND and watching them inspired Adele to take up the accordion. It serves her well to this very day.

The war saw her entertaining, as pianist and accordionist, all over Europe and the desert with ENSA, alongside NERVO AND KNOX, BRIAN REECE (PC 49) RICHARD HEARNE (Mr Pastry) and RUDY STARITA. A real pro never stops learning and, while in Italy, an opera singer advised her to have voice training. She did, and her post-war act was singing semi-operatic songs to her own accordion accompaniment.

Adele played Variety and summer season everywhere and was a popular Principal Boy in panto. She was once a guest artiste at the notorious Windmill Theatre where she *didn't* strip. She told me: 'It could have been nasty – playing the accordion!' She was part of THE SYD SEYMOUR NEW MAD HATTERS SHOW, playing piano with the band and doing her own spot.

In her first TV show (1947) she had an entrance to be reckoned with. The magician, N'GAI, introduced her by opening his hand where, she, and her accordion, were discovered.

Adele has now retired but her talents are still in evidence in the Lodge Room of the Lady Ratlings.

Henri French

Trick cyclist. Born Henry French, New Zealand, 1916. Henri's father was THE GREAT HENRI FRENCH, a music-hall favourite who did trick cycling, juggling and quick change routines. Henri junior took the act over from his father. He did so well with it that his brother, MAURICE FRENCH, did a virtually identical routine. He had a successful career too. Thank you Dad.

Freddie Frinton

Comedian. Born Frederick Hargate, Grimsby, 1911. Now not a lot of people know this but, every New Year's Eve, in Germany, Freddie's version of the sketch 'Dinner for One' is shown on TV. It's become a sort of tradition. I wish it would become one here. The sketch, written by LAURIE WYLIE and originally performed by BOBBY HOWES and BINNIE HALE in a West End revue, is a little masterpiece. The set-up is an old dowager duchess (MAY WARDEN) alone in her mansion. Every year she

puts on a dinner party with only herself there. The other guests all died long ago but she imagines they are with her and they must be served their dinners – and wine with every course. Freddie plays the butler who has to do the serving and make sure that all the wine is drunk! If you get to see it (and there are pirated copies around) you'll be witnessing a master of mime and comic invention and a superlative stage 'drunk' at his peak. Do try.

Freddie was destined to be a fishpacker in his home town Grimsby but loved to entertain and ran his own amateur concert party. TOM MOSS saw him and booked him, at twenty, to play Dame. He had seasons in concert party, professional now, until the war came along. Here he fell on his feet: GEORGE BLACK got him into *Stars in Battledress*. After the war Black featured him in the touring version of the SID FIELD vehicle *Strike a New Note* and in the revue *Sky High*. In his Variety single he invariably played a drunk and his bent-in-half cigarette became as well known as a catchphrase. According to Philip: 'He bought the rights to "Dinner for One", a sketch he had seen on tour and, using the original script, plus material that HARRY ROWSON had added and his own unique business, he created a music-hall jewel.'

He scored heavily in television as half of the husband and wife team (THORA HIRD was the missus) in the sitcom *Meet the Wife*.

I got to know him while he was playing a farce for the summer season in Torquay. I was in concert party in Babbacombe. He was amazingly quiet and unshowbusiness for someone who was steeped in the game. He played Bingo every day until it was time to go to work.

Sadly, Freddie never really had the chance to show us what he could have done. He died, just as he was being accepted as a first-rate character actor, in 1968.

Leo Fuld

Singer/writer. Born Lazarus Fuld, Rotterdam, 1913. Someone, I confess, I'd never heard of but Philip assures me that, after a Variety season in 1948 at the London Casino, where he was a big success, he became a number one attraction on the halls and on the concert platform. He was a

vocalist who could sing in fifteen different languages: 'and talk in eight'.

Before the war he had a successful career in Variety and revue in the UK, in America and in his native Holland. He left his homeland just four days before the Germans invaded and spent the duration of the war in the States. Here he did his bit for the Dutch Underground Movement with regular broadcasts to them from New York. He also wrote comedy material for vaudeville and radio. He toured his own productions in America and, once Hitler had bitten the dust, he came to the UK.

Will Fyffe

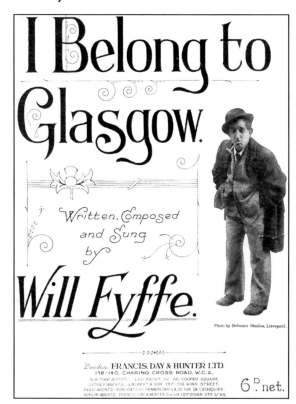

I Belong to Glasgow

Character comedian. Born Dundee, 1885. The man who through his song, 'I Belong to Glasgow' gave that much-feared (by English comedians) city its hard drinking image. Will just makes our period (he died, falling out of the window of a hotel, in 1947).

Unlike the comic who becomes an actor, he did

it the other way round, starting as an actor play-ing 'fit-ups' and all sorts of theatres all over Scotland till he became one of Britain's most popular music-hall stars.

His first brushes with the lighter side of the business came when he tried to sell songs ('Glasgow' was one) that he and HAYDN HALSTEAD had written, to the great SIR HARRY LAUDER. He rejected them so Will put them together in an act and did them himself. He never looked back. He made each song a little play in itself, complete with character make-up.

Philip remembers his opening at the London Palladium in the early 1920s when he was lauded as 'an overnight success'. He told Philip: 'I *was* an overnight success – after playing the dumps for more than twenty years!'

I never saw him 'live' but I have seen most of his films (he made ten) and he was years ahead of his time in his underplaying and total credibility.

His first wife, LILY BOLTON, was tragically drowned sailing from Scotland to Ireland in 1921 but his second, EILEEN (whom many of us music-hall fans met at meetings of The British Music Hall Society) lived till 1979. Their son, WILL FYFFE junior, is a superb accompanist and musical director. Will junior and ANTHEA ASKEY (Arthur's daughter) present an excellent show about their two dads which you must catch if it's in your neck of the woods.

___ G ___

Les Galantas

Roller balancer and juggler. Philip says: 'They were an attractive man and girl act, working on the diabolo pedestal and finishing with a fast acrobatic routine. They were an English couple who looked like a foreign act, hence the name (they were originally COOKE AND PARTNER).'

The Ganjou Brothers and Juanita

Romance in porcelain

Adagio dancers. Without doubt one of the finest adagio acts in the world. Three Polish brothers,

SERGE, BOB AND GEORGE with JUANITA (Joy) pre-sented a classy, brilliantly staged, great speciality act. George's wife ADELE was their musical director. Indeed the act, with Adele in the orchestra pit, is, thank heaven, on film. Their opening alone – a giant mantelpiece with a huge clock centre and Juanita swinging on the pendulum – was a show stopper in itself. The three lads, wearing powdered wigs and Georgian outfits, then proceeded to throw Juanita from one to the other in a succession of beautifully choreographed moves. Juanita was a classically trained ballerina and their throws and catches were copied by every act in the same field – but never with the same success. They played every number one venue in the world. Bob Ganjou died in 1972 and George in 1988.

The Three Garcias

Acrobatic dancers. Their leader was Carmen Garcia, born Glasgow, 1924. The three girls pre-sented an acrobatic and posing act (not nude) from 1940 on. They worked all through our period in cabaret, revue and Variety.

Gaston and Andree

Adagio act. Jimmy Gaston and Rosemary Andree. I remember the two names as the producers of those nudie revues that helped Variety towards the

crematorium but before this period, according to Philip, they had been a sensational adagio act, and were said to be the pair who introduced this style of dancing into Variety. Before they teamed up, Jimmy had been part of a two-man acrobatic team ART IN ATHLETICS. After the adagio period they presented a 'most artistic posing act. The nudity was such that no one was offended.' Jimmy died in 1966 and Rosemary in 1974.

Gay and Barry

Comedy magic and patter act. Cliff Gay born Truro, 1903 and Ivy Barry born Leicester, 1915. Cliff and his wife Ivy were a double act from 1934. They started in concert party, and because of the constant changes of programme required in that entertainment, they did all sorts of speciality acts: comedy, dance, patter, magic and acrobatics. Never big names, they and their sort were the life-blood of the business, stalwarts of the smaller shows and, during the war, invaluable to ENSA. Afterwards they appeared in numerous small revues and pantos. Good team players.

Jimmy Gay

Comedian. Born Liverpool, 1906. A highly underrated stand-up comic in the mould of ROBB WILTON. Unlike Robb, however, Jimmy was not a sketch comic, but a laid-back commentator on life whose immobility on-stage was a perfect example of relaxed control. His 'play on' music was a big laugh before he even spoke. The band would play the tune that matched the words: 'Have you ever caught your —s in a rat trap?' Jimmy's opening line was: 'Never!' He always smoked a Capstan Full Strength cigarette, leaving a pile of ash (about two inches across) behind when he exited. One classic line of his that I remember was: 'I played Scotland last week and business was so bad on the Saturday night they shot a stag in the gallery.' After years of knocking it out around the halls he got his big chance in the last Variety bill at the Prince of Wales. He was a success but the game was up. There was nowhere for him to go.

I did see him in a sitcom on television, as a director of a run-down football club. He was superb. Alas, poor Jim had a nervous breakdown and the last time I saw him he was an attendant at the Ace of Clubs nightspot in Leeds.

The Geddes Brothers

Comedy musicians. Thomas and Johnny Geddes born Scotland, Johnny in 1899. They stayed in their homeland and the north of England till after the First World War when their first trip abroad was to Russia – one of the first British Variety acts to play there. In the 1920s they came south where they broadcast from 2LO and played everywhere in the UK and South Africa, Australia and New Zealand as well as all over Europe. After the Second World War they

remained a popular act, particularly in their native Scotland.

Max Geldray

Electronic harmonica player. Born Max Leon Van Gelder, Amsterdam, 1916. Played all over Europe before the war and became known here while serving in the Dutch army. He was a member of the RAY VENTURA band but it was as solo broadcaster that he hit the jackpot. I remember him supplying, along with RAY ELLINGTON, the musical interludes in *The Goon Show*. He was a well-featured act in Variety all through our period.

Geraldo

Bandleader. Born Gerald Bright, London, 1904. Geraldo was the son of immigrant Jewish parents and began his career playing the piano for the silent films. His first 'name' band was THE GAUCHO TANGO ORCHESTRA who were resident at the Savoy Hotel. They broadcast and played all the number ones as top of the bill. After the war GERALDO AND HIS ORCHESTRA, with EVE BOSWELL as one of their vocalists, became even more popular. Philip says: 'Although he always wore beautifully tailored suits and was always immaculately turned out he never lost his "Cor blimey" accent. A well-known producer once suggested he take elocution lessons and he replied, "but I 'ave!" He was a first-class musician and his show was a first-class presentation.'

Gerry, as he was known, was one of the first to see the viability of the cruise ships and went on to present the very best sort of shipboard entertainment. He died in 1974.

Tony Gerrard

Comedian/compere. Born Anthony Driker, Bermondsey, 1898. Originally a stand-up Cockney comedian before he started his famous talent shows for Gaumont British and, says Philip: 'he must have played every cinema in the UK. He worked for a pittance and must have made the cinema circuit thousands of pounds profit.' HUGHIE GREEN, CARROLL LEVIS and BRIAN MICHIE, who followed in his flat footsteps, reaped the benefit of his pioneering. Flat feet? He was a victim of trench foot inherited from the First World War.

Gilbert and Partner

See Vogelbein's Bears.

Frank Ginnett

Dog trainer. Born Brixton, London 1921. Trying to trace who is related to whom in the circus world is impossible – everyone is related to each other somehow. Frank, though, is a member of one of the most well-known families, the Ginnetts (famous for their sketch 'Dick Turpin's Ride to York' which played all over the UK and the States). They are all descendants of Jean Pierre Ginnett, a French prisoner of war brought here after the Battle of Waterloo. Oddly enough, the founder of Lord George Sanger's Circus, James Sanger, was an English veteran of the same battle. Jean Pierre, beginning with four canaries and a kerbside show, built up to become the owner of his own sixty-foot-round big top and later several circuses. Fred Ginnett, Frank's grandfather, was a great showman and a King Rat of the GOWR. It was he who really put the circus on the map and, incidentally, built two theatres in Brighton – the Grand and the Hippodrome which, at the time, seated 5,000 people.

After the usual tough circus apprenticeship (he rode, trained dogs and horses and ring mastered), Frank devised his own act, FRANK'S FOX TERRIERS in 1947. This was the year, while appearing at the Victoria Palace with LUPINO LANE, that he met and married MIRIAM DEWHURST. She was a member of MANZ, CHICO AND LOPEZ, yet another circus family act. Frank and Miriam married on a Sunday night and opened in variety in Portsmouth, with the dogs, the next day. They worked the act till their son was born in 1953. With all the resourcefulness a circus upbringing engenders, Frank learnt hairdressing and the London cab drivers' Knowledge. Miriam carried on with just one dog and called her combination of canine capers, rope-spinning and acrobatics, MANDY AND SANDY. They worked on for twenty years and finally called it a day in 1973.

Gertie Gitana

The star who never fails to shine

Singer. Born Gertrude Mary Astbury, Longport, 1887. One of the great music-hall survivors whom I saw in the show her husband, DON ROSS (they married in 1928) devised, *Thanks For the Memory*. Gertie started on the halls at the age of four as 'Little Gitana'. At sixteen, as Gertie Gitana, she was a star, topping bills till her retirement in 1938. She featured, and made popular, some great music-hall songs: 'Never Mind', 'Silver Bell', 'When I Leave The World Behind' and, most famously, 'Nellie Dean'.

Don persuaded her to return to the stage in 1948 with *Thanks for the Memory*. The show, which also starred the music-hall veterans G.H. ELLIOTT, NELLIE WALLACE, BILLY DANVERS, RANDOLPH SUTTON, ELLA SHIELDS and TALBOT O'FARRELL, broke box office records everywhere it played. It was the star attraction at the Royal Variety Performance of 1948. Gertie was very popular in pantomime and a legendary show biz story tells of her sitting by the fire as Cinderella and saying: 'Here I sit all alone, I

think I'll play my saxophone'. She then reaches up the chimney, produces her sax and goes into her act. I wonder if it was true. Hope so.

Gertie died in 1957. An excellent book about Gertie and Don is *Thanks for the Memory* by Ann Oughton.

Archie Glen

Blotto as usual

Comedian. Born Manchester, 1889. The bill matter says it all. He was a 'drunk', evening-dressed, front-cloth comedian: a standard act who, after an apprenticeship with FRED KARNO, played all the number one dates. He was the uncle of the North Country comedian TONY DALTON. He died in 1966.

The Glenns

Acrobatic dancers. Wally Allen born Chicago, 1917 and Marie Allen born New York, 1920. I don't know anything about the third member. Wally and Marie were a husband and wife whose sensational trio was born in 1943. Marie was originally a single singer and dancer and Wally was half of a two man hand-to-hand balancing act, MARTIN AND ALLEN. Philip says: 'They were a great novelty with an act that combined ballroom dancing, lifts, spins and balancing tricks. They opened here at the London Palladium in 1949 and were a sensation.' They returned to the States where they played every number one venue in theatre and cabaret.

Tommy Godfrey

Comedian. Born The Cut, Waterloo, London, 1920. Tommy, who I had the joy of working with in *Underneath the Arches* (he played TEDDY KNOX) was a funny man. A fruity real Cockney voice, a good ad-libber and the thinnest legs in show business. A pal of mine, the press representative LAURIE BELLEW, reckoned it was worth the price of

admission just to glimpse Tommy's legs in Principal Boy's costume. We knew him, latterly, as a fine, always totally real, character actor on television and film but he had a sterling Variety background. He was an excellent tap dancer who started, as a boy, in a three-handed act, GODFREY, RANDALL AND DEANE. Randall was JOYCE RANDALL, the daughter of the redoubtable agent, MANNIE JAY, and DEANE was Sylvia Heath the wife of AL HEATH. As a single act he, according to Philip, pirated the act of AL SHERMAN: 'He even dressed the same.' He seemed to know everybody in show business, the great and the good as well as the deadbeat and decidedly dodgy. Tommy died, and what an old-fashioned London funeral he had, in 1984.

Gold and Cordell

Dancers. Al Gold and Lola Cordell were, according to Philip, 'A nice classy double dancing speciality. Al's great claim to fame was that his first dancing partner was LORD GRADE (Lew). They were GRADE AND CORDELL.'

Paul Goldin

Hypnotist. Born Ronald Paul Gold, Ilford, Essex, 1928. Like several others in the same line of business Paul began by hypnotising his brother airmen in the RAF. He had, before call-up, studied medicine and psychology. On demob he was 'discovered' giving a demonstration of his powers at Speaker's Corner in Hyde Park. He had a very successful stage career but I haven't heard of him for years. Philip says: 'He always had ambitions to start a clinic', so perhaps this is what he is doing now.

Nat Gonella

Georgia

Trumpet player and bandleader. Born Nathaniel Charles Gonella, London, 1908. Probably the most famous jazz trumpeter England has ever produced and the inspiration for so many brass players. He began in the Twenties as a member of a brass band, THE BUSBY BOYS (a featured act in an ARCHIE PITT revue), and played with most of the legendary names: ROY FOX, LEW STONE, IVOR MAIRANTS, JOE CROSSMAN and AL BOWLLY. In the Thirties NAT GONELLA AND HIS GEORGIANS got together. After the war they became THE NEW GEORGIANS and even HIS SWINGSTERS but with the same Gonella at the helm. He sang in LOUIS ARMSTRONG style and had a hit record with his signature tune, 'Georgia on My Mind'. Until just a few years ago he was a featured act in music hall with his 'Salute to Satchmo' spot. He is *the* memory man of British jazz and always the first person to whom historians of the era go for info, comments and gossip!

In 1994 HUMPHREY LYTTELTON led the celebrations when the square in front of Gosport Town Hall was renamed 'Nat Gonella Square'.

Eddie Gordon and Nancy

Comedy cyclist. Eddie was born in Hollywood and came to the UK in the late Thirties. Philip remembers him well: 'He worked, silently, as a miserable, bald-headed clown. Always with a very glamorous partner. His great claim to fame was that he would always get to the theatre early. In twice nightly Variety he would be in the place, made up, ready to go by four o'clock in the afternoon. His partner, who only needed to put on a leotard, would arrive at the usual time and, from the minute she arrived, he would be calling out, every few minutes; "Are you ready Nancy?" That phrase became known throughout the business.'

Eddie Gordon and Nancy

Freddie Gordon

Eccentric acrobatic tap dancer, vocalist and percussionist is how he described himself in the 1950s. Born Gordon Frederick Garrett, Northants, 1923. Freddie became a single act in the late Forties via stints as a drummer in every sort of band, from the pit orchestra of the New Theatre, Northampton to FREDDIE MIRFIELDS GARBAGE MEN. He drummed for BILLY MERRIN and CHARLES SHADWELL too. In the Fifties he added dancing to his percussion work and was a featured single act in Variety. His bill matter was, 'A Goof in Love'.

Gordon and Colville

Comedy double act. Vic Gordon born Gordon Horsewell, London, 1911 and Peter Colville born Brighton, 1918. Originally Vic was, along with GLADYS HAY (WILL HAY's daughter), ALBERT POTTER (Gladys's husband) and AL FERNHEAD (of later *Radio Revellers* fame) a member of the musical act THE SIX HARMONISTS. He was, again with future *Radio Revellers*, STAN EMENEY and ART REED in *The Four Aces*. With the outbreak of the Second World War the act broke up and Vic played leads in straight plays till he met Peter, in 1948, and their act was born. Peter worked in revue and in *Star*

in Battledress as a light comedian and feed, and continued feeding all sorts until he met Vic in a summer show at Clacton. During our period they headlined in summer season and, as principal artistes, in touring versions of GEORGE AND ALFRED BLACK's West End successes. Peter now lives in Australia.

El Granadas and Peter

Rope-spinning speciality. Born Cecil Prentice, West Hartlepool, 1903, Lila Prentice born London 1908, Peter Prentice born London, 1928 and Dorothy Prentice born Blackpool. A family act, and how! Cecil was the founder when, in 1929, via an early career in circus, doing everything from rope-spinning to comedy cycling, he and his wife Lila produced their double act LA-ROPE AND LADY. They later changed their name to El Granadas. Their son Peter joined them in 1943 and *his* wife

Dorothy became part of the team in 1949. With their rope-spinning and stock whip manipulation they were a good colourful speciality. Nobody slept when they were on.

The Grand Order of Water Rats

An organisation that will be mentioned many times in this book. Why? Well, for over a hundred years to be a member of the Order has been the great accolade for anyone involved in the light entertainment side of show business. It is difficult to become a Rat. A huge percentage of its membership has to be on your side and vote for your inclusion. The qualifications? You have to be male (the ladies have a separate organisation, the Grand Order of Lady Ratlings), be in show business, be known by the majority of the lads, be good at your job, a good mixer and have a charitable nature. If you are all these things you are in with a chance.

The Order began in 1889 in a typically eccentric show biz way. Three music-hall performers, JAMES FINNEY, JOE ELVIN and JACK LOTTO, bought an interest in a trotting pony, The Magpie. They raced the pony on a straight mile course on the Croydon Road – between Thornton Heath and the William the Fourth pub in Streatham. The pony was bright and easily taught. Joe Elvin described the method used to make him a champ: 'The pony was driven from its stables in Kennington to the finishing line in Streatham. Once there he was allowed to have a good look round so he'd remember where he was. His nose-bag was then put on. He was allowed just one mouthful before it was snatched off and he was driven to the starting line. Once he was let go here he went like lightning to the place where he'd left his "munjari" (food).' It worked a treat and The Magpie was unbeatable over this course.

More and more 'pros' gathered on Sunday mornings to watch him race, and make a few bob betting on him. One afternoon Joe Elvin was taking the little pony back to his stables after a particularly strenuous morning. He was bathed in perspiration and looked a sorry sight. A bus driver, spying the apparition, called out: 'What have you got there Joe?' 'A trotter,' replied Elvin. 'Blimey,' said the driver, 'it looks more like a bleedin' water rat.' From then on that was the pony's name and The Friends of The Water Rat was formed. Later it was known as the Select Order of Water Rats and finally, as today, The Grand Order of Water Rats. The objects of the group of friends were: 'Philanthropy, conviviality and social intercourse'. They remain the same today. Since its inception, in 1889, the members of the Order have met, had fun and raised enormous amounts for charity. To be made a Water Rat is the ambition of every true pro.

Billy Gray

Juggler. Born London, 1914. One of EDDIE GRAY's brothers who, before he became Eddie's stooge, was a greengrocer, fishmonger, butcher, baker, coalman, newspaper seller, milkman, rag and bone man, furniture remover, office cleaner, hotel porter, parcel packer and horse-breaker. As a Gray, pretty par for the course. He met his first wife, OLIVE AUSTIN (a great granddaughter of the famous circus proprietor LORD GEORGE SANGER), and they worked as a double act, AUSTIN AND GRAY. Just like Billy, Olive could turn her hand to most things and when show biz jobs were thin on the ground she would work as a ladies' hairdresser or salesgirl. No posh 'resting' for Variety pros!

When I met Billy he was a prop man for one of the big television companies. He left TV to be part of the team in *Underneath the Arches* at Chichester and the Prince of Wales. He didn't do a bad job at all, playing his illustrious brother.

Eddie Gray

Monsewer

Juggler. Born London, 1898.'Juggler': that one word can't even begin to tell you anything about the great 'Monsewer'. To try to describe what he did, what he was like and why he was so loved, is like trying to describe TOMMY COOPER. They had the same sort of appeal – both 'one-offs'. While comedians generally try to caricature real people there are some who, the second they walk on, draw you into their very own world where only they make sense. Both Eddie and Tommy were members of this special breed.

The ludicrous moustache, red nose and glasses and that Cockney accented mangled French chat combined with real juggling skill put Eddie into the W.C. FIELDS class.

He began as a 'boy wonder' juggler and toured in Britain, in America and in the Far East. In 1930 came the meeting that was to change so many people's perceptions of revue. He was on a bill with NERVO AND KNOX. They were as off-beat and anarchistic as he was and, within two years, all three opened at the London Palladium in George Black's *Crazy Week*. NAUGHTON AND GOLD and CARYLL AND MUNDY completed the cast. The Crazy Gang was born. FLANAGAN AND ALLEN joined later. Eddie was with the Gang, on and off, till their retirement in 1962. He carried on as a single act.

He was as unpredictable offstage as he was on and stories of his legendary practical jokes are told to this day (see my anecdote book – please!).

Patrick Newley tells of Eddie's last week in Variety, in 1969: 'He had finished a week in his home town, Brighton. On the Sunday he went to see ELSIE AND DORIS WATERS (Gert and Daisy) in a concert at Eastbourne. The girls, feeling sorry for, who they thought, was a forgotten man, invited him on to the stage. The entire audience stood and applauded.' No one could ever forget the 'Monsewer'. He went home with a standing ovation ringing in his ears. He died the following morning.

Larry Grayson

Shut that door!

Comedian. Born William White, Banbury, 1924. Lots of good comedians work a bit 'camp' – SID FIELD and FRANKIE HOWERD for starters – but Larry outcamped them all. He was the ever complaining, gossipy chorus boy and landlady rolled into one.

During our period he was first WILLIE WHITE, then a drag act, BILLY BREEN, and finally, as a stand-up comedian, Larry Grayson. He spent the Forties touring in a small all-male revue. He told me it was called *Come Peep Through My Porthole* but I didn't believe him. He just caught the dying days of Variety way down on the bill but always talked about by people in the profession as 'a real original … ahead of his time'. Nothing happened for him and when Variety stopped he went back to the Midland clubs where he had started as a lad. It was here that his cast of, never seen, characters were born: Slack Alice, Everard, Apricot Lil, Self Raising Fred (from a pub called 'The Friend in Hand') and Pop it in Pete the Postman.

In the early Seventies a miracle happened. PETER DULAY (the son of the magician BENSON DULAY) booked him for a week in a number four hall, the Theatre Royal in Stratford. There he was noticed and via an all-male West End revue (the show flopped but Larry scored), a stint at DANNY LA RUE's nightclub, Variety at the Palladium and summer seasons and panto, he had his own television series and became a national institution. His handling of *The Generation Game* (formerly the province of the hard-hitting, well-organised Butlin redcoat type of comic) was a pure delight.

He was a genuinely funny man, offstage as well as on, and he loved every minute of his star status. It was sweet indeed that he achieved all he had ever wanted so late in life. He died in 1995.

Larry Grayson and friend

Hilda Gregory

Comedienne/feed and dancer. Born Sheffield, 1922. Hilda was one of those invaluable Variety artistes who were the backbone of the business. She began, in 1937, as a dancer in the chorus of a touring revue, *Red Hot and Blue Moments*, which starred the, as yet undiscovered, SID FIELD. She graduated to principal dancer with the touring shows, *To See Such Fun* with NAUGHTON AND GOLD and *Mr Brown Comes to Town* with the giant xylophonist TEDDY BROWN and 'WEE' GEORGIE WOOD. She caught the end of ENSA where she teamed up with one of my favourites, JIMMY GAY,

HILDA GREGORY
AND
LYN ANDREW

as GAY AND GREGORY ('Gags, Grins, Grace and Glamour'). How I wish I'd seen them together. After the war Jimmy left to go principal comicking while Hilda continued all through our period as half of the dancing act GREGORY AND ANDREW (Lyn Andrew). After a lifetime's service to the profession Hilda is now retired and living, with her vibrant memories, in Carmarthen.

George and Lydia. The Gridneffs

Acrobats. George Gridneff born Russia, 1914 and Lydia Herman. 'A very classy act,' says Philip. George was originally a member of his family's act, THE AMAZING GRIDNEFFS, and first appeared here in 1938. After wartime service with the RAF he met and married Lydia Herman (of THE FOUR HERMANS). George then devised the unsupported ladder act that played all over the world. Philip says: 'They were renowned for their fantastic leotards and never appeared in the same outfits two shows running.'

___H___

Halama and Konarski

Dancers. Alicia Halama Bardzinska born Poland, 1918 and Czeslaw Konarski born Poland, 1914. Philip says: 'They were probably the most stylish ballroom type dancing act to play Variety. They were a handsome couple, beautifully gowned and dressed and their immaculate lifts and turns were evidence of their ballet training in Poland.' Indeed Czeslaw's first London appearance was as a member of the Nijinska Ballet.

They were a top speciality act with seasons at the Palladium and a Royal Variety Performance among their many credits.

Adelaide Hall

Singer. Born Brooklyn, USA, 1901. One of our favourite imports. Adelaide was a great singer of jazz and sentimental ballads. She came to the UK in 1931 after her early years with all-black shows and as the singer with DUKE ELLINGTON at the Cotton

Club. At one time her pianist was ART TATUM. She recorded here and then moved to Paris where she appeared at the Moulin Rouge, ran her own nightclub, and then came back to make her home in the UK. She ran her own radio series. During our period she recorded, topped Variety bills, and played in musicals, both in Britain and in the States.

She was married as a teenager to BERT HICKS, who remained her husband and manager until his death in 1963. I heard her sing at a charity show just a year before she died in 1993.

Alec Halls

A cavalcade of junk

Comedian/musician. Born London, 1904. Died 1984. A genuine eccentric whom I met when I first joined the Water Rats. His letters to the Rats, explaining why he couldn't attend, ranked alongside those of LES DAWSON's as miniature masterpieces.

Trained as an electrical engineer, he soon abandoned that and joined the ERNIE LOTINGA show as a drummer and stooge. He eventually played five musical instruments – and the bagpipes! During the Second World War he toured twenty-two countries with ENSA. He gave his all, even performing extra shows to hospital patients

the lady in half, a 'Girl in the Air' suspension and his 'Zig Zag Lady' illusion.

My memory of him, though, is the paper bird that flapped its wings when you pulled its tail. Robert died in 1978.

Robert Harbin

in his spare time, and was the only ENSA artiste to be awarded the MBE. He played circus, Variety and pantomime often with a boy assistant. His first assistant was REG MATTHEWS who was a stalwart of the Entertainment Artistes Benevolent Fund. 'Alec was,' says Philip, 'a naturally funny man.'

Robert Harbin

Magician. Born Edward Williams, South Africa, 1909. Do you remember a friendly uncle sort of bloke, on children's television, demonstrating origami (folding paper to make animals, birds, etc)? It was Robert Harbin. That's all I knew about him until I talked to historians of magic. He was a very famous name to them, coming to the UK in the late Twenties where his first job was in the magic department of Gamage's store. He learned all he could there, launched his single act, in Variety, within a year, and won the first Magic Circle Maskelyne Award. Tricks that magicians still talk about included his own version of sawing

Norman Harper

Singing cowboy. Born Toronto, 1920. Norman arrived here in the late Forties and, with his horse Starlight, was part of BIG BILL CAMPBELL's *Rocky Mountain Rhythm* radio and stage show. I saw him later with the TEX MCLEOD Western revue *Rhythm on the Range*.

Dump Harris

Comedian and xylophonist. Born Ralph Harris, Bristol, 1907. Long before I saw him he was a semi-pro drummer after being a baker and a butcher. At round about twenty stone he was always being confused with the other, more famous, giant xylophonist, TEDDY BROWN.

It was his amazing likeness to OLIVE HARDY that was earning him a living when I first saw him. In a show called *Hollywood Doubles* he toured the number twos with a STAN LAUREL look-a-like billed as DUMP HARRIS AND STAN – 'Britain's Laurel and Hardy'. They weren't.

Will Hay Junior

Character comedian. Born William Edward Hay, Manchester, 1913. The son of one of our finest, Will junior, from twelve years of age to twenty, played the Cheeky Boy in his father's act. When Will senior retired he took the sketch 'The Fourth Form at St Michaels' on the road. Alas, he was merely a small chip off the old block. Dad was an impossible act to follow.

Arthur Haynes

Comedian. Originally a member of CHARLIE CHESTER's *Stand Easy* team, Arthur became a big success on television with his own show. With help from the writer JOHNNY SPEIGHT (later to invent the monstrous 'Alf Garnett' for WARREN MITCHELL), he created the 'know-all' tramp who drove NICHOLAS PARSONS crazy. His success on TV led him to top Variety bills all over the country and play revue at the London Palladium. I always remember his version of 'Le Rêve Passe' ('The Soldier's Dream') where he would play the wounded soldier. He died, at the end of his year's reign as King Rat of the GOWR, in 1966.

Richard Hearne

Mr Pastry

Character comedian. Born Norwich, 1909. 'Mr Pastry' was the character he created: the silly old man whose exploits, always involving lots of

tumbling and slapstick, endeared him to children and their parents everywhere. Those skills were drilled into him from an early age (he'd worked with his dad in circus from the age of nil). His classic comic character evolved through his playing old men in West End musicals and revues. Many people thought that, like CLIVE DUNN, he was a real old man and marvelled at his gymnastic ability. He featured an excellent one-man Lancers which he always attributed to its originator, TOM D. NEWELL. He made 'Mr Pastry' a national figure through television and capitalised on his success with his touring revue, *Mr Pastry Comes to Town*.

I did one of my very first pantomimes with Richard and found him to be a gentle, painstaking perfectionist. We did his famous shoe shop sketch and for this he taught me how to fall backwards off a chair. Very useful.

He retired from the business too early, being 'totally disillusioned with the vulgarity that has crept into our business', and spent his last years raising thousands of pounds for spastics organisations. He died in 1979.

Hilda Heath

Comedienne. Born Hilda Cree, Manchester,

1910. Philip says: 'Hilda was a very versatile performer who did the lot; tap, acro, contortions, cat in panto, impressions, and old *man* characterisations. She played low comedy sketches at the Windmill before becoming part of an adagio act, HEATH, NEUMAN AND WHEELER.' She worked with an act called THE THREE ARISTOCRATS which entered show biz folk lore. Whenever anyone told a particularly obscene or disgusting gag (off-stage) the enquiry would always come: 'Didn't you used to be with the Three Aristocrats?'

She worked as half of the act AL AND HILDA HEATH and during our period was a solo turn, 'The Versatile Comedienne'. She was a strong comedienne and a good panto Dame.

Miss Hella and Her Sea Lions

A Cologne-born former hotelier who sealed her fate by marrying the animal trainer RICHARD DECKER. She learned the business with the Circus Krone in Munich. I saw her, and her fishy breathed friends, at Olympia with the Bertram Mills Circus. Of all circus animals it seems to be dogs, chimps and sea lions who enjoy themselves the most.

Dick Henderson

The Yorkshire Nightingale

Comedian. Born Hull, 1891. We now remember Dick as the father of our own DICKIE HENDERSON and the singing sisters, THE HENDERSON TWINS, but he was a big star long before his clever children ever trod the boards. I saw him as a member of the DON ROSS music hall revival show, *Thanks for the Memory*. He was a fat little man wearing a tiny bowler hat and smoking a cigar. His delivery was attacking and his subject matter all the usual music-hall targets: wives, sweethearts and mothers-in-law. He even sang the occasional sentimental ballad like 'Pal of My Cradle Days'. His big finish was, 'Tiptoe Through the Tulips'. He did a Royal Variety Performance in 1926. The King laughed at: 'I went to get married and asked the parson how much it was. He said "what you think it's worth." I gave him a shilling. He took one look at the bride and gave me twopence back!' Another classic line of his was his opening.

He would stand sideways showing his enormous belly and comment: 'I was standing outside a maternity hospital, minding my own business…'

He died in 1958, just a few days before he should have appeared in his third Royal Variety Performance.

Dickie Henderson

Comedian. Born Richard Matthew Henderson, London, 1922. Perhaps the most versatile and certainly the smoothest, most laid-back comedian it has been my pleasure to see. It was always a pleasure to see this consummate pro in everything he did – and he did everything.

He began, as a lad, playing in films in Hollywood, notably *Cavalcade*. Back in England he worked with, and learnt from, his dad (see above) but their style couldn't have been more different. Dick was the archetype music-hall comic while Dickie was the epitome of mid Atlantic sophistication. From the late Forties he was a huge favourite in revue, musical comedy and straight plays. His Variety spots were always beautifully observed burlesques and his crooner with Sinatra-style ambitions was a classic. He danced, sang and delivered one-liners wonderfully, and even his prat falls were, somehow, classy.

He had a run of a 120 Dickie Henderson shows on television plus countless appearances on *Sunday Night at the Palladium*, proving, yet again, that he was the master of every medium he tackled. He played pantomime, notably as Buttons in *Cinderella*, and he was, without doubt, the best I ever saw.

Dickie was a six handicap golfer, a Royal Variety Performer fourteen times and a tireless worker for charity. He was the complete pro and a smashing bloke an' all.

He started to write his autobiography which is the first part of a book called *Sincerely Dickie* by Peter Cotes. He died in 1985.

Joe 'Mr Piano' Henderson

Pianist. Born in Glasgow. At first glance, Joe was another in the long line of 'all together now' pianists but he was more than that. Certainly he was a popular variety act but he had been a pianist and accompanist from the age of fifteen, had his own music publishing company and was a prolific composer. His most famous tune, 'Trudie' won him a Novello Award.

He was accompanist and musical arranger for ALMA COGAN before he embarked on his solo career, doing countless radio series, recording fifteen LPs and a stack of singles.

I did a summer season with him in Bournemouth where, always worried about his weight, he had a steam cabinet in his dressing room. Between shows he would sit inside the cabinet while I would sit outside and chat with his sweating head – and feed him whisky at the same time. He was a nice, gentle man who died far too soon.

Margo Henderson

Piano/entertainer. Margo was born in Clydebank, Scotland and did an act at the piano with her husband, SAM KEMP. I never saw the double act. They played mostly theatres north of the Border throughout the Forties and Fifties. The vivacious Margo was a solo act when she came to fame in the UK via radio, television, cabaret and, especially, through her seasons with the fantastically popular *Black and White Minstrel Show*. She had a great personality and seemed to ooze fun with everything she did, especially with her wickedly accurate impressions.

Margo retired in the Seventies and opened a restaurant near Brighton. She and Sam now live in Spain.

Charles Henry

Producer/stage director. Born Putney, London, 1890. A name familiar to those who looked at posters and programmes beyond the performers' names. Charles produced hundreds of shows from *Rockets* at the London Palladium in 1922 through to *Sunday Night at the Palladium* on television. He produced touring revues and pantomimes all over the country and, at the Palladium, looked after all the big American stars who came there just after the war (DANNY KAYE sighed a photograph, 'To Charles – if you hadn't pushed me out on the stage I would never have appeared in London.'). He knew comedy sketches and gags better than almost anyone and his cool, calm approach led to his long association with THE CRAZY GANG. CHARLIE NAUGHTON told me; 'He was the only one the boys would listen to.' He died in 1968.

Frankie Higgins

Comedian. Born Islington, 1913. A Cockney comic who, after performing in the London Fire Service show *Fireman Smith Entertains* became a popular Variety and pantomime regular. Philip says: 'He always did a strong spot but never acquired the fame a successful radio or TV series would have brought him.'

Benny Hill

Comedian. Born Alfred Hawthorn Hill, Southampton, 1924. After CHAPLIN and STAN LAUREL, probably the most famous British comedian in the world. It was, of course, Benny's TV shows that did the trick. Who would have believed that his mixture of familiar gags, over the top characterisations and plain rudery would capture America and most of the world? They did. So much so that he left over seven million pounds in his will.

Why should it have been Benny who reaped these incredible rewards and not any of the other equally creative and talented comics in these pages? Was it just a case of the old show business cliché, being in the right place at the right time? He certainly was that. In the mid Fifties, when TV had just one channel and was desperate to find new, young faces, Benny was there. His early shows set the standard for all that followed. He used all the expertise of the make-up department, exploited the technical side with recorded inserts and under-cranking and, unforgettably, made old jokes look new. It's a shame that his last shows became so uninventive and obvious . But here our subject is Variety and Benny did begin in the golden period.

He was, in 1948, a member of the HEDLEY CLAXTON summer show *Gaytime* company, had been feed to REG VARNEY and made it, via television, to topping bills in the West End and everywhere else. I saw him several times live and he never seemed totally at home with an audience. In my book, not a great Variety comic but seven million quid tells you what I know. He died in 1992.

Ronnie Hilton

Singer. Born Adrian Hill, Hull, 1926. Ronnie became one of our most popular top of the bill singers from the mid Fifties on. His recording of 'The Windmill in Old Amsterdam' is still a hugely popular one with children of all ages. He began, in 1951, by winning a local singing competition. He

broadcast with the BBC Northern Variety Orchestra and was the resident vocalist at a Leeds dance hall. His first recording contract came about in an odd way. A friend had written a song of which Ronnie made a private recording. The boss of HMV records heard it, signed him and a string of top ten hits catapulted him to headline status in Variety. Ronnie held the position and was also versatile enough to become a popular male Principal Boy in panto.

He is now semi-retired in Sussex but recently presented a series of highly popular nostalgic record programmes for BBC Radio Two.

Joan Hinde

Trumpeter. Born Eckington, Derbyshire, 1933. A superb instrumentalist who, whether she's playing a rousing, 'Post Horn Gallop' or a bluesy jazz standard, never fails to pull the place apart wherever she appears. Joan came from a family of musicians and learned the cornet at six years of age. A great background in silver bands (nearly all the best seem to have had that training) led

her, as a child prodigy, into broadcasting, Variety and touring with ELSIE AND DORIS WATERS ('Gert and Daisy'). Since then she has taken her talent all over the world and the fact that she is constantly employed by KEN DODD, MAX BYGRAVES and SIR HARRY SECOMBE says everything. Master Variety performers always use the very best.

Betty Hobbs Globe Girls

Speciality act. A very unusual act with a troupe of girls 'walking' on huge globes. They were mostly used as a speciality in the big revues.

Michael Holliday

Singer. Born in Liverpool, 1928. The ex-merchant seaman whose amazing vocal similarity to BING CROSBY and laid-back, relaxed way with a song made him a recording and Variety star in the Fifties.

He began by winning a talent competition in New York, where his merchant ship had docked. Out of the Navy, he worked as a singer guitarist with the ERIC WINSTONE Band around the Butlin camps. I started as a redcoat in Clacton and stories of his anything but laid-back way with troublesome punters were legion.

It was NORRIE PARAMOR, in 1955, who signed Michael for Columbia records and a string of top

ten hits was the outcome. He topped in variety, had his own TV series and even appeared on film in 1962 with THE CRAZY GANG in *Life Is a Circus*. His image as an avuncular, cuddly, ultra-ordinary man singing cosy songs took a bit of a bashing when he died in 1963, as the cause of his death was thought to be a drug overdose.

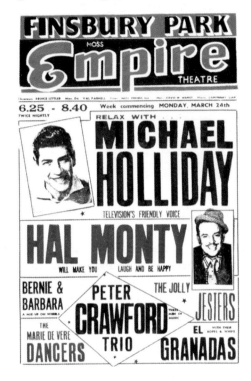

Stanley Holloway

Actor. Born Stanley Augustus Holloway, Manor Park, East London, 1890. It does seem incredible that someone we all seem to know actually started as a performer, in pierrot troupes, before the First World War. I only knew Stanley towards the end of his life. To me he was Victorian man, never the wrapped-up-in-his-own-little-world specialist of today. During his long career he tackled, successfully, almost everything. His concert party days gave way to musicals. The 1920s saw him as a member of *The Co-Optimists*, an up-market version of the shows of his earliest days. In 1929 he first appeared at the Palladium where, thinking he should break up his songs with something different, he put in the very first

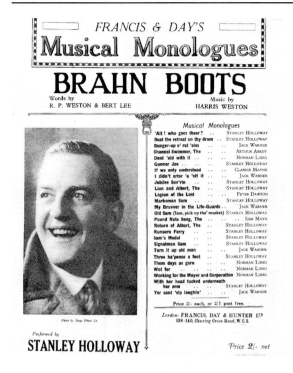

monologue he had written, 'Old Sam': 'Sam! Sam! pick up tha musket'. With the help of MARRIOTT EDGAR, BOB WESTON and BERT LEE he gave us a continuous supply of classic pieces that are still very much remembered today: 'The Lion and Albert', ('What waste all our lives raising children, to feed ruddy lions? Not me!') 'The Runcorn Ferry' ('per twopence, per person, per trip') 'Brahn Boots' ('fancy comin' to a funeral in brahn boots'). Oddly enough, most of the monologues were North Country based but Stanley was a Cockney.

One of his first film parts was in a GRACIE FIELDS vehicle *Sing as We Go*, and it was Gracie who persuaded him to take his talents into Variety. Radio, records, musicals, revue, character parts in films – he did the lot.

By the mid Fifties he was winding down. He'd made a lot of money and seemed quite content to do just what he felt like. He had met ALAN J. LERNER in London and, while in America with the Old Vic Company in 1955 they met again and chatted about a new musical. The rest, of course, is history. *My Fair Lady* is, in my book, one of the most perfect musicals. Stanley had been waiting all his life for a part like Doolittle. It had everything he was best at, philosophical speeches,

roguishness and, best of all, cracking songs that suited his rich music-hall baritone like a glove. After the success of the show and the film, both here and in America, he flitted happily between the UK and USA doing television, films and a one-man show.

His life story *Wiv a Little Bit of Luck*, as told to Dick Richards, was published in 1967. He made his last film in 1974 and his stage appearance was in the Royal Variety Performance of 1980. I had the pleasure of escorting him on and off the stage.

Most people today only remember Stanley as the superlative singer of 'Get Me to the Church on Time' and 'Wiv a Little Bit of Luck' but, to me, he will always be the man who made 'Albert' a national hero. He died in 1982.

Holt and Morice

Comedy duo. I never saw them but Philip says: 'They were an old-fashioned two-man double act. Corny stuff but they were such nice guys you had to use them. Their bill matter, 'Shredded Wit' tells you all you need to know.'

Percy Honri

A Concert-in-a-turn

Concertina player. Born Percy Harry Thompson, Banbury, 1874. A legendary music-hall star. Could a concertina player top the bill today? Unfair, because Percy was much more than this. He was a presenter of shows. His touring revue *Concordia*, employing a hundred performers, was one of the first in the field in the early 1900s and he was the

Mary and Percy Honri

original user of film back projection in a Variety act. He was also the very first artiste to be recorded by HMV. During our period he did a double act with his daughter, MARY HONRI. He retired in 1951 and died in 1953. Mary died at the age of seventy-seven, in 1988. Percy's grandson PETER HONRI is a working actor and concertina player. He has written the story of his family in *Working The Halls* and has a fascinating new book, a history of the Variety Artistes Federation, (the Union we all belonged to till it was swallowed up by Equity) *Music Hall Warriors*, just published.

Hope and Keen

Comedians. Mike and Albie Harrison. Mike Hope born 1935 and Albie Keen born 1935. Two real cousins whose dads were a well-known Variety act in the Thirties and Forties, SYD AND MAX HARRISON. Following in their father's footsteps, and with their advice, Mike and Albie learned everything. They dance, sing, are

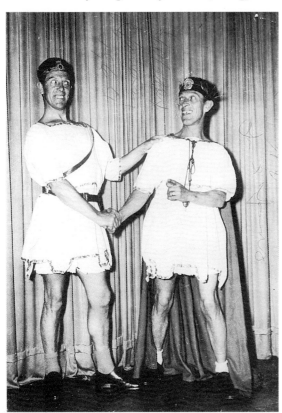

Hope's and Keen's fathers – Sid and Max Harrison

excellent acrobats, play a fantastic number of instruments and are a great straight man and comic combination. Follow that!

Both Mike and Albie are qualified Olympic gymnastic instructors. You'd believe it if you saw their act. They joined the RAF for National Service with the hope of becoming PTIs but the powers-that-be thought they'd be better employed as typists! They did, however, make the ceremonial parade band and this is where their act began to take shape. After demob, in 1956, they turned pro and their first gig, so they say, was in Dartmoor Prison! On-stage, not in the audience. Three years' hard graft in Variety followed. They added lots of comedy to their already impressive list of musical and acrobatic skills and they were away. They were featured on Variety bills, in summer season and pantomime (what a Captain and Mate they are) everywhere from the London Palladium to all the number one venues. I don't have to tell you they are extremely successful in America too.

They have taken the best of old-time show business and modernised and honed the old routines to perfection.

The Hortobagyi Troupe

Springboard act. There were lots of these sort of acts in Variety. One member of the troupe would stand on the end of a see-saw while another would land on the opposite end. The first would then be catapulted on to the shoulders of a 'bearer'. This routine would continue till a human pyramid was formed. The Hortobagyi Troupe played all the top theatres in the world and the youngest of them had the distinction of being the one at the top of the pyramid from the age of seven.

Renee Houston

Comedienne/actress. Born in Renfrewshire, Scotland, 1902. Another great survivor. Renee, from a theatrical family (her father and mother were JAMES HOUSTON AND COMPANY), after a tough apprenticeship in concert party, became half of the top of the bill Variety act, THE HOUSTON SISTERS. The other half was her real sister, BILLIE. They

Renee Houston and Donald Stewart

...were a headline act in the 1920s. In one of their ...pots they played two children, the tables and ...hairs they used on stage being made larger than ...ormal to create the illusion. They parted in 1936 ...hen Billie (who was always dressed as a boy in ...e act) became ill.

Renee, whose ad-libbing and rapport with an ...udience were her greatest assets (and manage-...ent's greatest worries!) carried on alone and ...ad great success in musical comedy. The double ...ct was revived with Renee's third husband, ...ONALD STEWART, playing the boy's part. They ...ecame an equally big draw in Variety until ...onald's death in 1965.

The beautiful Renee battled on. She was a ...opular, outspoken panellist on radio in the all-girl ...uestion and answer show *Petticoat Line*, and she ...layed dozens of memorable dramatic and ...omedy roles in films and on television. She wrote ...terrific autobiography, *Don't Fence Me In*. Billie ...ouston died in 1972 and Renee in 1980.

...en Howe and Audrey Maye

...wo funny four words

...omedy double act. Water Rat Len and Lady

Ratling Audrey came together from totally differ-ent backgrounds. Len's family were publicans while Audrey's were dyed-in-the-wool theatre people. Her dad was SYLVESTER STUART from Cardiff where he ran his own shows for many years. Her mum was a well-known actress MAY WARDEN, never to be forgotten as the hostess of the dinner party in FREDDIE FRINTON's classic sketch, 'Dinner for One'.

They both worked for Sylvester in his concert parties and married in 1949. Their act was a mélange of double patter, audience participation, singing, dancing and mime comedy. They played everywhere from the Palladium to Collins Music Hall and all stops between, touring Australia and New Zealand for eighteen months and even working in Pakistan and India. Yet again, as Variety crumbled, two experienced pros adapted their talents to suit conditions. Audrey directed panto and played comedy parts while Len took to 'book' shows like a duck to water. He does a great drunk and his unforgettable face is often featured in TV adverts.

They still sometimes perform their Variety act which I will rush to see the next time they do.

Frankie Howerd

Titter ye not

Comedian. Born Francis Alick Howard, York, 1917. Frank, during the war, was rejected once for the Army Entertainment Organisation ENSA, and for the Army show *Stars In Battledress* no fewer than *four* times. One man, Colonel RICHARD STONE (later to become a famous theatrical agent) saw his potential and put him into a touring concert party. On demob, he was no luckier until an agent, STANLEY 'SCRUFFY' DALE, spotted him and he was taken on by the bandleader JACK PAYNE. His big break, as with so many others, came with radio. He became one of the two regular comedians on *Variety Bandbox* (DEREK ROY was the other) and, after twenty years of amateur shows, and disappointments, he became a star overnight.

'Scruffy' Dale (Frankie had freed himself from Jack Payne after an acrimonious court case) looked after his business and did very well for him. Together they started Associated London Scripts, a writers' set-up that nurtured the talents of GALTON and SIMPSON and, especially, ERIC SYKES. Eric was the man who wrote all Frank's early radio scripts, capturing his unique style perfectly. He was soon topping Variety bills everywhere, doing films, radio and television shows and making highly successful forays into the legit. He had a hit as Bottom but then, suddenly, everything went wrong.

A couple of disastrous West End shows and several badly received television series meant, that in just a couple of years, he had become a show biz leper. In 1961 the head of Television Light Entertainment told Ray Galton and Alan Simpson, who wanted to write for Frankie, 'Forget him, he's finished.'

I remember seeing him, for the very first time, wander clumsily on to the stage of the Croydon Empire. He looked like a man who had just woken up from a nap. Ill-fitting creased suit, enormous lugubrious face, topped off with a toupee you could spot from the back of the gallery – within a minute he had us eating out of his hand. He was the next door neighbour who knew all the gossip. Outrageous and outraged when we laughed at his confidences. I suppose he was very camp, but to us he was just an eccentric who made it up as he went along. What a tragedy it would have been if 1961 had seen the end of him. Of course the rest of his story is well known. His 'comeback' in TV's *That Was the Week That Was*, the lead in *A Funny Thing Happened on the Way to the Forum* (the inspiration for *Up Pompeii*) his excellence on chat shows and his acceptance by the yuppie set. A wonderful book, *Star Turns –*

the life and times of Benny Hill and Frankie Howerd by Barry Took tells the stories of the two great comedians in painstaking detail and with great love. Frank died in 1992.

Hutch

Singer/pianist. Leslie A. Hutchinson, born Jamaica, 1900. It is only now, long after the death of Variety, that I've learned to really appreciate 'Hutch'. I have all of his 78rpm records (those that have been transferred to LPs). I did see him in Variety but he wasn't really up a lad's street: I only really liked the comics. I do remember him sitting at the grand piano, mopping his brow with a white handkerchief (I could never work out why – he'd only sung one song) and the ladies in the audience hanging on every note. His handsome looks, lazy sophistication, unique creamy voice and excellent piano playing did add up to something special.

He came to the UK, via New York, in the 1920s and, from 1927 on, was the darling of London's West End cabaret. Philip, a great fan says: 'He was the toast of London during and after the war. He was the first black entertainer to be accepted, indeed worshipped, by Society. He was immaculate in dress, style and delivery and a great ladies' man.'

He made an LP just before his death in 1969. He was, if anything, better than ever.

Vic Hyde

Multi-instrumentalist. Born Chicago, USA. Vic began playing his act during the intervals of an American tenting show, performing in the playlets as well. He became a 'gofer' for OLSEN AND JOHNSON, doing everything from blowing up balloons to playing the gorilla in their show. It was RUDY VALLEE who gave him his big break on American radio. He came to the UK in 1948 where he featured his playing of almost every instrument you can think of in the West End and in Variety. His big finish was playing four trumpets, with four separate mouthpieces, at the same time. JOHNNY LAYCOCK later did the very same finish.

the song in a pantomime where Friar Tuck, ARTHUR TOLCHER, provided the harmonica backing.)

I worked with Frank in both summer show and pantomime (he was the best, most believable, male Principal Boy I ever saw) and he never failed to score. His fresh-faced, outdoor type personality and terrific country and western style voice made him special. Just like DONALD PEERS before him Frank always made an audience feel better for having seem him. His big finish was his high-speed, guaranteed to get the audience 'high', yodelling. Sadly, for us, he now lives in Australia but the good news is that, after a long battle with ill health, he may be coming back here to work again soon. Everything crossed.

___ I ___

Frank Ifield

Singer. Born Coventry, 1937. Frank just makes our period. He came back home, after a show biz apprenticeship in Australia, in 1959, springing to prominence with his own version of an old song, 'I Remember You'. At one time the record was selling a thousand copies a minute! (He included

___ J ___

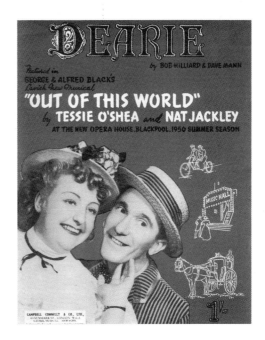

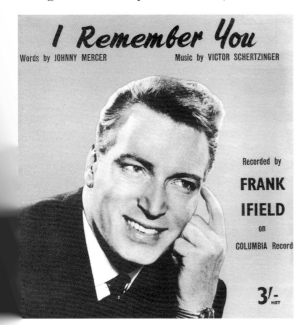

Nat Jackley

Rubber Neck

Eccentric comedian and dancer. Born Nathaniel Jackley-Hirsch, Sunderland, 1909. Of all things, a straight man who, when it was discovered he was funnier than the comedian

(JACK CLIFFORD), swapped roles with him. Neither of them ever looked back.

He was a tall, thin, excellent dancer who, with his off-beat delivery of gags, bird-like neck movements and 'educated' legs, became a star. He had a great pedigree. His grandfather, Nathan, a circus performer, had his own troupe, THE JACKLEY WONDERS, and George, his father, was a popular panto and Variety top of the bill. Nat began as a member of the EIGHT LANCASHIRE LADS (the starting point for so much talent) and progressed to a double act with his sister Joy. His apprenticeship with Jack Clifford led to his solo career. Well, not really solo as he usually had a handful of feeds with him, DICK BEAMISH, SAMMY CURTIS and ARTHUR VOLLUM among them. He often worked with his first wife MARIANNE LINCOLN. Their relationship was one of the stormiest in show business and stories about them are legion, none repeatable here!

Nat had the honour of three Royal Variety Performances to his name and topped seasons at the Palladium and all the top seaside resorts. I worked with him in panto where he was an extremely unorthodox Dame though his Girl Guide and military line-up sketches fitted in a treat. He actually did fifty pantos, his last in Newcastle (1980) on the very stage where his dad had done the previous last panto to be staged at that theatre. Late in life he became a highly respected TV character actor, notably as the Grandad in *Spoils of War*. He died in 1988.

Jimmy James

Comedian. Born James Casey, Stockton-on-Tees, 1892. Truly the comedian's comedian. The last time I saw Jimmy was in a week's Variety at the Wimbledon Theatre. The theatre bar was packed with comedians, and as Jimmy's play on music was heard, the room emptied and thirty or forty worshippers at the shrine crammed into the back of the stalls. As Jimmy exited, thirty or forty comics did too – back into the bar.

Of course you remember the classic 'lion in the box' routine. Jimmy would be joined on-stage by a stuttering question mark on legs, Eli (JACKIE CASEY) and a man in a huge hat and a down-to-the-ground overcoat. Overcoat (see ROY CASTLE)

carried a shoebox under his arm and, after establishing that it wasn't Jimmy who had been 'putting it around that I'm barmy', proceeded to explain what was in that box. Ten minutes or so later, when the whole situation had been painstakingly explained to the slightly confused Jimmy, a volley of 'fah! fah! fahs!' would somehow get the trio into their finishing song. I remember 'Kisses Sweeter Than Wine' as a favourite. It is impossible to pin down in mere words the timing of the great man and Eli, the 'throwaway' observations, the inspired lunacy of their logic and the visual delights of their tiny, beautifully choreographed, movements and bits of business. If you never saw that sketch you have missed out, badly. The great news is that Jimmy's son, JAMES CASEY (a BBC Radio producer: see JIMMY CLITHEROE) and the real Eli are doing the act again and it really is a bit special. Rush to wherever you see them on a bill. How Jimmy ever concocted the classic sketch we'll never know. I would think a thread of a plot and a thousand ad-libs was the route. He had been a great ad libber since his early days. He began as a juvenile performer, 'Terry – the Blue-eyed Irish Boy' but, after being gassed in the First World War, couldn't sing any more so turned to comedy. He developed his drunk sketches (he didn't drink), added stooges and became a real original. His solo routine where he explained the dangers of being a chip frier was another classic.

Twice he was brought to Variety's Mecca, the London Palladium, to save the day. Once when LUCAN AND MCSHANE failed there and again when MICKEY ROONEY 'laid an egg'. He did one Royal Variety Performance, in 1953, and stopped the show. I don't think he ever was a huge top of the bill but he was loved and admired by everyone who ever shared his surreal, yet totally accessible, world. He died in 1965.

Jane

of the Daily Mirror

Model. Born Chrystabel Leighton-Porter, Chandlersford, Hants, 1919. Now, did this lady start the nude show period? She might well have. Philip remembers she was one of the first to appear at the posh number one Moss Empire halls. LEW LAKE produced the show which had 'Jane', her dachshund 'Fritz', and three supporting acts as its first half. The second half was a re-jig of the FRED KARNO sketch, 'A Night in an English Music Hall'.

Miss Leighton-Porter became 'Jane' via a modelling career and the winning of the Miss England title (and a hundred pounds). Pett, the man who invented the famous strip cartoon, used Miss LP as his model for the girl every soldier, sailor and airman longed to meet. All her posing for him was done in the afternoon and at week-ends, which left her the rest of the time to play Variety. I remember seeing her in Cambridge and very decorous she was. She opened in silhouette and recited:

I'm Jane, Jane the model – that's plain.
I can't sing – I can't even croon,
And the dog that I fondle, is also a model,
That you've seen in a popular strip cartoon.

She was very nice and mumsy – worse luck.

Audrey Jeans

Comedienne. Born Portsmouth, 1930. Audrey was just too ahead of her time for this country. There wasn't much room for comediennes of her type in the golden days of Variety. Most top funny ladies on the halls were grotesques like HYLDA BAKER, GLADYS MORGAN and NELLIE WALLACE. Audrey was an attractive, beautifully dressed real woman who could dance, sing (straight and point numbers), play sketches, deliver one-liners, get laughs and act. In America she would have been a star.

She began her career, at sixteen, as part of the chorus in the SID FIELD revue *Piccadilly Hayride* and from then on, with encouragement from the great Sid, worked at comedy. She toured Australia with ARTHUR ASKEY and then, as so often happens

PROGRAMME

PICCADILLY HAYRIDE

1. **LET'S HAVE A PICCADILLY HAYRIDE** (Dick Hurran)
   The Country Girl .... TRISS HENDERSON
   The Yokels .... THE REGENT CHORISTERS
   and the Hey-Hey Makers
   Dances by Jack Billings. Costume and Decor by Berkeley Sutcliffe
   Music arranged by Arthur Fenoulhet
2. **RETURN OF SLASHER GREEN**
   JERRY DESMONDE introduces "THE COAT" .... SID FIELD
3. **SHAKESPEAREAN EPISODE** (Frederick Burtwell)
   King John .... SLASHER GREEN   The Chamberlain ..GEORGE HAMILTON
   The Sentries .... SYD RAILTON and PETER MORTON
   Simnel (a Cook) ...... TERRY THOMAS   Robert Fitzwalter .. JERRY DESMONDE
   Charlie Stevens .... ALFIE DEAN   Lady-in-Waiting ...... PAULINE TYLER
4. **IN TOWN TO-NIGHT** .... with TERRY THOMAS
5. **BON VOYAGE**
   Anchors Away!
   The Sailor .... ALAN LUND   The Girl on the Quay ..BLANCHE LUND
   His Friends........VICTOR RANGER, GEORGE GERHARDT and AUDREY JEANS

– nothing did. She packed it in and worked behind the counter of a friend's shop in Portsmouth. The agent KEITH DEVON persuaded her to go back into the biz and, with his guidance, she became a good middle of the bill act and an excellent feed for the comics, playing her Variety and cabaret act in the UK and all over the world.

My first big summer season was with Audrey in Torquay and her advice, on and offstage, was invaluable. I was an idealist, blissfully ignorant of the devious politics of show business. I would always say what I thought, and still do. Audrey did manage to make me hold my tongue at least for that season. After one particularly unpleasant run-in with the powers that be she took me on one side and said: 'Listen. Keep that (pointing to her nose) out. That (pointing to her mouth) shut and who's got a packet of fags on Friday? You have!' I'm still waiting for the packet of fags! Audrey was married twice and, tragically, was killed by a hit-and-run driver while on her second honeymoon in Paris.

The Jerry Builders

Also known as WILLIS, WEST AND MCGINTY, they were a classic slapstick act who played all the top Variety dates both in the UK and abroad.

Jewel and Warriss

Comedy double act. Jimmy Jewel born James Marsh in Sheffield, 1906. Ben Warriss born Sheffield, 1909. Perhaps the most famous double act of the Forties and Fifties, Jimmy and Ben were cousins – born in the same bed. Jimmy's dad was a well-known comedian – Jimmy took his name, JIMMY JEWEL, and his apprenticeship with his father (who had started in the game as a set designer) included not only feeding Jimmy senior but making scenery, props and stage managing too. What a beginning.

Ben's start was an early one too. He was a single turn from the age of ten. He was a pioneer broadcaster from Savoy Hill and a black-faced act with ALEXANDER AND MOSE and as a solo act in Variety.

In 1934, the lads were together in a revue at the Palace Newcastle when one of the acts failed to turn up. They went on and the famous double act was born.

During their thirty-year partnership they did the lot: seven Royal Variety Performances, twelve summer seasons in Blackpool, films, pantos everywhere for the top management HOWARD AND WYNDHAM and their own shows on tour and at the Palladium. Their radio series 'Up the Pole' was the icing on the cake. It ran from 1947 till 1952 and made them the highest-paid double act of the day.

The set-up of the act was one that goes back into the mists of time. The smart, know-all man about town constantly conning his lovable, daft partner. Ben was a terrific straight man, sharp, incisive with great attack. Jimmy was a good comic. He looked funny, talked funny and was a great timer. Their spots were mostly situations rather than jokes. they were totally different characters off stage too. Jimmy was a great worrier, a bit of a loner, for ever anxious that everything should be just right. Ben was, what was called in the days when English was a beautifully descriptive language, a gay blade. He was always the master of the revels, a gregarious irresponsible flirt who loved life and his fellow pros.

They stayed on top till 1966 when, depressed by

the lack of Variety and the proliferation of club work, where they were expected to do 'blue' material, they called it a day.

Ben embarked on all sorts of ventures but eventually came back to perform in Old Time Music Hall and pantomime. Jimmy had a fantastically successful Indian summer. He became a wonderful actor with triumphs on television, in films, at the National and in the West End. Ben died, skint, in 1993 and Jimmy, very comfortable, in 1995.

Jo, Jac and Joni

Three-handed comedy dance team. The act were originally three dancers, Johnny Burslem, Tommy Scott and Norman Littlehales. They met in a TOMMY TRINDER revue in 1950, where the act was born. They, all three, had white faces and wore bowler hats, black tights and tails (à la MAX WALL) but plus spats. With the help of JOAN DAVIS they concocted a mélange of eccentric dancing, music, harmony singing and great visual gags. Their big break came, in 1952, when they deputised for the multi-trumpet player, VIC HYDE, at a Water Rats Ball. They were a sensation: so much so that they did the first of their the Royal Variety Performances that very year. From then on they played every conceivable Variety date in the book plus seasons at the Lido in Paris and in South America. In 1955 Norman left the act and Johnny's wife June took over. I never knew one of them was a girl. They played Las Vegas, Reno and *The Ed Sullivan Show* on American TV. Johnny

and June left the act in 1957 and carried on as a double dancing act in Paris.

Tommy Scott is still with us, running a theatrical agency in Blackpool, and Johnny and June (who is an examiner for the Royal Academy) still teach dancing in Wickford, Essex. I can't think of anyone more qualified.

The Jovers

Comedy burlesque acrobats. Tommy Jover born Florencio Tomas Jover, Villena, Spain, 1895. The Jover name is still represented in the business but it was Tommy who began the whole thing back in the 1910s. He, like all circus family members, learnt *everything*. He even did a bit of bull-fighting when times were hard. He led the Jover family for at least five decades in their routines. His two sons RAF and JULIAN were a highly successful act from 1950 onwards. Their big trick, on the trapeze, was a half-standing back somersault into an ankle catch. Julian married TED RAY's partner, KITTY BLUETT, in the radio show *Ray's a Laugh*.

Betty Jumel

The Bundle of Fun

Comedienne. Born Fairhaven, 1901. Betty was a tiny, effervescent, eccentric and versatile comedienne who, from her early days as part of her dad's Variety act, rose to become a well-known face in those funny old Mancunian British films with FRANK RANDLE, NAT JACKLEY, etc. Pantomime was one of her specialities: she was

Norman Evans and Betty Jumel

the perfect Humpty Dumpty and one of the few ladies to successfully play Dame. Once again radio helped her career quite a lot and she was featured in several series of *Good Evans!* and *Over the Garden Wall* with NORMAN EVANS. She was an important part of Norman's touring theatre revues too. She died in 1990.

___K___

Eva Kane

Siffleuse (lady whistler) and soprano. Born Isle of Man 1923. 'Eva,' Philip says, 'was the English counterpart of NORA WILLIAMS the whistling songstress from DAVE APPOLLONS band which was an American outfit that did so well in the UK on its brief visits. Apart from a most melodious whistling routine of pops she would then break in to a coloratura vocal and usually stop the show. Her act was one of the first to be televised after the Second World War. Her family owned hotels on the Isle of Man to where, I believe, she retired.'

Kardoma

He fills the stage with flags

Magician. Born Leonard Crompton Clifford,

Bradford, 1891. His bill matter, above, is well remembered and still referred to, in a jocular way today. He began, as LEON CLIFFORD, 'Britain' Youngest Illusionist' in 1911. The 'filling the stage with flags' came about as a result of one of his original routines, in which his big finish was to completely cover the stage with flowers which made it look like a giant garden. When war came he simply substituted flags for flowers and had great, patriotic finale. I last saw Leonard demonstrating magic tricks at Ellisdon's in Holborn.

The Three Karloffs

Comedy hand-to-hand balancers. Three Geordie lads from Consett. They were all gymnasts who got together as an act in 1926. They played circus in Ireland and returned to Variety and revue in the UK when they came back from war work.

Billy Kay

Comedian. Born William Henry Stephenson Leeds, 1898. A diminutive, less than five feet high highly inventive comic, who originally worked as TUBBY STEVENS! Under his new name he ran his own shows both as producer and principal comic In 1948 he was part of the famous OLSEN AND JOHNSON show, *Hellzapoppin* at the London Casino and Princes Theatre. When Olsen and Johnson returned home to America Billy went with them.

Danny Kaye

Entertainer. Born David Daniel Kaminski, New York, 1913. 1948 was the year Danny scored one of the greatest triumphs in Variety that London had ever seen. His films had been successful in the UK and so he, like almost every American film or recording star of the time, was booked for a stint at the London Palladium. Now some Americans had scored and some certainly hadn't Most were an unknown quantity so the Palladium was taking a chance every time. Danny Kaye's London début* (in 1948) was a smash. His mixture of tongue-twister songs, his sense of satire, audience participation and, most of all, his totally relaxed approach (he even sat, with legs dangling in the pit, and drank a cup of tea) had never been seen before and he became London's darling. His tour of the number one halls all round the country had exactly the same effect. Of course his success was no fluke. His early years were spent in holiday resorts in the Catskill Mountains (America's Butlin's) where he first found out he could be funny. His meeting, in 1939, with SYLVIA FINE, whom he later married, was the big break. She wrote material tailored especially for him and Broadway and Hollywood success followed.

The comedian, and life-long Kaye aficionado, TED ROGERS, does a wonderful tribute show to Danny. Do catch it if you can. Danny died in 1988.

*He did own up later that he had been to London before. In 1938 he had done cabaret at the Savoy Hotel and 'died the death'.

Dave Kaye

See IVOR MORTON and DAVE KAYE.

Davy Kaye

Comedian. Born in London's East End. A diminutive Jewish comic who has done the lot: Variety, cabaret, musicals, TV and stage drama and films. He started in the game in 1936 as half of a double act KAYE AND VALE. They played the smaller number twos in a show called *The Year's Discoveries* for MANNY JAY and SIDNEY MYERS. The act split and, after the war Davy was booked as principal comedian in TEDDY HINGE's revue *Fanny Get Your Fun*. This title became the subject of a court case which achieved nationwide press coverage. The impresario EMILE LITTLER was presenting the famous musical *Annie Get Your Gun* at the London Coliseum and he accused Teddy Hinge of pinching his title. Emile Littler lost the case and *Fanny*, after its posters were overprinted with the message, 'The Show They Tried to Ban!' did terrific business.

(Emile Littler ran the Palace Theatre, Shaftesbury Avenue when I appeared there in a revue with DANNY LA RUE. At the opening night party Mr Littler, at the end of the do, emptied the salted peanuts that weren't eaten into a large can, sealed the top with sellotape and took them back home with him.)

Davy did a long stint as resident host and compere at London's Embassy Club where a visiting American star dubbed him 'a substantial midget'. He was, and still is, a glutton for work and while at the Embassy Club he doubled as a replacement in *Guys and Dolls* at the London Coliseum and played a lead part in a wonderful musical (killed by the critics), *Belle – the Story of Doctor Crippen*.

He will always be remembered for his one-man band routine (the idea sold to him by JIMMY LEE) to 'Macnamara's Band'. Davy developed the idea to its present perfect form where he plays drums, cymbals and hooters while knocking seven bells out of himself. The last time I saw him perform the act, at a Water Rats dinner, was at the request of JOHN MAJOR!

Irving Kaye

Violinist. Born Isidor Kalusky, South Africa. Irving left home for Europe in the early 1930s to study violin, came to London, played with ALFREDO and his Orchestra and toured the halls as half of KAYE AND EDNA. On radio (in ARTHUR ASKEY's show *Bandwagon*) he introduced the speciality that kept him in business well into the Eighties. He whistled, in harmony, while accompanying himself on the fiddle. I saw him many times and he never failed to tear the place apart.

The Kaye Sisters

Vocal trio. Sheila Jones born Lewisham, 1936, Shirley 'Shan' Palmer born Hull, 1938, and Carole Young born Oldham, 1930. The act was formed in

1954 and originally called THE THREE KAYES. It was a TV spot in 1956 that made their names. With their good three-part harmony singing and distinctive fringed hair styles (which made them look like sisters) they became a very popular act. They often supported MAX BYGRAVES in Variety and summer season, recorded with FRANKIE VAUGHAN and covered several hits in their own right.

Sheila left the act in the late Sixties but they carried on with a replacement lady, GILLY. Carole, who was married to the comedian LEN YOUNG, became an actress in the late Seventies. The original three got together again in 1992 for the tour of a tribute to GLENN MILLER.

The Kemble Brothers and Christine

Comedy knockabout act. The two lads were the sons of LARRY KEMBLE and, says Philip: 'They were an excellent speciality act using unicycles and ladders. They played all the number one dates here, and on the Continent.'

Neville Kennard

Comedian/writer. Born Eastbourne. One of the most famous names associated with that long-gone, and much lamented, entertainment-concert party. Encouraged by the great music-hall comedian, SAM MAYO, Neville's early years in the business were with alfresco concert parties. (To my knowledge the last of these, 'if wet in the Pavilion,' shows was, *The Ramblas Concert Party*, run by GORDON HENSON on Clacton Pier in the Sixties.)

After seasons at the Windmill Theatre in the Thirties (before its 'naughty' days I should think), weeks in Variety, as half of KENNARD AND WELLS, and tours with FRED KARNO's *Mumming Birds*, Neville became a popular principal comedian in pantomime, revue and summer show.

We were still doing his sketches in *Out of the Blue* in the early Sixties. He wrote all sorts of stuff and, along with FRANK WILCOCKS and ROBERT RUTHERFORD, his new material was eagerly awaited by concert parties all over the UK. He wrote some very off-beat items. I remember a sketch called 'The Tale of a Tail' which featured the comic as a man who grew a tail.

Bill Kerr

I'm only here for four minutes

Comedian/actor. Born Cape Town, South Africa, 1922. So many remember Bill as TONY HANCOCK's sidekick on radio but before this he had scored in Variety with his 'miserable' style of comedy. He would always preface his turn with 'I'm only here for four minutes.' He would follow this with a diatribe, pointing out to his audience things like the dangers of having a seat in the circle: 'It doesn't look too safe to me' and 'While you're all here enjoying yourselves your homes are probably being burgled', etc.

Bill had begun his career as a child actor in Australia and he returned there when Variety died. Even now there is hardly an Oz film that doesn't include Bill.

Bobbie Kimber

Ventriloquist. Born Ronald Victor Robert Kimberley, Birmingham, 1918. Bobbie, with the dummy 'Augustus Peabody',* was a popular act on early TV and we were all totally shocked when 'she' announced she was actually a man. He did look good on the box. He began as himself but the going into drag was the gimmick that made him. He fooled everyone; even HANNEN SWAFFER gave the 'female vent' a good notice. Although no one knew it at the time, he was the first female impersonator to appear in a Royal Variety Show (with DANNY KAYE in 1947). Whether it was his 'coming out', or the demise of Variety, I don't know, but he did seem to disappear from the scene during the Fifties.

I met him many times in the late Eighties. He had given up the business and spent his time painting miniature pictures of the old Variety turns. There are some on the walls of Brinsworth House. A nice memory of a very nice *man*. He died in 1993.

*'Augustus' was made by the variety comedian BILLY RUSSELL.

Chris King

You take two pieces of paper

Comedy magician. Born Bow Road, London. I knew Chris as an entertainer at Butlin's. How often BILLY BUTLIN gave young hopefuls a first chance and older pros an extended career. He knew what he was doing – this combination of enthusiasm and experience made for great entertainment during the high days of the holiday camp.

Chris began his career in the USA where, he always said, playing on bills with, and watching, the great W.C. FIELDS influenced him greatly. I know several beginners, at the time, who learned an enormous amount watching Chris. He played all the leading halls till Variety faded and is still operating as a children's entertainer.

Dave King

Comedian/singer. Born 1929. He was originally a member of the MORTON FRASER HARMONICA GANG. His flair for comedy led him into a solo career and his laid-back style and PERRY COMO-type singing voice brought him a BBC TV series and top billing in Variety. He was one of the first British acts to headline at the Palladium in the late Fifties. I wish I knew why he turned his back on Light Entertainment to become a successful straight actor.

Hetty King

Male impersonator. Born 1883. Truly a music-hall great who spent an incredible seventy-five years as a 'pro'. How lucky so many of us were that DON ROSS had the idea that led to the famous

touring revue *Thanks for the Memory*. Just after the war the show, with a collection of music-hall greats including GERTIE GITANA, G.H. ELLIOTT, RANDOLPH SUTTON and HETTY, gave those of us who were fascinated with the golden days the chance to experience true show biz magic. As a lad I didn't think any of the cast were old codgers. They all had a laid-back, intimate, relaxed style of singing and pattering that was so different to the new wave of just demobbed, anxious-to-please, attacking young performers. The carefully characterised telling of the stories in their songs fascinated me.

It didn't even seem strange that one of the most memorable performances was by a lady dressed up as a man. A tiny sailor, complete with kitbag, swaggered on to the stage and told us, confidentially and confidently, that 'All the Nice Girls Love a Sailor'. The half-sung, half-spoken words were beautifully enunciated and the chorus was a joyous signal to join in. Even I sang along, and I didn't know it. The band repeated the chorus while the tiny tar produced tobacco, pipe and matches. Taking all the time in the world, he filled his pipe and, striking a match on his backside, lit and smoked it. Another verse and chorus and this little creature was gone. I turned to my Gran:

'Who was he?' I asked. 'Hetty King,' she replied. I nodded sagely. I couldn't let her know *I* didn't know the funny little sailor was a girl.

I had witnessed a performance by a lady who had started, in drag, in music hall before the turn of the century. Her career had taken her, as a top of the bill, from the London Music Hall, Shoreditch to every number one hall in the country via South Africa, Australia, New Zealand and, notably, America. Old pros, who had seen the lady over the years, have raved to me about her painstakingly, perfect portrayals of the characters she created for her songs: the man about town, the down and out, the army sergeant. How I wish I'd seen these. The amazing Hetty wove her magic till her last summer season, in Eastbourne, in 1972, at the age of eighty-nine. She died at the end of that year.

Joe King

Always Jo-king

Comedian. Born Cecil Emmott, Keighley, 1900. It always amazes me where comics come from. So many, especially today, don't come from a show business background. Joe was, wait for this, a bus driver and full-time rabbit catcher before he became a pro in 1937. He was a popular Yorkshire version of the BILLY RUSSELL type of 'working man's comedy'.

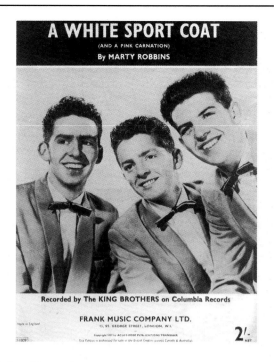

The King Brothers

Vocal and Instrument trio. Mike King born Barking, Essex, 1935, Tony King born Barking, 1937, and Denis King born Hornchurch, Essex, 1939. Three real brothers whose happy personalities, tight singing and excellent playing – Mike on guitar, Tony on bass and Denis on piano – made them a much in demand middle of the bill variety act during the 1950s.

A spot on the BBC TV show *Shop Window* in 1952 encouraged them to do it for a living. Their first variety date, with HUTCH topping the bill, was at the Empress, Brixton (long gone I'm afraid). Throughout the decade the brothers played everywhere, including the London Palladium with HOWARD KEEL.

The success of their recordings, 'A White Sports Coat' and 'Standing on the Corner', added to their popularity and at one time they seemed to be almost permanent guests on every television Variety and popular music show. As Variety died the lads moved into the working-men's clubs. But, as Denis says, 'It was never the same'. They finally disbanded in 1969.

Denis has become one of our most successful composers with a string of musicals and TV themes to his credit.

Kirby and Hayes

Comedy double act. Sidney Joseph (Sid Kirby) born Bristol, 1926, and Michael Hochrad (Mickey Hayes) born Bow, London, 1927. Sid, from theatrical parents, auditioned as an eccentric dancer and singing ukulele player in 1942, for ENSA. He was accepted and spent time entertaining factory workers and troops and in a revue with the rope-spinner BUCK WARREN. His own call-up came in 1944 and the next three years were spent with *Stars in Battledress*.

After demob he worked in revue for HINDIN, RICHARD AND HICKS and met Mickey in 1950. Their double act was the very stuff of Variety. They were a visual comedy act who not only got laughs but played guitars, sang in close harmony and opened and closed with fast song-and-dance routines. They were successful as principal comedians in the Butlin revues and well featured in pantomime. Between seasons their Variety date book was a full one: a supporting act with impact was always required. Alas, by 1958, they could

see the writing on the wall. They called it a day and went their separate ways. In the 1980s, Sid who had made a new career in telecommunications, bumped into his old partner who was then working in Dutch TV. Sid is now retired but still keeps his hand in by writing 'undiscovered musicals'.

Joe Kirby

Not famous as a performer but as the Kirby of KIRBY'S FLYING BALLETS. Joe's father GEORGE KIRBY was the man who really put the speciality on the map. His company was used from 1904 onwards for the 'flying' in *Peter Pan*. Their special effects were seen all over the world. I still wince when I remember 'flying' for the first time. I was given a female harness to wear (not by Kirby's I assure you!). It took several hours for my voice to return to its normal 'butch' bass baritone. For such a simple idea, based on the pendulum principle, Kirby's effects were, and still are, quite magical. The 'flying' out to the front of the circle still gets gasps from the audience.

Knie's Chimpanzees

Presented by Alfred Smith, born Moscow, 1905, and Theresa Smith, born Austria, 1908. The debate goes on as to whether it's right to have animal acts in circus and light entertainment. Personally I always feel a bit uneasy when lions and tigers are shown but I am a lot happier when dogs and chimps are on. I've never seen a dog act where the stars weren't constantly wagging their tails or a chimp act where it seemed the monkeys weren't having a ball. Nor have I ever met anyone who handled these gregarious creatures who didn't love them like their own kids.

I saw Alfred and Theresa's act in the fabulous BERTRAM MILLS circuses at Olympia. Both the Smiths had impeccable backgrounds and that enviable versatility that is the hallmark of true circus folk. Alfred juggled, rode horses and trained them before concentrating on the chimps while Theresa had been a rider, trapezist, ballerina and acrobat.

Koba and Kalee

Acrobats. Dickie Koba born Vishnu Pather, Durban, South Africa, 1912. Eastern acrobatic tumblers and balancers. Dickie learnt his trade with the German acrobatic troupe THE REMOS FAMILY before forming his own act after a year with the SEVEN ROYAL HINDUSTANIS. His first partner was MAISIE ROGERS of THE THREE DYNAMITES but he is best remembered from KOBA AND KALEE. Their gimmick was all the usual tricks but performed on roller ball.

Jack Kodell

Magician. Born John Koudelka, Mankato, Minnesota, 1929. One of the great originators in magic, lauded by magicians and magic societies worldwide. He invented 'bird manipulation', producing live budgerigars, cockatiels, pigeons, parrots and macaws seemingly from his bare hands.

At the age of seventeen he was presented, by the International Brotherhood of Magicians, the 'Most Original Act of Magic Award' and became the first magician to play Las Vegas. His list of engagements – which I've seen – is just amazing. He headlined in fourteen countries and was the first to present his act on ice (at London's Empress Hall in *Ranch in the Rockies* and again in their panto).

In 1953 he married the beautiful British leading lady MARY NAYLOR and returned to the States to work, again on ice, in Chicago. A year later he was back in London working with Mary in VAL PARNELL's *Champagne on Ice* – the last show presented at the London Hippodrome (the theatre became The Talk of the Town and is now the giant disco Stringfellow's). Between 1953 and 1962 he split his time between the USA, the British Isles, France, Monaco, Italy, Germany and Morocco.

He was the most creative of magicians. He would do the trick where a growing number of billiard balls appear between the fingers of his hands – but with live budgerigars! He performed, for the first time ever, the Indian Rope Trick: but, in his version, a parakeet would climb a magically rigid rope and, once at the top, disappear in a puff of smoke. His most spectacular effect again

concerned birds. At the end of his routine he would turn his back on the audience. As he walked off fifty pigeons would fly from the back of the room, or theatre, and follow him off. How about that?

In 1962, Jack clocked the way the business was going, theatres and show venues closing and not being replaced so, at just thirty-three, he started something else, quite revolutionary.

He formed a company called Incentive Travel, which presented shows on board ships. Almost single handedly he built a stage over a ship's ballroom floor and produced full-scale professional musical productions. Since then cruise ships have been a great source of work for so many. Thank you for that, Jack.

In 1997 this amazing man retired and now lives in Orlando, Florida.

Bob and Marion Konyot

Comedy adagio. Bob was born in Budapest, 1915. Brilliant 'cod' adagio dancers and acrobats. Their 'Painter and His Model' routine is a classic. Bob, from a famous circus family, began as a horseman, then toured Europe with his own solo springboard act before he devised the famous comedy acrobatic duo. His first partner was his

sister. His second, from 1945, was, and is, his wife MARION OLIVE. Incredibly, fifty years later, they are still at it.

Harry Korris

Eeee! If a man ever suffered!

Comedian. Born Henry L. Corris, Isle of Man, 1891.

> We three we're not highbrow
> Working for the BBC
> Ramsbottom and Enoch and me

Remember that one? The signature tune of *Happidrome*, the radio show which catapulted Harry Korris from run-of-the-mill radio concert party entertainer to nationally known comedian. The other two of the team were ROBBIE VINCENT (Enoch) and CECIL FREDERICKS (Ramsbottom). In Variety the team capitalised on their radio popularity but, alas, when they went their separate ways, the magic had gone and, although Harry formed a double act with ELVA SHERIDAN, the three lads never regained their top of the bill status. Harry died in 1971.

Krista and Kristel

KRISTA & KRISTEL

Twin trapeze act. Born Thomasen, Copenhagen, 1929. They began in circus and Variety all over Scandinavia. Kristel had a terrible accident when their apparatus collapsed: five ribs, both arms and hips broken. With typical circus tenacity, after nearly three years in hospital, she worked and worked and eventually got back with her sister. It was all worthwhile as their first appearance in the UK was in 1948 at the London Palladium. They were such a success that they were included in that year's Royal Variety Performance. Do they make 'em like that any more?

Charlie Kunz

Clap Hands! Here comes Charlie

Pianist. Born Allentown, USA 1896. The immaculate, tail-suited, terribly English-looking

piano stylist was actually an American who came to the UK in 1922. He was, in America, a church organist and bandleader and here led a band for SANTOS CASANI (a famous ballroom dancer). In the mid Thirties he became a soloist and, via his beautifully arranged piano medleys, on radio and records, he became a number one draw on the halls. He was the forerunner, never bettered, of a long line of star Variety pianists. He died in 1958.

L

George Lacy

Dame comedian. Born London, 1904. When pantomime addicts get together there is always a discussion about Dames. Who was the best, the funniest, the most inventive? Alongside DAN LENO, CLARKSON ROSE, DOUGLAS BYNG and, of course, today's greatest, JACK TRIPP, George Lacy is always at the top of the list.

Jack Tripp himself will happily do twenty minutes remembering George's characterisations and 'business'. George played in over sixty pantomimes, mostly as Dame. His greatest role (the 'Hamlet' of panto for the Dame) was Mother Goose. Like Buttons for the male comic, it's the combination of fun and pathos that makes it so special. Although people remember him in the seasonal shows, George was a highly successful summer show and revue comic too. He wrote scenes, sketches and songs and was a powerhouse of ideas. I still do an adapted version of his concerted number (based on 'If I Were Not Upon The Stage'), 'Automation'.

The incredible George, like all the very best Dames, was a consummate actor and played in every form of 'legit' from musical comedy to farce and thrillers. He always stole the show. He died, and some of panto's magic with him, in 1989.

Johnnie and Suma Lamonte

Double juggling act. Suma born Suma Deguchi, London, 1927 and her brother Johnnie. Originally part of her mum and dad's act, THE LAMONTE JULIE

TRIO, Suma teamed up with her brother and they became a never-out-of work speciality at all the number one halls. Suma now spends her time looking after her husband, the impressionist VICTOR SEAFORTH.

Robert Lamouret

Comedian/ventriloquist. Born Paris, 1912. Robert scored a huge success in London in the SID FIELD vehicle *Piccadilly Hayride* in 1946. His 'Dudulle the Duck' dummy (who constantly misplaces his eye throughout the routine) was a winner. Since then he has played all over the world, especially the United States. Whenever he returns here for TV or a Royal Command Performance he still transfixes 'em.

Laurel and Hardy

Comedians. Laurel born Arthur Jefferson, Ulverston, Lancs 1890, Hardy born Oliver Norvell Hardy, Harlem, Georgia, USA 1892. There is nothing more that can be said about Stan and Olly, the most recognisable and loved double act of all time. They have a place in this book by virtue of their tours, arranged by Bernard Delfont, of our Variety theatres in the 1950s. An

excellent book about the immortal pair is *The Laurel and Hardy Encyclopedia* by Glenn Mitchell.

Lee Lawrence

Singer. Born Manchester, 1920. The son of two Carl Rosa Opera Company singers, he studied opera in Italy for four years and it showed when he came in to Variety in 1950. He had done mostly cabaret until he began to be featured on radio on shows as diverse as *Welsh Rarebit* and NORMAN EVANS's *Over The Garden Wall*. He headlined in Variety till, once again, rock and roll kept us from hearing real voices. He died in 1961.

Johnny Lacock

Multi instrumentalist. Born Middlesbrough, 1925. The ebullient Johnny was one of the stalwarts of Variety, playing everything, and beginning in a Salvation Army band at the age of seven.

After wartime service with the Royal Navy he joined the FREDDIE PARKER'S ACCORDION BAND in a revue. When he asked the producer of the show, JACK GILLAM, if he could have a solo spot Gillam agreed and got rid of the band! By then he was playing accordion, xylophone, sax, trumpet and trombone. Inspired by CHARLIE CAIROLI, he introduced playing two saxophones together and, later, a trumpet and sax. It was watching VIC HYDE that gave Johnny his best gimmick. 'Vic' says Johnny, 'played three trumpets at once, but his technique was wrong, so I practised for a year to play three trumpets together in three-part harmony.'

He was forever adding new things to his act and, when Variety was at its height, he used fourteen different instruments, plus the three in unison trumpets, playing trombone, sax and bass drum all at the same time. He supported, to great effect, every number one star in the business. Alas, it was a week with CLIFF RICHARD that led to Johnny packing it in. He says 'All the clever things I did didn't mean a thing. I realised that the trumpet was becoming old-fashioned next to the guitar.' He became an agent, one of the first to bring top turns to the working-men's clubs and later, through the *Star Wars* movies, one of the leading agents for little people (in size not in talent).

Sadly for us, his brother Water Rats, he retired to Spain in 1988. Need you ask – he still comperes and plays the organ over there. Lucky old Costa del Sol.

Turner Layton

Piano Entertainer. Born Washington DC, 1895. Better known in the 1930s as half of the ten-million record-selling double act, LAYTON AND JOHNSTONE, Turner Layton had a successful career as a solo artiste throughout our period. Layton and Johnstone, with their beautifully blended voices, immaculate evening-dressed appearance, royal patronage (the Prince of Wales never stopped 'plugging' them) and their 'acceptable' jazz style duets, became enormously popular.

Turner Layton had had fascinating career up to the birth of the famous double in 1922. He rubbed shoulders with W.C. HANDY (the composer of 'St Louis Blues') and wrote, with TED CREAMER, 'After You've Gone', 'Way Down Yonder in New Orleans' and quite a handful of classic songs.

Layton and Johnstone parted company in 1934, when the tearaway, CLARENCE JOHNSTONE, got mixed up in a nasty divorce case and returned to America where he died, in poverty, in 1953. The

Layton and Johnstone

pianist, Turner, coped very well on his own and via radio and recordings was always a featured act on the halls until he retired in 1961. He died in 1978.

Benny Lee

Vocalist. Born Glasgow, 1916. Benny really was *the* radio singer. He had done over 2000 broadcasts by the early Fifties! He sang with all the leading bands and was featured as an actor as well. He hosted the very first TV programme especially for under twenty-ones, fed TERRY-THOMAS and was one of MICHAEL BENTINE'S team in 'It's a Square World'.

It was BERNARD BRADEN who featured Benny in those two mould-breaking radio shows, *Breakfast With Braden* and *Bedtime with Braden*. All this exposure led to his headlining in Variety.

I did several series of the CHARLES CHILTON show, *Roy Hudd's Vintage Music Hall* on radio with Benny. Here I saw just how brilliant he was. He never read the music, he would hear a tune once, then sing it, note perfect. When the halls closed, Benny the great survivor, carried on as if nothing had happened. He hosted radio's *Time for Old Time* and appeared in musicals until his last, *Windy City*, in 1983. He died in 1995.

Gerry Lee

A kitten among cats

Animal impersonator. Born Bicester, Oxon,

"MUSHIE", THE LION AT BUTLINS

1917. Gerry was, for many years, the very best pantomime cat in the business. He would always ask to include his own Highgate Hill scene in *Dick Whittington* and those who knew a good thing would always acquiesce. His performance was funny, touching and totally real. He used to do an interval speciality where he would run around the circle, slide down ropes and jump into the boxes. How's that for value!

His early days were fascinating. He started at twelve playing child parts in melodrama, then on to concert party, musicals, cine-variety – the lot. In 1939 Gerry met his wife, ELLEN HARVEY, the daughter of Captain JACK HARVEY (presenter of THE RACING CHEETAHS which would compete against greyhounds at the local stadiums), while he was in the circus. Ellen had her own legendary act, MUSHIE THE FOREST BRED LION AND MISS ELLEN. Gerry would be the 'volunteer' from the audience who would face Mushie at close quarters, at the risk of getting a nasty suck! The Forties and Fifties were Gerry's great pantomime years. He worked all the best dates with all the best Principal Boys.

He packed in the cat business in 1953: 'I was no longer at my best,' he said. In his long career he has been, among many other things, a theatrical agent (with HAROLD DAVISON), a bareback rider, a part-time mortuary attendant and a successful songwriter (DAVID ESSEX recorded his song 'Goodbye-First Love').

He did return to his old trade for a TV pantomime in 1963. Gerry, although now retired, is still writing and living in Cromer.

Ann Lenner and Bob Harvey

Vocal duo. Bob born Chichester, 1918. Just after the war Bob auditioned for, and got, a spot on radio's *Variety Bandbox*. He teamed up with vocalist Ann in the late Forties and, via radio, they became standard 'hits of the day' duettists in Variety.

Leonard, Semon and Sonia

Magicians. A good novelty act. Three Dutch midgets, whose 'pot-pourri', as they called it, was seen all over the world. They could patter in several languages.

Claude Lester

Comedian. Born Claude Forrester, Stafford, 1893. Now we are talking legends. If you ever noticed, next to the stage door of every Variety theatre was a pub: the brewers knew what they were doing. Most performers' acts were, top whack, twenty minutes long (unless you were top of the bill). Twenty minutes on-stage, twice nightly, where could the turns go between appearances? Exactly. There were some hard drinkers in the Variety world but amazingly few real terrors. Claude was one of the latter. He, was sadly, an alchoholic, and this, naturally, led to his downfall. Philip says: 'He was one of the great comics of all time bought down by the bottle. His drinking bouts were legendary.' (One amazing story of how he was locked in his dressing room, to keep him away from the booze, yet still managed to become paralytic is, of course, in my book of anecdotes!)

He was a tall, painfully thin man who would walk up and down expertly twirling a cane (indeed he taught DICKIE HENDERSON the skill). CHARLIE CHESTER described him 'dressed in skin-tight trousers, to emphasise his skinniness', and, commenting on his trip to Brighton, would say: 'As I walked along the sea front all the winkles shouted 'Back in your shells boys, here comes a pin!'

His second wife, and stage partner, was DOREEN ANDRE who wrote a fascinating piece about life with the eccentric genius for The British Music Hall Society's magazine *The Call Boy* in 1986. As poor Claude got worse the managements refused to book him and his golden days of playing the Palladium and the Holborn Empire turned into sporadic appearances at the number twos and threes. His last job was as an attendant at Golders Green Cemetery. He died in 1955.

Harry Lester and His Hayseeds

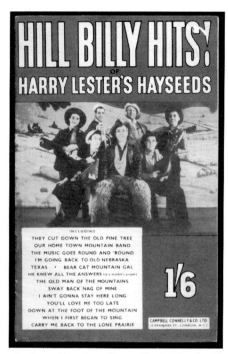

Comedy bandleader. Born Fort Worth, Texas, 1895. Harry's childhood was spent, in the days just following the real Wild West, performing all over the United States. He, and his family, did circus, rodeos, dramatic repertory, medicine shows and even shows on the Mississippi river boats.

In the UK the family produced dozens of different acts and shows from *The Upside Down Band* to Blackpool's *Midget Circus and Town*. The Hayseed's was Harry's own act and their combination of comedy and good music was very popular on radio in the Forties. But they had to be seen to be really appreciated and were, in their own road show, *Your Country Cousins*, a big draw everywhere. Harry retired in 1957 and died, just before his ninety-eighth birthday, in 1993.

Levanda

Foot juggler. Born Moxon, Norbury. Levanda was a member of the famous juggling Moxon

family. I worked with a later member, JUDY MOXON. LEVANDA worked with her father and brothers till, at nineteen, she produced her own solo act and played here and all over the world. In the late Forties she incorporated her fifteen-year-old daughter into the act and became LEVANDA AND VAN.

Carroll Levis

Truly the discoveries of today are the stars of tomorrow

Compere. Born Toronto, Canada, 1910. 'Stardust' was the tune that introduced the show that made Carroll a household name. Well before *Opportunity Knocks*, his 'discovery' shows on radio and in Variety, were a popular feature, although the only discoveries I knew who made it were BARRY TOOK, ANNE HEYWOOD (VIOLET PRETTY when she was with Levis) and JIM DALE (originally JIM SMITH). Not a good average when he claimed to have auditioned more than a quarter of a million turns.

He began as a boy actor, was a journalist, a hypnotist and an all-in wrestler, and then became a radio announcer, all in his home country, Canada. The 'discovery' shows happened by accident when, finding he had time to fill on a live broadcast, he dragged a schoolboy up from the audience to sing a song. Incredibly, for a man with (to me) nothing more than a transatlantic accent, he became on of Variety's highest paid performers. His great trick was to discover talent from near at hand. Rather like using local children in pantomime, it's a great way of putting bums on seats. He suffered a nervous breakdown in his late forties and his brother CYRIL LEVIS took over the show. In the Fifties Carroll tried again but the demise of Variety led to his hasty retirement. He died in 1968.

Josef Locke

Singer. Born Joseph McLaughlin, Londonderry, N. Ireland, 1918. The legendary Irish tenor who, only recently had a re-birth with the film based loosely on his shenanigans *Hear My Song*. He was originally trained, in Italy, for grand opera but his personality and showmanship led him to our side of the business. He did have a terrific voice and

he also sang a chorus of 'I'll Take You Home Again Kathleen' to us all. They really don't make 'em like that any more.

The last sighting of him was somewhere in the wilds of Ireland.

Johnny Lockwood

Comedian. Born John Sidney Lockwood, London, 1920. Philip says: A standard act with smart patter and good acrobatic dancing to finish. Johnny began, in 1935, as half of the BISTO KIDS, a juvenile act he did with a girl partner, MIMI LAW. He was, 'discovered' by BRYAN MICHIE via a radio show, *Monday at Seven*. The new talent spot within the show was called 'Youth Takes a Bow' and such was its success, JACK HYLTON took a version on the road. Johnny toured with the show and with the stage version of 'ITMA' until the war broke out. During hostilities he was with ENSA and afterwards was back in Variety as a solo act.

He became a Water Rat in 1947 and a couple of years later the Rats presented a big charity show, *Rats Revels.* Topping the bill should have been DANNY KAYE but he had to pull out at the last minute and Johnny took over his spot on the night. He paralysed 'em. So much so that he was included in that year's (1949) Royal Variety

the style to knock the crowd for six. His version of 'Goodbye' from *White Horse Inn* never failed to impel his audience to wave their handkerchiefs as he marched up and down.

He was, to say the least, a character. The mere fact that he did seasons with FRANK RANDLE must make you believe that! He claimed his first job was as a policeman. Whether this was true or not we'll never know but he did get to know the law pretty well during the passing years. He fled from tax problems in the UK and the legends surrounding him grew and grew. He was, supposedly, seen playing the clubs here, wearing a mask and calling himself 'Mr X' (a story blown away in the famous film). He was flown into the UK for a *This Is Your Life* TV show – and then flown straight out again before the powers that be could catch him. All must have been settled because he did sing at the London première of *Hear My Song,* accompanied by the son of the great Scottish comedian, WILL FYFFE junior.

He was worshipped by his audiences and I have, here in front of me, a little 'throw away' photo of the great man that he tossed out of his dressing room window when he was playing the Croydon Empire. He not only gave out his photo,

Performance. Philip remembers that night very well: 'Johnny had a gag in the act where he would run into the audience. He did it that night. Alas, he slipped on the revolving stage and finished his spot with a handkerchief clutched to his bloody nose.'

In 1957, he went to Australia for a few weeks. He scored so heavily he's still there. He became a star in Variety, revue and musicals and was one of their very first TV soap personalities. He did return to England to play Fagin in *Oliver!* for two years (1962-3). The Water Rats, particularly, look forward to Johnny's all too infrequent visits.

Jimmy Logan

Comedian. Born Glasgow, 1928. Jimmy really is Mr Scottish Show Business. A man who has spent his entire life in the business he loves. He was the third son of the well-known music-hall duo SHORT AND DALZIEL. His aunt, Ella Logan, was the original star of *Finian's Rainbow*, and his sister is the international jazz singer, ANNIE ROSS.

At the age of seven he was selling programmes at his father's summer show in Northern Ireland. He was soon on the other side of the footlights and rapidly established himself as one of Scotland's top Variety comedians. I saw him several times as the star of the legendary *Five Past Eight* revues (he was with the show for ten

seasons). He was one of the few Scots turns to do well south of the border, particularly at the London Palladium.

Jimmy is a true man of the theatre whose enthusiasm and great talent has enabled him to succeed in every branch of the business he has tackled. Just read this lot: he has appeared in thirty-five pantos and is rated one of the very best Dames. He has made five coast-to-coast tours of Canada and America including three appearances at Carnegie Hall. He presented and played the leads in thirty-four comedy plays as well as scoring in major dramatic roles (everything from Willie Loman in *Death of a Salesman* to Elwood P. Dowd in *Harvey*). He wrote and starred in the one-man show, *Lauder* (the story of SIR HARRY LAUDER). This piece, and his presentation of *Scottish Variety in the Fabulous Fifties*, were both enormous hits at the Edinburgh International Festival. He has made films, appeared in nine Royal Performances and, in just the last twelve months, appeared in sixty-four churches all over Scotland bringing what he believes in, 'genuine laughter, entertainment and song', back to real family audiences.

Jimmy is a shining example of a true Water Rat – a kind-hearted, fun-to-be-with, master craftsman. He is connected with, and works hard for, more charities than any other artiste I know and has more letters after his name than Albert Einstein. In 1996 he was awarded the OBE for his services to entertainment. For how he has kept the Variety flag flying north of the Border he deserves at least a knighthood.

Norman Long

A smile, a song and a piano

Piano entertainer. Born Deal, Kent, 1893. Alas, I never saw the jolly Norman but I did hear him on radio. He sang, to his own piano accompaniment, piano numbers with great titles: 'Back I Went to the Ministry of Labour', 'Why Is the Bacon So Tough', 'Never Have a Bath with Your Wristwatch On' and 'Where Does Poor Pa Go in the Blackout?'. He was a brilliant pianist and would often play popular tunes in the style of various classical composers. I always liked his opening line: 'I'm Norman Long – all teeth and

trousers'. It became a catchphrase in my family.

He began, after studying violin and piano, as the accompanist to concert parties – The Brownies, The Impromptus and The Chocs. He graduated to a solo turn after service in the First World War and first appeared on the halls at the Lewisham Hippodrome in 1919. He was popular on radio from his first broadcast (from Marconi House in 1922) right through to the late Forties. He was in the very first Royal Variety Performance to go out on the air (from the Victoria Palace in 1927).

By 1950 he was making just occasional broadcasts as he spent most of his time helping to run the Bolt Head Hotel in Salcombe, Devon. He died in 1952.

Mario 'Harp' Lorenzi

Harpist. I remember him very well from his many broadcasts but, alas, I have little information on him. He claimed to be the first to use the harp as a vehicle for ragtime, jazz and swing. He was a popular attraction on the halls and abroad. Philip remembers him as a brilliant musician. It was arthritis that forced him into retirement in the late Fifties. He died in 1967.

Ernie Lotinga

Jimmy Josser

Comedian. Born Sunderland, 1876. An immaculate theatrical heritage, his family were THE SIX BROTHERS LUCK, and he was part of that act in his early days. As early as 1909 he was writing and presenting his own revues and this he continued to do until the late Forties. His shows usually featured the character he had created, 'Jimmy Josser'. Alas, he was a pioneer of the stationary nude (he gave PHYLLIS DIXEY her start) in those revues that did such damage to family Variety.

Philip says: 'He was always in some sort of conflict with local Watch Committees for using 'blue' material. It was unnecessary as he was a very funny man.' His first wife was the great male impersonator HETTY KING and his second, his leading lady in revue, KATHLEEN BARBOR. He died in 1951.

Marie Louise and Charles

Aerialiste. Marie Louise born Marie Caban, London, 1918. Unusually Marie *didn't* come from a circus family but was completely self taught. CYRIL MILLS of BERTRAM MILLS CIRCUS discovered her and she played the act everywhere from the Palladium to the Palace, New York.

Lowe and Webster

Comedy duo. An old-fashioned, patter only, two-man comedy team. They were very much in the mould of MURRAY AND MOONEY where the comic keeps interrupting the straight man with silly question and answer gags. They, believe it or not, are credited with being the first to use the phrase, 'I say! I say! I say!' Murray and Mooney certainly did use a phrase that has become part of the language, 'I don't wish to know that – kindly leave the stage!' *Kindly Leave the Stage!*, incidentally, is the title of an excellent book on the history of Variety by Roger Wilmut.

Len and Bill Lowe

Len, whom I know very well through the Water Rats, has had one of the most fascinating careers of all. He was trained in drama at the Italia Conti Stage School and was on the boards from childhood. (He was in the original West End productions of *White Horse Inn*, *Cavalcade* and *All God's Chillun* and appeared in the first two seasons at the Open Air Theatre in Regent's Park.)

He sang with the JACK HYLTON band and toured America with them in 1935 before becoming a Variety act with his brother Bill. They were a featured act at all the number one halls both here and all over the world.

Philip says: 'They were one of the foremost double acts of their time. They were the forerunners of the smart double act. Where the comedian, as well as the straight man, wore a Savile Row suit – no baggy trousers and grotesque make-up. Later MORECAMBE AND WISE adopted the same style.'

When the brothers dissolved the act, in 1950, Bill became a personal manager, then went to Hollywood where he was an associate director in

television (how sensible to have an ex-pro doing that job). He is now happily retired in Honolulu. Len produced a new double act with yet another brother, DON (see DON SMOOTHEY), LOWE AND LADD. They were together till 1956, playing the Palladium and all the number one dates, summer shows and pantos. They worked all over Australia and New Zealand as principal comedians in *The Folies Bergère*, *The Latin Quarter* and their own revues.

Don developed his own single act while Len went into TV as an ace straight man and feed. In 1959 he returned to Oz for more Variety and revue. He had his own weekly TV series over there too, which he wrote, produced and appeared in. Back home again he continued to appear in revue and musical comedy. On TV he played parts in series as diverse as *Colditz* and *The Benny Hill Show*.

He is a Past King Rat, now Preceptor of the GOWR and the fount of so much knowledge about the Order. His mind is also a treasure house of gags, crossovers and sketches and his brains are constantly being picked by lesser mortals. Like me.

Lucan and McShane

Old Mother Riley and her daughter Kitty

Comedy double act. Arthur Lucan born Arthur Towle, Boston, Lincs, 1887 and Kitty McShane born Dublin, 1897. Recently the play *On Your Way Riley!* provided a vehicle for MAUREEN LIPMAN and BRIAN MURPHY and what a good job they made of it.

The tales of Arthur and Kitty's life together, offstage, are the stuff of melodrama but I shan't go into them here. The unlikely pairing, on and off stage, in 1913, of Arthur and the sixteen-year-old Kitty was just the beginning of their legendary partnership.

The honeymooners toured all over Ireland, Australia and New Zealand with their rapidly developing mother and daughter sketches. They made it to the Palladium in the Thirties and from then on they were a top of the bill act. They made a string of very successful movies and, happily, their best sketch, 'Bridget's Night Out', is on film too. It is still a masterpiece.

Their private life was a mess and the violent 'arm waving' they did in their sketches they did just as well at home. They sadly split, Arthur working Old Mother Riley on his own and Kitty with his understudy ROY ROLAND (who was terrific). Neither ex-partner did as well separately and Arthur died in the wings of the Tivoli Theatre, Hull in 1954. Kitty battled on for a few years with Roy but the magic had gone and she retired. She died in 1964.

Ted Lune

The Lad from Lancashire

Comedian. Born Bolton, 1922. Imagine a stretched out MARTY FELDMAN, without teeth and with a frame that made Twiggy look like Charles Atlas. Stick a flat cap on top and you have an idea of Ted Lune. His gentle, daft, humour (he worked rather like JIMMY CRICKET with a Lancashire

accent) was popular in the working-men's clubs of the early Fifties. A Variety booking at the Hulme Hippodrome led to radio dates and he was away. By the mid Fifties he was sharing top of the bill in summer shows in Blackpool. It was TV's *The Army Game* that made him a national figure and things looked great. Alas, he was dogged by ill health and, in 1962, bronchitis forced him to leave the cast of *Humpty Dumpty* at the Liverpool Empire. He never worked again and died in 1968.

Ted Lune

Laurie Lupino Lane and George Truzzi

Comedian. Laurie was born in 1922, the only child of the legendary LUPINO LANE. What a family the Lupinos were – part of a theatrical dynasty that went back to the 1500s. He first appeared, at the age of eight, in a children's theatre company run by his uncle, STANLEY LUPINO, alongside his cousin IDA, who became a Hollywood star and film director Laurie played, on tour, his father's famous role in *Me and My Girl*.

He made his great contribution to Variety when he teamed up with George Truzzi, a member of the famous Truzzi circus family. Together they revived the slapstick routines of the music-hall star WILL EVANS. They performed them as an act, and the addition of George's juggling with the props made them a unique team. They were a number one act both at home and all over the Continent. How I wish someone would revive their routines: the heartiest laughter you will ever hear, especially in pantomime, is from a good, old-fashioned messy 'slosh' scene. A memory etched into my brain is seeing Laurie and George perform as policemen in a flying ballet at the Adelphi Theatre in the Strand – a routine devised by Laurie's dad. Laurie died in 1986 and George in Brinsworth House in 1995.

Vera Lynn

The Forces Sweetheart

Singer. Born Vera Welch, East Ham, London, 1917. Surely our most popular Dame outside panto, she first sang in her local working-men's clubs at the age of seven ('three songs for seven shillings, and sixpence plus one and six for an encore').

She began as a pro with the CHARLIE KUNZ Orchestra and with that great spotter of vocal talent, AMBROSE. Success on record and in radio led to her own single act in Variety. Of course it was during the war that she became a National Institution. She was the girl next door that the lads had left behind. Her records, her radio shows and her live concerts, here, and with the troops, established her, firmly as 'The Forces Sweetheart.' The image still persists. When the Gulf War was about to erupt KEN DODD said: 'It must be serious – Vera Lynn's started gargling!'

Such was Vera's association with the Second World War that incredibly, she was all set to retire in 1945, believing that the type of ballads she had sung during hostilities were outdated. She couldn't have been more wrong. Her first post-war hit was the biggest she'd ever had, 'Auf Wiedersehen Sweetheart.' It reached number one both here and in America. Happily she resisted the temptation to move to the States permanently. She did tour there with great success, and also in Scandinavia, Holland, Australia, South Africa and Canada. She still, occasionally, played Variety and scored heavily in a revue at the Adelphi, *London Laughs*, with a couple of up-and-comers, JIMMY EDWARDS and TONY HANCOCK.

London Laughs, 1952

She proved how well she could handle any material with her amazing LP, 'Hits of the Sixties,' and, my favourite, an album of country and western songs recorded in Nashville. Her pure, straight down the line voice, with its perfect diction, knocked the cowboys sideways.

Her autobiography, *Vocal Refrain*, is the fascinating story of a totally professional, dedicated, somewhat reluctant, star.

Jimmy Lyons

Comedian. Philip says: 'He was a standard front-cloth comic [one who could do his act in the small space between the footlights and the first back cloth. Today we call them 'stand ups']. He had an old fashioned, aggressive delivery perfectly suited to the character he created, 'Jimmy Lyons MP' He always did well.' He was the husband of the comedienne IRIS SADLER.

___ M ___

Macari and His Dutch Serenaders

Band leader. Born Anthony Macari, Liverpool, 1896. Yet another performer from a circus family. His mother, wait for this, was billed as 'The Only Clock Eyed Lady in the World' – what did she do? Macari was a terrific accordionist who, after his début as a boy, played for fifteen years as one half of an accordion double act, THE MACARI BROTHERS.

He formed his highly successful show and broadcasting band in 1931. Where the Dutch bit came from I don't know but the whole band were dressed in full national costume against a backdrop of windmills. Macari's sons and daughter, LARRY, JOE and ROSE, were all, at various times, members of the band. They continued as a big draw in Variety and cine-variety until economics forced the dissolution of the big show bands.

Will Mahoney

Knockabout comedian and xylophonist. Born Montana, USA, 1896. Will had been a huge hit here in Variety well before our period. He married the beautiful American entertainer, EVIE HAYES, in the late Thirties and they emigrated to Australia in 1938. There they became popular and influential both as performers and promoters.

Will's great specialities were his falling down routines and his use of a giant xylophone. With hammers attached to his feet he would play tunes by dancing on the instrument. 'No one,' says Philip, 'has ever tried it again with any success.' I'm not surprised!

Will died in 1967 and Evie in 1988.

Manley and Austin

Comedy acrobats. Tommy Manley born Burnley, 1909 and Florence Austin. Tommy toured in various circuses until he met the great granddaughter of the famous circus proprietor, LORD GEORGE SANGER. Together they produced the double act. Philip says: 'It was a very physical act and the amount of beatings Tommy endured was a wonder to behold. Their hefty falls and breakaway violins made them a must at all the number one halls. They were hilarious.' Tommy died in 1975.

The Maple Leaf Four

Vocal group. As so many Variety acts did, they came together through wartime service. The founders were two brothers from a theatrical family, JOHN AND NORMAN MACLEOD. They teamed up with a fellow Royal Engineer, Joe Melia, and were part of the, *Stars in Battledress* organisation.

On demob, as DUFFY, ROSS AND MACLEOD, they

111

joined a touring revue, *Canada Calling*. The tenor in the show, Alan Harvey, used to join the three for offstage harmony singing and, after a one-night try-out on-stage they formed themselves into THE MAPLE LEAF MELODYMAKERS. In 1947 the lads were part of a NAT MILLS AND BOBBIE revue that played all the major Moss and Stoll dates in the country.

In 1948 their entry into summer season brought about their final change of name. In Blackpool they became THE MAPLE LEAF FOUR. The shorter the name the more prominence on the posters. Loads more top summer shows, Variety and panto followed. On-stage they wore great suits. Their musical arrangements were impeccable and their perfect harmonising of the hits of the day made them one of the most popular acts of their type. They had a great finish which didn't rely on the vagaries of the hit parade. The baritone of Norman would lead the lads in a full-blooded version of 'Largo al factotum' from *Barber of Seville*. Their own TV series and their Sunday afternoon radio show, *Smoky Mountain Jamboree*, helped the box office too. When Variety declined they adapted the act for old-time music hall, very big in the Sixties, and called themselves THE GLADSTONES.

Eventually, in the late Sixties, they dispersed. John went into song writing and producing and Norman, as a singer and actor, into musicals.

Alfred Marks

Comedian. Born Alfred Edward Touchinsky, London 1921. By the time I worked with Alfred, in the mid Nineties in a RAY COONEY farce, he had given up the stand-up comicking. By then he was content to be a superlative actor, good baritone singer, excellent after-dinner speaker and wonderfully dry-witted workmate.

His first appearance in London was a one-nighter at the Blue Hall Islington in 1936. He studied singing in Italy for three years before joining up in 1939. In the RAF he organised ENSA concerts in the Middle East for four years.

Like so many mad keen apprentice comedians he became resident comedian at the nude revue Windmill Theatre. 'It was tough there,' Alfred told me, 'you didn't get many laughs. The loudest

sound from the audience was the popping of fly buttons!' He stayed there for 20 months.

He began broadcasting around the late Forties but his greatest triumph, he said, was being acclaimed by the Brighton Critics as the star of *Montmartre* at the Grand, Brighton. What made it so special to Alfred was a congratulatory backstage visit from his childhood hero, MAX MILLER. Television followed, notably the sketch show, *Alfred Marks Time*.

His switch to the legit, in the Sixties, was hugely successful and he had a string of notable roles in straight theatre from *Spring and Port Wine* through farce and Shakespeare to musicals. He was equally at home in films and on television and his rich, unique voice was perfect for radio. His last radio series, *'Muir on…'* (Dissertations by FRANK MUIR on all sorts of subjects) was illustrated by Alfred telling stories and delivering one-liners in an amazing range of voices and accents. His contributions were a master class in the art of joke telling.

I last saw Alfred at a friend's memorial service. As he moved to the lectern to deliver the address, he tripped on the steps. His muttered: 'That'll go better second house!' was much appreciated by the entire congregation and set the mood for yet another of his brilliant monologues. He died in 1996 leaving a widow, the comedienne PADDY O'NEIL and a highly talented son GARETH MARKS.

Margery Manners

Singer. Born Coventry, 1926. I knew Margie, towards the end of her career, as a top-notch music-hall chorus singer. She had a great voice and an indefinable gift that enabled her to get an audience to join in without ever having to resort to begging. Her long career (she started in the clubs at the age of eight) embraced summer show, stints with BIG BILL CAMPBELL's Western show, ENSA – she was at one time the youngest of their artistes – and, most notably, pantomime. She was a stunning-looking Principal Boy with a personality that even *little* boys responded to. Margery died in 1997.

Marqueez

Exotic dancer. Born Laily Saldin, Lincoln, 1918. She was the daughter of a Ceylonese tea merchant and a white mother. Philip says: 'She

was a beautiful olive-skinned girl who mostly appeared as a speciality dancer in big revues at the Palladium, the Prince of Wales and in the Folies Bergère at the London Hippodrome.' She did play Variety as half of the act (with MAURICE COSTELLO), MALKA AND MARQUEEZ.

The death of Variety didn't really affect her as she carried on as a single act in cabaret worldwide. She played the biggest clubs all over the UK and in the West End. She worked for that doyen of cabaret producers, LEW LANE, at London's Churchill Club where he described her as 'the Pavlova of the music halls'. She died at her home in Tenerife in 1992.

Dorothy Marno

Multi-instrumentalist. Born Sydenham, 1915. Another name familiar to me from radio though even I didn't hear her first broadcasts – from 2LO! Dorothy was a child prodigy who won a scholarship to the Royal College of Music at thirteen and was running her own band at fourteen. She became a single act in the late Forties featuring the accordion, cello, vibraphone and marimba xylophone. She was a terrific turn.

Al Marshall

Comedian. Born Odessa, 1900. From a famous family of pantomimists he came to Britain in 1904. As so many show biz families do, they put him into a 'proper' job. He became a tailor but all the time practised his comedy dancing and eventually became a pro as half of ANTONET AND BEBE. With various partners he played all the number twos and, in revue, the West End. He played in pantomime and, as principal comedian, in touring revue. After a bad accident, which kept him off the boards for two years, he returned to Variety as half of a double act with DAWN WHITE (of GLAMAZONS fame). He was five foot tall and weighed eight stone while she was five foot ten and weighed twenty stone!

Cliff Martell

Comedy piano act. Born Clapham, London, 1892. Cliff began as a dancer with EDIE GRAY AND HER BOYS before becoming a solo dancing turn.

He put together an act in which he did comedy items both at and from the piano. Philip says: 'He just missed somehow and never made the big time. With the right chances he would have been a star.'

Veronica Martell

Juggler. Philip says: 'The Martell family were famous throughout Variety. JACK MARTELL, Veronica, etc, all being first-class juggling speciality acts. They played, between them, all the number ones both here and abroad.'

Len Marten

Front-cloth comic. Born Leonard Hart, Manchester, 1920. Len had the great training that only the old-fashioned 'rep' could provide. He began as a child actor and continued as a thespian, ASM and 'gofer', until, during the war, when he was seconded to GEORGE BLACK's Central Pool of Artistes. Here he met CHARLIE CHESTER and a long-standing association was born. They appeared together in *Stand Easy*, the famous radio and stage show.

In later years, as well as writing, Len reverted to his former trade and played parts on television, notably in *Coronation Street*. He was the associate producer on HUGHIE GREEN's *Opportunity Knocks* where his wise counselling helped many a young hopeful into the business. He died in 1990.

The Martin Brothers

Vocal, instrumental and comedy trio. George Frederick Martin (accordion and piano) was born in Aldershot 1921, Bob McGowan (bass) was born in Edinburgh 1921 and William James Martin (guitar and piano) was born in Aldershot 1927.

A real family act. George and Bill were brothers and Bob, whom George met in the RAF, was their brother-in-law. George and Bob formed the act, MARTIN AND McGOWAN, which Bill joined after the Second World War. As the Martin Brothers they played, via the Windmill and a season in Scotland, most of the number twos but, while playing in Germany, George broke a leg and the act split up.

Bill Martin, Bob McGowan and George Martin

Bill went to work on in Variety as BILL VINDEN, the Guitar Playing Comedian, eventually going into management and finally returning to comicking. He is now the most sought after, and best, warm-up man for television shows. Bob ran a club in the Martin Brothers' home town, Aldershot. George's long and fascinating career follows.

George Martin

The Casual Comedian

Comedian/scriptwriter. After the break up of THE MARTIN BROTHERS, George auditioned as a solo comic at the Windmill and, amazingly, clocked up 2,280 performances playing to, what was generally recognised as, the toughest audience in London.

Directly from that long baptism of fire, he went into his own television series. Faced with writers who were unable to capture his style, he started writing his own material and did so for the rest of his career.

George's great gift was being able to pick stories from the day's newspapers and weave gags around them. No one else was doing it at the time and this unique ability, plus his warm, pipe-smoking, laid-back personality, soon brought him countless radio broadcasts and featured billing in Variety at the Palladium and all the number ones. As our period closed he became a pioneer, on television, of the advertising magazine shows like *Jim's Inn* (with JIMMY HANLEY). George had his

wn, 'By George', which lasted until the government took them off the air, declaring that such blatant advertising was undesirable. Today there re whole channels devoted to the idea.

Disillusioned with the way his beloved Variety was going, he took on a pub but thankfully he was empted back into the game, this time as a television scriptwriter. His credits are legion: he wrote for all the top names in comedy, was the leas man and associate producer for all DAVID IXON's magic shows and, through his thirteen ears of providing IVAN OWEN with songs, gags nd stories, made BASIL BRUSH a star. All through his period the tireless George still performed as comic and, most effectively, as a masterly after-inner speaker. George had all the qualifications o become the top notch Water Rat he was, ecoming a most popular King Rat in 1971. In 986, he suffered a crippling stroke and spent his st years in the Star and Garter Home in ichmond. For someone as witty, loquacious and ll of bonhomie as he was, the loss of speech and obility was a tragic blow. George was married vice, first to Joan and, much later in life to ARGARET MITCHELL, a past lead soprano in the 'Oyly Carte Opera Company. He died in 1991.

I am grateful to George's son, the current cribe Rat of the GOWR, MIKE MARTIN, for the etails of his dad's life and career.

'Skeets' Martin

Character comedian. Born Bernard Martin, Liverpool, 1886. Skeets served in the Boer War, was believed to be the youngest bugler in the Army during the First World War and was among the first artistes to tour with ENSA in the Second. He continued his career as a character comedian all through our period. Philip remembers: 'He always worked in character and, like BILLY RUSSELL, made a feature of the BRUCE BAIRNSFATHER cartoon creation, 'Old Bill'. Napoleon was among his other characters. What a career. His first appearance, as a pro, was in 1906 and his last, in Blackpool, in 1969. He died just a year later.'

Topper Martyn

Juggler. Born London, 1923. Topper is the son of a well-known Australian act, MARTYN AND FLORENCE, and the brother of the lady juggler, DECIMA MARTYN. He claims to have been the first juggler to adapt his act for ice shows and indeed played in many throughout the late Forties and Fifties. I heard from Topper only the other day. He is now resident in Sweden and is still in great demand all over Scandinavia with his juggling and magic.

Horace Mashford

But of course!

Entertainer. Born Cleethorpes, 1908. Horace described himself in *The Performer – Who's Who in Variety*, 1950, as 'light comedian, juvenile lead, vocalist, raconteur, dancer and feed'. He must have fitted in somewhere! I remember him best as the chairman in his own music-hall show, *All Pals at the Palace*, at the Alexandra Palace but he began his career in concert party – the place where, to be a success, you had to be able to do all the things Horace said he could do. He did play Variety as half of HORACE AND EDNA with his first wife but summer season and panto were his main things.

In 1947 he began to be regularly featured in ERNEST LONGSTAFFE's radio show *Palace of Varieties*. He re-created the songs of the famous music-hall light comedians FRED BARNES, WHIT CUNLIFFE and RANDOLPH SUTTON. For most of the rest of his long career he concentrated on the music-hall revival type of show. He died in 1985.

Kitty Masters

Singer. Born Katherine Masterson, Salford, 1902. A long and distinguished career with dance bands, on record (one of her first accompanists was MANTOVANI) and as a solo turn. I saw Kitty as part of DON ROSS's *Thanks for The Memory* company. She sang the song she made a hit when resident singer with HENRY HALL on radio, 'Little Man You've Had a Busy Day.' She toured in Variety, first with her male counterpart in the Hall band, LES ALLEN, and later as a solo turn with the blind jazz pianist JOE SAYE as her accompanist.

Her first appearance was, at four, finishing off, solo, 'The Red Flag' at a Socialist rally. The last time she sang was at a meeting of the British Music Hall Society in the late Seventies. During our period she was a featured artiste on number one bills. She became a resident of Brinsworth House and died there in 1995.

Billy Matchett

Comedian. Born Liverpool, 1890. A Liverpool comic of the old school. I saw him as Chairman in Old Tyme (don't you hate it being spelt that way?) Music Hall. He had all the attack and gusto of the music hall, having learned his trade the traditional Scouser way, via smokers, working men's clubs and concert party. He graduated to play variety, revue and pantomime (always as Dame) at almost every theatre in Britain. He was a regular broadcaster in John Sharman's Music Hall. He died, in his beloved Liverpool, in 1973.

The Two Maxwells

The Bright Pair

Comedy acrobats. Max Kitson and Lou Sachse, both from South Australia. Getting together towards the end of the Second World War, they were a fairly ordinary comedy acrobatic team until a suggestion by the comedy tramp cycle act, EDDIE GORDON, turned them into a genuine speciality. Eddie suggested they work in slow motion and deadpan. They took his advice and were a hit in

their home country and in the UK. They adapte their act to work on ice and they had a good ru here and in the States in the big ice spectaculars They went home in the mid Fifties where Max sti works with his wife.

Bill Maynard

Comedian/actor. Born Walter Frederick Georg Williams, Farnham, Surrey, 1928. For those of yo who only know Bill as the rascally Claud Greengrass in TV's *Heartbeat* it will be a surpris to know he was a top of the bill Variety star fort five years ago. Bill, who is stage-struck to this da began in the working-men's clubs of Leiceste shire at nine years of age as 'Little Billy Williams Leicester's Own George Formby.'

He became a pro in 1951, as second comic t TERRY SCOTT in a Butlin's revue. He did have a amazingly quick journey to the top. In the ne three years he was principal comedian at th Windmill Theatre, doubling Variety, and *The Foli Bergère* revue at the Prince of Wales plus cabaret a the Astor Club. 1954 saw his big television brea with TERRY SCOTT in *Great Scott – It's Maynard*. Th success of this series catapulted him to top of th bill status in Variety. His strange sort of crew-cu hair style and big woolly sweaters were th gimmicks, plus talent, that helped him get away.

His own television series, *Mostly Maynar*

didn't work but he capitalised on his popularity as a comedian by going into plays. Something he'd always wanted to do. A long story of triumphs, flops, financial disasters and artistic successes followed till, eventually, he became the much in demand household name he now is. Two amazing careers. You can guess that one of my favourite plays is John Osborne's *The Entertainer*. I've seen all the greats play Archie Rice and Bill's performance, in Edinburgh, as the dead-beat comedian was the very best of them all.

For full details of Bill's fascinating life, read his autobiography, *The Yo-Yo Man*, published by Golden Eagle, up-dated in 1997.

Chas McDevitt

Guitar player. Born in Glasgow 1935. Skiffle, Chas's kind of music, just about squeezed into our period. He, and LONNIE DONEGAN, were the two most famous exponents of this catchy, folk-tune based music.

Chas began as a banjo player with various trad bands and was spotted, in 1956, backing TOMMY STEELE in a Soho coffee bar. Those were the days when things happened very quickly in the recording business and within a year Chas, along with his group and NANCY WHISKEY, had made the charts with 'Freight Train'. They did TV, at home and in America, broadcast and topped the bill in Variety. Nancy left the group for a solo career and SHIRLEY DOUGLAS took her place.

Chas is still very much at it and has just written a book on the fascinating history of skiffle published by, would you believe, Robson Books.

Owen McGiveney

Quick change artiste. Born Preston, Lancs, 1884. Along with music hall's R.A. ROBERTS and CHARLOTTE PARRY, OWEN MCGIVENEY was described as a 'Protean actor,' after the sea-god Proteus who could assume any form he pleased. He was, indeed the most sensational of acts, not only here but, with even greater effect, in America. He shared top billing at the Palace, New York with SARAH BERNHARDT and W.C.FIELDS and played that famous theatre no fewer than twenty-one times.

He was originally a straight actor until he devised his sketch 'Bill Sykes' where he played five characters. He quickly rose to headline status. I saw him on television in the early Fifties and was mightily impressed. I leave it to Philip to tell you exactly what he did.

'His amazing quick changes were done in full view of the audience with a skeleton set and four black-clothed assistants (so they couldn't be seen) who, literally, threw him back on stage. His closing trick was sensational. He would exit, as Bill Sykes or Scrooge in full costume and, while the curtain was slowly descending, he would be walking down centre stage in full evening dress, top hat, tails, the lot. He would be at the footlights as the curtain hit the stage behind him.'

He last appeared in the UK at the Finsbury Park Empire in 1952, returning to the States to roles in films. On his retirement his son continued with the act but without the élan of his father. (I'd love to find out how it was done and have a go myself.) Owen died, at the Motion Picture Hospital, California, in 1967.

Kenneth McKellar

Singer. Born Paisley, near Glasgow, 1927. The natural successor to the popular Scottish tenor ROBERT WILSON, Kenneth, like Robert, began in light opera before he became, both at home, in England and in Canada, Australia and New Zealand, the epitome of the kilted, romantic Scots

THE
TARTAN

SONG

WORDS BY
SYDNEY BELL

MUSIC BY
KENNETH McKELLAR

BROADCAST AND RECORDED BY

KENNETH
McKELLAR

Lawrence Wright

2'6

minstrel. He first sang in public at the age of thirteen and continued, as an amateur, through school, university and his early career in forestry. He gained a BSc. in the subject from Aberdeen University.

As a pro his great success was in the unique, all-Scottish pantomime, *A Wish For Jamie*, written by one of the cleverest of Scots writers, JOHN LAW.*

Kenneth partnered most of the top Scottish comics of the day usually at the, now long gone, Glasgow Alhambra. He would have enjoyed this, for he was an inveterate practical joker with a great sense of fun. Often, between the beautifully sung ballads, he would tell stories and recite humorous monologues – (often those made famous by WILLIE MCCULLOCH from Paisley). In 1957, he helped sound the death knell of Variety when he appeared in the opening night spectacular to mark the beginning of Scottish Commercial Television. Commercial television was the final nail in Variety's coffin.

He was a quite exceptional tenor and I have a much-played, superb LP of him singing Handel. Kenneth still does concert tours, recently in Australia and New Zealand.

*John was MICHAEL BENTINE's writing partner on the mould-breaking TV show *It's a Square World*. I played in a brilliant 'silent' TV film he wrote, *The Maladjusted Busker,* which won the Press Prize at the Montreux Festival.

McKenzie Reid and Dorothy

A top Scottish accordion act, still working today. They rarely venture down south but, when they do, they paralyse 'em.

Tex McLeod

Spinning ropes and telling yarns

Rope-spinner and raconteur. Born Alexander Donald McLeod in Austin, Texas 1888.

Philip says: 'Probably the best of all the cowboy entertainers with a combination of rope spinning and very funny, topical patter à la WILL ROGERS.

The McLeod name came from his father, a Scottish farmer who emigrated to the States. It was there that young Tex became a champion rodeo rider, steer thrower and lariat spinner. He graduated to vaudeville via several seasons with the legendary 'Buffalo Bill's Wild West Circus'. When he came to England in 1919, he remained a popular top of the bill in West End revue, Variety and in his own touring shows till he retired in 1957.

He was married to the horsewoman VERA CODY. He died, while running a hostel for down and outs in Brighton, in 1972.

Norman Meadow

Singer/straight man. Born in Wigan 1918. Norman, another of those unsung heroes, the straight men, made his first impact as a singer in 1935. He did a broadcast from the famous old theatre, the Argyle Birkenhead, and was hailed by the press as 'a new Bing Crosby'. Four days before the broadcast he had been a butcher's boy.

He became a feed, the hardest job in comedy, to, among others, DON ARROL and, most famously, to SANDY POWELL. For many years the pair of them were practically resident on Eastbourne Pier. When Sandy retired from summer show, Norman became the manager of the Pier and, until very recently, was still working there in the public relations department.

He is a dyed in the wool pro who, as he always has, continues to raise funds for The Grand Order of Water Rats Charities with his show biz talks to spellbound audiences.

Medlock and Marlowe

Novelty dancing act. Vic Marlowe and his wife Bobbie Medlock. They were a very different sort of dancing act. Their fast-moving routines were a mélange of types of national and popular dances. The gimmick was that the pair wore complete face-masks and costumes to reflect each dance: thus Chinese mask and moustache plus pigtail and cotton jacket equalled an Oriental routine. They also wore masks of popular personalities such as LAUREL AND HARDY and (popular and unpopular) politicians. Vic died in 1987.

Felix Mendelssohn

Bandleader. Born London, 1911. No, it wasn't a stage name. He was a descendant of the famous composer. Originally, in turn, a clerk, an actor, a nightclub owner (Club Felix) and a publicity agent, he formed his famous FELIX MENDELSSOHN AND HIS HAWAIIAN SERENADERS. They were a number one attraction till Variety faded and the pressures of trying to keep a big band together made him throw in the towel. He died in 1981.

Eddie Mendoza

Bandleader. Born Edward Middleton, Aberdeen, 1913. Eddie began as a solo accordion vocal act then, he said, 'got ambitious and started a band, EL CUBANOS'. After ENSA and *Stars in Battledress* he formed EDDIE MENDOZA AND HIS ARCHER STREET SPIVS with BETTE CAROLE.

Hal Menken

Speciality dancer. Born New York. He worked all over his native America in vaudeville with various dancing acts but in 1930 he claimed to have originated the staircase dance. 'So,' says Phil, 'did THE ASTAIRES, THE ASCOTS, THE HARRY DENNIS FOUR, KEITH DEVON, HAL MONTY, ASCOT AND ASCOT and some more!' He was a good strong act and, in the late Forties, played all the Moss and Stoll dates.

Tom Mennard

Comedian. Born Beeston, Notts, 1918. The wicked Tom, whose surreal offstage activities and practical jokes made him a modern-day EDDIE GRAY, was, in my book, a great comic. His ROB WILTON style monologues, particularly on radio, were masterpieces of observation and oblique thinking.

Tom's father was an undertaker (well, knowing Tom he would be!). Tom didn't get the show biz bug until he moved to Brighton and got involved with an amateur revue company. He created such a stir in the town that the singer DONALD PEERS, who was playing Variety there, made a point of going to see the show. He was so impressed he arranged for Tom to audition for television. He got a spot in *The Centre Show,* a showcase for newcomers compered by BENNY HILL. He gained return bookings and Benny sent him along to the Windmill Theatre for an audition. After three attempts he made it, with his road-sweeper routine, and stayed there for a year. Variety followed, The *Fol de Rols* summer show (I wonder what their audiences made of him) and a tour with Harold Fielding's *Music for the Millions* alongside his idol, ROBB WILTON. Tom was amazed that Robb helped him so much but I've always found the bigger they are the more inclined they are to encourage talent.

It was radio in Manchester that put him on the national map. MIKE CRAIG, that indefatigable nurturer of comics, featured him in chat programmes, sit coms, Variety and his own fifteen-minute solo shows.

He really hit the jackpot in *Coronation Street* in the Eighties. Sadly, just as he was being recognised for the excellent actor that he was, cancer struck and one of the real originals died in 1989.

Mike Craig has kept recordings of over fifty of Tom's solo radio shows and has become his Boswell. To read, in depth, about the man I recommend Mike's book *Look Back with Laughter*, Volume One.

Miki and Griff

Singers/comedian and comedienne. Miki, born Barbara Macdonald, Ayrshire, Scotland, 1920, Griff born Emyr Morus Griffith, Holywell, Wales, 1923, I first met Mike and Griff when I was a redcoat for Butlin's in Clacton. They were part of the revue company, with WALLY DUNN and DEREK DENE, and their act used to stop the show. It was a combination of broad visual comedy and superb harmony, country and western type singing.

They first met as members of the GEORGE MITCHELL CHOIR and married in 1950. It was their harmony singing, in the dressing room, that led to LONNIE DONEGAN using them on his TV series. They were a hit and Lonnie not only arranged their first recording contract – he produced most of their early records as well. They backed him on several of his hits too. They became the most recorded UK country and western act and were a success in America as well.

Their albums sold particularly well but I still preferred the perfect blend of music and comedy that their Variety act was. Miki died of cancer in 1989. Griff never worked again.

Bernard Miles

The finest bit of sharpening stone in Hertfordshire

Comedian. Born Uxbridge, Middlesex, 1907. Yes it's the same one, Lord Miles, the founder of the Mermaid Theatre in London and character actor supreme.

It doesn't happen very often but Bernard was

originally a straight actor who had a very successful run on the halls in the 1950s. He would be discovered on-stage, a knowing yokel, leaning on a farm cartwheel from where he would regale us with tales of life in his Hertfordshire village. His monologues were beautifully observed and a bit saucy too: 'Old Charlie was a rare one for the girls. He used to say "I believe in spreadin' my Maker's image about a bit afore I goes." And he did. The new vicar says to me, "I can't understand it. All the children in this 'ere village look alike to me" – well I laughed – but he never seemed to follow so I give it up.' In fact, he was a sort of early BILLY BURDEN.

He died, after many years back in the legit, in 1991.

Max Miller

The Cheekie Chappie

Comedian. Born Thomas Henry Sargent Brighton, 1894. If you ever saw Max, the bes front-cloth comic of all time, you need no word from me to convince you of his appeal. If yo didn't I'll put in my two pennorth. Much mor important people than I have extolled his virtue – well JOHN OSBORNE and LAURENCE OLIVIER fo

Max with evacuees on Brighton beach, September 1939

didn't overshadow his personality. He came across as the eternal commercial traveller. He was the admired, independent 'Jack the Lad', the man who, leaning on the bar, always has a good story and, if he felt like it, could pull every bird in the place: barmaids, landladies, sweethearts and wives. He was a great flirt, either preceding, or following, a cheeky one-liner or complicated story with a glance to the gallery from those periwinkle blue eyes. The ladies loved him and the men envied him.

His technique, when I saw him, was the opposite of our greatest living stand-up comic, KEN DODD. Whereas Ken will pepper his audience with gags, Max would take his time. 'The Mirth Miser', someone once christened him. He could make a story last and, if the tag didn't get all he thought it should, he would wait until its point sank in. Like Ken, he featured songs. His were mostly funny ones but he would always include a 'sincere' ballad to prove, for all his crumpet chasing (and catching), he was a good lad at heart. 'Be Sincere – in Everything You Do' and 'I Ain't Arf Proud of My Old Mum'. John Osborne said that 'Mary from the Dairy' (his signature tune) was 'an overture to danger'. Right. The reputation he had cultivated so carefully – that he didn't care what he said – preceded every appearance. 'Would he go too far?' He did, to my knowledge, do it only once. The memorable folk joke about the girl on the narrow mountain pass. I know you know it! His was the art of suggestion, innuendo, the unspoken. He died, in his beloved Brighton, in 1963.

The only biography of the great man is *Max Miller – the Cheekie Chappie* by John M. East.

starters – but, as someone who adored him years before I knew why, I'm allowed.

He began in 1919 in seaside concert party, JACK SHEPHERD'S ENTERTAINERS in Brighton. He was the light comedian and married the contralto, KATHLEEN MARSH. It was Kathleen who, in 1920, renamed Harry Sargent Max Miller. In the 1930s Max became a top of the bill star in Variety and on record. His recording career went from 1935 through to 1963 when he did his last single, 'The Market Song', with LONNIE DONEGAN.

Although he came from the south coast everyone thought he was a Cockney and it was London where he was most popular. He confessed he didn't like playing further north than Birmingham but today even the Scots seem to remember him with affection. He made a string of successful films, notably as Evans in Edgar Wallace's *Educated Evans* stories.

I first saw Max at the Croydon Empire just after the war and, as a small boy, he impressed me greatly. Not, as you many think, by the rude jokes everyone says he did, but by his appearance: the gaudy plus-foured suit, the black and white correspondent shoes, the snow white homburg, the outrageous kipper tie. All this 'over the top' gear

Nat Mills

Let's get on with it!

Comedian. Born Nathan Miller, London, 1900. Half of the legendary act, NAT MILLS AND BOBBIE (BOBBIE MCCAULEY). How well I remember, on radio particularly, Bobbie's stream of irrelevant questions halted by Nat's exasperated 'Oh let's get on with it.' Philip says they were the forerunners of HYLDA BAKER's double act with 'Cynthia', 'except that Bobbie would constantly stop Nat's complaining monologue with her

squeaky, nonsensical interruptions.' I always felt they were a sort of dafter BURNS AND ALLEN. They teamed up, on and off stage (they were husband and wife) in the early 1920s and were as popular in pantomime as in Variety. Nat was, according to eye witnesses, one of the great Dames – particularly in *Mother Goose*. Their long and highly successful career (and marriage) lasted until Bobbie's death in 1955.

Nat tried to carry on with other partners but his heart wasn't in it and he eventually left the business to work as a carpet buyer for his brother in Manchester. He married his second wife, LILY GRACE NICHOLSON, in the Sixties.

Although retired for many years he never lost touch with show business, mainly through his membership of The Grand Order of Water Rats, and I believe his last public appearance was, quite rightly, on the stage of the London Palladium (the theatre where he regularly appeared, eight times a year, in the Thirties). 1989 was the centenary of the Water Rats and a high-spot of the celebrations was a star-studded *Rats Revels* at our most famous Variety theatre. There wasn't a dry eye in the house as Nat, wheelchair bound, led his Brother Rats and a packed house in the song he had written with FRED MALCOLM, 'Nice People'. He died in 1993.

Sid Millward and His Nitwits

Comedy band. Sid Millward born London, 1909. More than an English version of SPIKE JONES AND HIS CITY SLICKERS, Sid's band were, to me, a much cleverer burlesque of classical musicians. The tabs would open to reveal an idiot conductor in ill-fitting tail suit with mad hair and a Hitler moustache. He would introduce the members of his orchestra individually and a bunch of lunatic-looking, senile delinquents would take their places on the stand. From then on musical mayhem would rule, wild versions of classical lollipops were the order of the day interspersed with lots of great visual gags. They paralysed audiences.

It was the radio show *Ignorance Is Bliss* that brought them national fame in 1946. They went on to be a top attraction in Variety in the UK; they did long seasons in Paris and in Las Vegas too.

Their conductor, Sid Millward, was a straight woodwind player who had been a student at the

Royal College of Music and played with all the top bands of the Thirties. He had his own band, a forerunner of The Nitwits, in 1937. It was while he was with *Stars in Battledress* during the war that he met his future partner, comedian and dancer WALLY STEWART. They got The Nitwits back together again for the radio show in the mid Forties.

Wally died in 1970 and Sid, in the middle of a season in Puerto Rico, in 1972. One member of the band, CYRIL LAGEY, is still playing music 'in the Millward manner' with the band NUTS AND BOLTS.

The Three Monarchs

Harmonica players. One of the most remembered acts from our period, and well after. The two driving forces were ERIC YORKE and LES HENRY. Eric began in 1936 as 'The Harmonica Kid' with radio's *The Carroll Levis Show*. He stayed with the touring version until he was called up for the Second World War. Les formed his own harmonica group, which won the Open Harmonica Band Championship at Butlin's Holiday Camp in 1938. The following year he won the Open Harmonica Solo Championship. This started him in show biz in *Brian Michie's Radio Stars of 1939*.

In 1946 Eric formed THE MONARCHS. The originals were Eric and Les plus JIMMY PRESCOTT and JOHNNY CROWE. Within six months they were three. Johnny left to join his father-in-law's bookmaking business.

Eric says: 'It was radio that really established us. We were resident on *The Forces Show* every week for six months.' It was during this stint that the character 'Cedric' (Les) became well known. They were suddenly different: three terrific players, one of whom was an idiot. His shuffling gait, lugubrious expression, tiny black beard, brilliant comic timing and unmistakable voice (pre-dating by years JOE PASQUALE) turned them into a top-rated Variety act. Throughout our period they did the lot, season after season at the London Palladium, supporting all the great tops of the bill, revue in London and South Africa, cabaret in Las Vegas, royal performances and, of course, Variety. After the game finished they became an almost permanent fixture in the spectacular *Black and White Minstrel Show*. Sadly 1981 was the year Eric and Les parted company, having been partners for thirty-five years. Eric is now retired and living in Dorchester but the unquenchable Les (as CEDRIC MONARCH) works on. His solo act is an irresistible combination of wild 'off the wall' bits of visual comedy and one-liners plus, naturally, great harmonica playing. I have never seen him fail to tear the place apart.

The Mongadors

Jugglers. Where to begin? The Mongadors were a French act who juggled with clubs. Their descendant, NINETTE MONGADOR, who was indeed a Variety act of some repute – NINETTE MONGADORS AND ANNE (Anne was Ninette's mum), gave a fascinating talk to The British Music Hall Society some years back – and what a show biz history the family has.

It began in the 1760s as part of ASTLEY'S CIRCUS. PHILIP ASTLEY was the father of British circus. His permanent venue in London was in the Westminster Bridge Road a few yards from the famous Canterbury Music Hall. It's now covered by St Thomas's Hospital. Astley, a great horseman, began his circus activities in Paris and brought the Monagadors over here as a top-line attraction.

The family played all over the world right through to the days of Variety. Ninette, I think, the last of the line, has now packed her clubs and is a successful journalist.

Bob Monkhouse

Comedian. Born 1928. A top of the bill brilliant stand-up comedian whose long career is, if anything, at its peak today. Bob has done everything. Originally a cartoonist, then the script-writing partner of DENNIS GOODWIN (they worked in radio and Variety as a successful American-style double act), he is a consummate actor in plays and musicals and, along with BRUCE FORSYTH, one of the master game show hosts.

Bob is one of the great survivors, adapting his material to suit whatever the public demands.

Hal Monty

Comedian/dancer. Born Albert Sutan. I remember well Hal Monty's touring revues at my local, the Croydon Empire. As I was only a kid, I remember his balloon sculpture more than anything else. Philip tells me he knocked the idea off an American, WALLY BOAG.

I've found out hardly anything about Hal except that in his early days, 1929, he teamed up with a pal, BORIS WINOGRADSKY to do a knockabout comedy dancing act. It was the agent SIDNEY BURNS who christened the lads THE DELFONT BOYS, although they were only together a couple of years. Hal went on to present his own shows even, on one occasion, topping at the Palladium. His partner, whose Christian name eventually became Bernard, did all right too.

Billy Moore

Yodelling accordionist. Born in Barking, Essex, 1926. Billy, says: 'I was never a top of the bill. I was always a strong supporting act among the "wines and spirits".' When Variety was at its best, people like Billy were its life-blood. The ideal Variety show would engage its audience from the overture on. A 'variety' of acts was essential and the running order of a show was very important: it should build up to the all-important star spot and every act should increase the sense of anticipation.

Billy was nearly always early on. His accordion playing, both sing-a-long and solo, plus his yodelling and his 'double voiced' duets with himself, were guaranteed to put the crowd in a good receptive mood. Acts like Billy's were invaluable. Still are. His mum and dad were both working men's-club pros and Billy's first, unscheduled appearance was joining his parents, to their great surprise, on stage in Leicester when he was four.

Billy's formative years were spent in a stockbroker's office in the City. He didn't like it an

when he was called up to be a 'Bevin boy' during the war, he chose the pit that was nearest the biggest collection of clubs. He worked them all. In 1950, he became the resident accordionist/entertainer at a Butlin's camp. He was a pro at last. He went back every summer for five years. In between he played Variety, revue and pantomime. A high spot was a yodelling duet with NORMAN WISDOM in the film, *Man of the Moment*. In the mid Fifties he did numerous tours, here and abroad, with HAL MONTY. When he married YVONNE PRESTIGE, they formed a double act. Sadly the marriage ended in divorce and, with theatres closing hand over fist, Billy went back to office work. Need you ask, he was spending every free evening playing in clubs and theatre music halls. It was at the inaugural meeting of the British Music Hall Society that he met Ena, whom he married in 1966. Since his retirement from 'proper' work he has become a full-time pro again. Old supporting acts never die – unless they play the Glasgow Empire.

Max Moran and His Mannequins

Speciality act. Max was a lightning dress designer. He would create, with the help of three or more girl models, dresses of the day using only bolts of cloth and pins.

Morecambe and Wise

Comedy double act. Eric Morecambe born John Eric Bartholomew, Morecambe, 1926, and Ernie Wise born Ernest Wiseman, Leeds, 1925. Own up, *the* double act. How lucky we are to have so much of the priceless pair on video: they are as popular today as when they first did the shows. Their comedy, like that of CHAPLIN, LAUREL AND HARDY and BUSTER KEATON, is timeless. It relied not on jokes but on the personalities of the partners. Ernie the stingy know-all with delusions of grandeur and Eric, the seemingly gormless, randy, pricker of pomposity.

They had both already served time in Variety as single acts when they got together in 1940. For years they were a well-respected, great value for money, standard turn until television turned them into the legends they became. For all the gen about our most loved coupling there are many books on the market, including their autobiography *Eric and Ernie* and *Morecambe and Wife* by Eric's widow. Truly the whole nation mourned when Eric died in 1984.

Ivor Moreton and Dave Kaye

Piano duettists. Both London-born, Ivor Moreton and Dave Kaye were one of the first piano double acts in Variety. They were both nightclub pianists till they teamed up as a duo, THE TIGER RAGAMUFFINS, with HARRY ROY'S band. They were a headline act in Variety and on radio both here and all over the world throughout our period.

Robert Moreton

and his Bumper Fun Book

Comedian. Born in Teddington 1922. Now here was an original. An original in all sorts of ways. His comic persona was as original as his journey to stand up comicking.

He was, firstly, a straight actor in rep and films. He must have been a good one, he was the juvenile lead in an Old Vic tour before he became a scriptwriter for LUPINO LANE and TOMMY HANDLEY.

During his period in the RAF, he carried on writing, and it was here that he devised his own, unique comedy character. On demob he did several more plays before the birth of his 'Bumper Fun Book' routine on TV in 1948. In 1950 he was the first tutor to the dummy Archie Andrews in the radio show that made so many reputations, *Educating Archie*. It certainly 'made' Robert Moreton.

The actor JONATHAN CECIL, who often writes with perception, and love, about Variety, pantomime and comics has described the Moreton style better than anyone: 'He resembled perhaps a subaltern from the Education Corps who knew joke-telling was a good thing but had only the dimmest notion of what a joke actually was.'

He would scan the pages of his *Bumper Fun Book* for a suitable joke and then proceed to tell it to us. In his rather posh, 'oh this is a good one', hesitant voice he would look up from the book just before the punchline, turn over two pages, start again and generally get himself into a terrible mess. In a lesser performer, irritation would have set in but with Robert he knew just how far to take his confusion. You loved him because he was trying so hard to please. When, by some circuitous route, he did arrive at a kind of tag and got a laugh, he would cry out in triumph, 'Get in there Moreton!'

He always finished on a song, something totally unsuitable. I remember him desperately trying to be 'with it' and singing a BILL HALEY number: 'You take a brim bram broom and mip map mop and you swim swam sweep out the rim ram room cos my bim bam baby's coming out tonight – oh yeah! yeah!'

As so often happens, the public tired of this one-joke approach and, in a fit of depression through lack of work, he committed suicide in 1956. His agent revealed, the day after his death, that a good contract was being sent to him that very day.

Gladys Morgan

The Laugh

Comedienne. Born Swansea, 1898. Even if you never had the pleasure of seeing Gladys on-stage you'll surely remember her toothless, ear-splitting infectious laugh from radio's *Welsh Rarebit*. She started in a juvenile troupe and began in Variety as the feed to her husband FRANK LAURIE. The act didn't take off until someone suggested they swap places. Gladys became the comic and Frank the straight man. To make their act more generally acceptable Gladys swallowed her broad Welsh accent. This was fine until she auditioned for *Welsh Rarebit*. She was told the show only used Welsh performers so, via a week at the Town Hall Pontypridd, she proved to the produces she was indeed a 'taff' and was given a two-minute spot on the show.

Her great chum WYN CALVIN (a *Welsh Rarebit* regular) tells me: 'Her maniacal laugh created such a furore it practically filled the two minutes.

She became the show's resident comedienne, sharing top billing with a young HARRY SECOMBE. Once away, she topped bills at all the number one theatres from the Palladium onwards.

She soon expanded her act to GLADYS MORGAN AND FAMILY. It included Frank, her daughter JOAN LAURIE (still at it and a terrific performer) plus her son-in-law and manager BERT HOLMAN. They were as successful in South Africa, Australia and New Zealand as they were in the UK but, alas, in her seventies, she retired to Worthing, suffering with arthritis. Big, broad, lovable performers like Gladys are hard to replace and she never has been. She died in 1983.

Morris and Cowley

Comedy double act. Harry and Frank Birkenhead, born Darlaston, Staffs. Two ancient Chelsea Pensioners chatting about the old days. First Pensioner: 'D'you remember, in the Boer War, that stuff they used to put in our tea to stop us thinking about women?' Second Pensioner: 'Yes I remember.' First Pensioner: 'D'you know, I think it's beginning to work!' That was the gag that always led into MORRIS AND COWLEY's finish, usually, 'Boys of the Old Brigade.'

They were real brothers who started way back in 1906 with their mother, another brother and two girls as THE BIRKENHEAD FAMILY. Their first

double act was THE VESTA BROTHERS but in 1923, things really started to happen for them when Frank spotted their unforgettable name on the front of a car. As a kid I always thought the car had taken its name from them! They ran, with JOHNSON CLARK the ventriloquist, their own touring revue, *The Squire's Party* ('The Squire' was the nickname of Johnson Clark) for five years before they returned, as a featured act, to the Variety bills.

They were one of my favourite Variety acts who I remember seeing almost every year at the Croydon Empire between 1945 and 1960. Harry, who for many years was Scribe Rat of the GOWR, died, at seventy-seven, in 1972. Frank died, a resident of Brinsworth House, in 1985.

Dave Morris

Don't laugh – meet the wife

Comedian. Born in Middlesbrough, 1896. One of that rare breed who, I'm told, was as funny off stage as he was on. He became Lancashire's favourite Yorkshireman. Dave, with his pebble glasses, boater and cigar was as much a part of Blackpool as the Tower or the Pleasure Beach. He lived there, was a comic hero there and did season after season there. It was said the summer didn't start until Dave was seen making his myopic way along the Prom at the beginning of the summer. He was of the ROBB WILTON, JIMMY

JAMES school with a caustic throw-away style.

He had a tough baptism. He started entertaining 'in every public house in Manchester'. He spent time with the juvenile troupe PHIL REECE AND HIS STABLE LADS and was launched as a solo act via an audition for RICHARD THORNTON (one of the original owners of 'The Water Rat' trotting pony). He gained much more prominence through his radio series of the Fifties, *Club Night*. His feed in this show, and on stage, was the voice of the Hovis TV ads JOE GLADWIN. One of its writers was REX DIAMOND who, at over ninety, was still writing gags for *The New Huddlines* a couple of years back.

Dave's brother GUS MORRIS was a comic too but he never achieved the laughs on-stage that Dave did. Philip tells me: 'Gus was a brilliant dressing room comic but did much better selling gear in the markets.' Dave died in 1960.

Ken Morris and Joan Savage

Comedy double act. Ken, an original member of CHARLIE CHESTER's 'Stand Easy' Gang, was born in Ferndale, Rhondda Valley, Wales, 1922 and Joan in Blackpool. They met while on tour with a GEORGE BLACK revue, *Music and Madness*, formed their double act and, with Ken at the piano and Joan's beautiful voice well featured, they played successfully in Variety. They were early into TV with the forerunner of *The Arthur Haynes Show* (Arthur was another of Charlie's lads) and a 'live' twenty-two week series for the BBC, *Hi Summer*. Their love of comedy was well catered for in *The Black and White Minstrel Show* on TV and in theatre where they aided and abetted LESLIE CROWTHER.

They did a long season at the London Palladium and several Royal Variety Performances. Ken died, at the height of his powers, in 1968. Joan worked on as a solo artiste and is still heard regularly on radio and seen in theatre. Just last year she was JACK TRIPP's sparring partner in the revival of *Divorce Me Darling* at the Chichester Festival. She is an excellent actress with a gorgeous voice and a rare gift for comedy.

Lily Morris

Comedienne. Born Lilles Mary Crosby, London,

1882. Another music-hall star who made it into our period. Lily, a genuine Cockney, graduated to low comedy after a long career as a soubrette and Principal Boy in pantomime. In the early 1900s she recalled: 'I had a production number to lead with the whole company dressed as Dutch boys and girls, 'By the side of the Zuyder Zee'. The pantomime was Aladdin!' By 1917 she had established herself as a chorus singer with classics like 'Why Am I Always the Bridesmaid?' and 'Don't Have Any More Missus Moore'. She played, with great success, all over the UK and scored enormously in America. She continued as a solo act (she never did revue) till her retirement, well before our period starts.

It was, once again, the silver-tongued DON ROSS who persuaded yet another music-hall star to go on the road with his revival show, *Thanks for the Memory*. She joined the show on the death of NELLIE WALLACE. Alas, I never saw her 'live' as she was taken ill the week before she was due to play my local, the Croydon Empire. Luckily she appeared in several films and she is probably the most effective, in this medium, of them all. I've watched them with very young people and, when she picks up her skirts and does her eccentric dance, all hearts are hers. Lily died in 1952.

Tom Moss

Comedian. Born Wigan, 1898. a producer and revue comedian whose mother, Philip tells me, was a professional mourner! Tom began as a tenor in one of his own shows but, when his principal comedian was taken ill, he took over the comedy and stuck with it from then on.

His first show, *Contrasts*, toured for five years and he had a string of successful revues. He made money, so much that he bought racehorses and packed the game in. Alas, the horses didn't do the business and Tom went back to what he knew – revue and pantomime. He claimed to hold a record for panto, having done four consecutive years at the Aston Hippodrome. (It may have been a record but pales compared to BRYAN BURDON's residency at the Theatre Royal, Windsor.)

Tom, King Rat of the GOWR in 1943, continued working till the late Seventies with his one-man show, *Behind the Footlights.* He was married to the ballerina VALERIE WYN. He died in 1980.

Jack Muldoon

Tap and comedy dancer. Born Jack Grayson, Middlesbrough. Opened as one of THE FIVE BOMBAYS at the London Shoreditch in 1920. In 1923 he joined THE FOUR KEMPTONS and in 1926 went solo. He met and married Hilda and they became JACK AND HILDA GRAYSON. Together they worked all the halls in the UK and toured South Africa and Holland. In 1934 he formed THE MULDOON FOUR. Philip says: 'They were a four handed flash act who played everywhere, even on ice!'

Alex Munro

The size of it!

Comedian. Born Alexander Horsburgh, Glasgow, 1911. He was just five and half feet high, hence the bill matter. He began, with his brother Archie and sister June, as an acrobatic act, THE STAR TRIO, soon changed to THE HORSBURGH BROTHERS AND AGNES. They were part of FLORRIE FORE's company with FLANAGAN AND ALLEN and it was Bud and Ches who advised wee Alex to try comedy. He did and shared the principal comic-king with his brother in the revue *Good Night, Good Night.*

After wartime service he toured with the RAF show, *Contact,* and had his own radio series, *The Size of It.* He earned a good living in Variety and panto until the theatres closed. Where others jacked it in, Alex battled on and found a very special niche. For nearly thirty years he was the resident host at the Happy Valley open-air theatre in Llandudno. There was no admission charge and the customers sat on the grass in the open air (if wet, in the Pier Pavilion). Alex was the principal comedian and compered talent shows, glamorous grannie competitions and the Variety bill. He became 'Mr Llandudno', lived in the town and was a real local celebrity. His daughter was the British film star JANET MUNRO. He died in 1986.

Joe Murgatroyd and 'Poppet'

Comedian. Born Rotherham, Yorkshire. I haven't been able to find out Joe's real name. He did have the strangest of careers, going the opposite way to that of most comedians. He began as a straight actor. He called himself MARK STONE in the 1920s and appeared in good, hefty roles in several West End plays including an appearance as Shakespeare's famous clown WILL KEMP opposite LESLIE HOWARD. He went into pantos as Buttons and Dame and into radio. On the air he always called himself Joe Murgatroyd, as he did when he went into Variety with his partner, 'Poppet'. They played all the number ones but Joe/Mark always kept one foot in the legit and in 1949 joined EDITH EVANS at Wyndhams for the long run of James Bridie's *Daphne Laureola.*

This clever bloke spent the rest of his career alternating between the straight theatre and Variety.

Murray

Even Hitler could not hold him

Escapologist and illusionist. Born Norman Murray Walters, Melbourne, Australia, 1901. The mere mention of his name is enough to set magicians talking about the amazing Murray. Rae Hammond in an article in *The Call Boy* in 1988 covered all the major happenings in this gentleman's amazing life and career. The following is just a précis.

He began as a teenage escapologist in a New York Coney Island side show. Before he was twenty-two he had 'escaped' all over Alaska, Singapore, India, South Africa and his native Australia. He added illusions to his repertoire and arrived in England in 1926 after touring with his own show in Java, Siam, Cambodia, Malaya, Japan, Manchuria, India, Afghanistan, Egypt, Malta and China (where he escaped from being manacled to the railway lines seconds before the Shanghai Express arrived).

His first week in the UK was in Manchester as an unknown. The very next week he was topping the bill at the London Coliseum. Here he pulled off one of his greatest stunts. During the rebuilding of the Swan and Edgar store (now Tower Records) he escaped from a straitjacket while suspended from a crane a hundred feet above Piccadilly Circus. Murray was fined £25 for obstruction but the publicity he gained helped him to play to capacity business all over the country.

He wandered the world again and made perhaps his most important escape in 1939. He caught the last train from Berlin to the Danish border and, on a borrowed bicycle, made it just before the Second World War started. Hence his bill matter.

He worked in the UK and in Scandinavia until, in 1953, illness forced a premature end to his career. He took a little magic shop in Blackpool which became a Mecca for magicians and show people all anxious to meet and talk with the great man. He died in 1988.

Murray and Mooney

Comedians. Harry Murray born 1891, Harry Mooney born Harry Goodchild, Richmond, Surrey, 1889. Everyone's idea of what an old-fashioned double act should be. Murray would start to recite a poem: 'It's a funny old world we live in…' when he would be interrupted by Mooney with a ridiculous enquiry: 'How do you

make a Maltese Cross with two matches?' 'I've no idea.' 'Light 'em and stick 'em up his jumper!' Exit stage right. There was no rhyme or reason for any of the gags but they were done with such attack and panache that, eventually, you had to laugh. The two Harrys were together for over twenty-five years and, apart from playing all over the UK, they had two Royal Variety Shows to their credit (1934 and 1938). When the team split, VICTOR KING joined HARRY MOONEY to become the act I so well remember, particularly on radio, HARRY MOONEY AND VICTOR KING.

I met Harry's daughter in the Seventies and she told me he was retired and lived for the horse racing on the telly. Apparently he was a keen student of form and actually made money from it! He died in 1972.

Chic Murray and Maidie

Comedy double act. Chic born Greenock, 1919. Now we are talking great comics. The deadpan approach, that of a sort of surreal ROBB WILTON, the SPIKE MILLIGAN logic and the ever present, for no reason at all, tartan bonnet, all added up to the most original Scots comic of them all.

It was his meeting, just after the war, with Maidie Dickson, who had been on-stage since childhood, that led to him becoming a pro. I remember seeing them first as a double act with the tiny Maidie downstage desperately 'selling' her accordion playing while the tall Chic, standing behind, sent her up. It was during the mid Fifties that the two of them really established themselves.

I did prefer the later Chic, when Maidie, fed up

with all the travelling, stayed at home to raise their family, left him to a solo career. Now there was nothing to detract from his inspired, wandering monologues. They invariably started in a quite ordinary way: 'I got up this morning (fair enough) – I like to get up in the morning – it gives me the rest of the day to myself.' We were off. Perhaps Chic's patter, written down, doesn't read funny but imagine it done in that rather up-market, Morningside-accented, matter-of-fact delivery and it starts to happen. His day continues: 'I went into Boots. I asked the assistant if she'd got any laces. She said 'No.' I said 'That's terrible – boots with no laces!' and so on.

He became a cult figure, the first of the 'alternative' comics. There were more people working doing impressions of him than he was himself.

Late in life he started to carve a new career, as an actor, (playing himself of course). He was terrific as the teacher in the film *Gregory's Girl* and, how I wish I'd seen him, on-stage, as Bill Shankly in the play of the great football manager's life, *You'll Never Walk Alone*.

I had the privilege of introducing his last television appearance in *Halls of Fame*. His spot, which was different at every rehearsal, had one line that I, and the band, loved: 'I was sitting on a park bench when a man came and sat beside me. I thought 'If he offers me a sweetie I'm off!' Chic died, all too soon, in 1985.

There is an excellent biography of Chic, *The Best Way to Walk* by Andrew Yule.

Rob Murray

Juggler. Born Sydney, Australia, 1926. Probably the last of that eccentric breed – the laid-back, melancholy, irritable, technically brilliant, juggler. Rob's approach was based on that of another Australian juggler, REBLA. He studiously reproduced all of Rebla's routines and adopted his nonchalant style of presentation too.

After an apprenticeship in Australia he caused a sensation in the UK in 1948 on the DANNY KAYE bill at the Palladium. His comedy plus his finishing trick – gold clubs *and* golf balls balanced on his head – guaranteed his constant presence in Variety as a very special speciality act. Through-

out the Seventies and Eighties he did numerous seasons with *The Black and White Minstrel Show*.

He did his last television with yours truly in *Halls of Fame* in the Eighties. Sadly he was a sick man and died in 1988.

Rob's inspiration, Rebla

Ruby Murray

Softly softly

Singer. Born Ruby Florence Campbell Murray, Belfast, 1935. On-stage, Ruby was the epitome of the shy Irish colleen. Her totally recognisable, soft, husky-voiced way with a song brought her enormous fame during our period. She holds one record that has never been equalled – she had five hit singles simultaneously in the UK pop charts.

She was, after performing as a child in amateur shows in her native Belfast, a pro from fourteen onwards. She toured all over Northern Ireland in Variety and did a summer season in Glasgow, all before she was twenty.

1954 saw her in a revue, *Yankee Doodle Blarney*, at the Metropolitan Music Hall, Edgware Road, London. Here she was spotted by RICHARD AFTON, a BBC TV producer looking for a regular singer for a series, *Quite Contrary*. Her first appearance on the show led to a recording contract with Columbia. Her entry into the Hit Parade was with

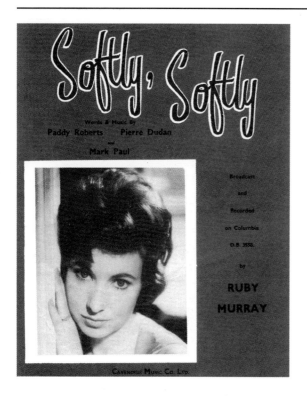

a song called 'Heartbeat', which went to number two. By March 1955 it had been joined in the top twenty by 'Softly, Softly', 'Let Me Go Lover', 'Happy Days and Lonely Nights' and 'If Anyone Finds This I Love You'. These were the times when one hit record led to topping the bill in Variety so Ruby was a headliner five times over. She was a huge crowd-puller. The summer of 1955 was spent in a resident revue, with NORMAN WISDOM, at the London Palladium and, in the autumn she made the Royal Variety Performance.

She did a film with FRANKIE HOWERD and DENNIS PRICE and was voted Britain's favourite female vocalist. In 1957 she married BERNARD BURGESS of THE JONES BOYS vocal group. In the early Sixties they toured the country in *Snow White* with Ruby as the heroine and Bernie as the prince. Not too long after our period things started to go wrong. Poor Ruby took a far too strong liking to the drink. She and Bernie were divorced in 1977.

She shared the last twenty years of her life with RAY LAMAR, an ex-dancer and theatre manager. They married in 1993. Happily Ray encouraged her to keep working and she did. Though the golden days were gone she remained a much loved favourite wherever she played until her death in 1996.

Musaire

Electronic musician. Born Joseph Forrest Whiteley, Leeds, 1894. Joe, whom I knew from his Vice Presidency of the British Music Hall Society, spent his early years as commercial traveller in Canada before he discovered the 'Theremin', a strange-looking box on wheels invented by a Russian, Professor Leon Theremin. This instrument produced sounds, imitations and tunes. Musaire himself described it in his his advertising brochure: 'Its six octaves of beautiful tone and great volume fill the air or fade away as Musaire moves both hands in space, touching nothing. It is the musical sensation of the century.'

Not quite as, despite many broadcasts, lectures, demonstrations, and exhibitions it disappeared without trace.

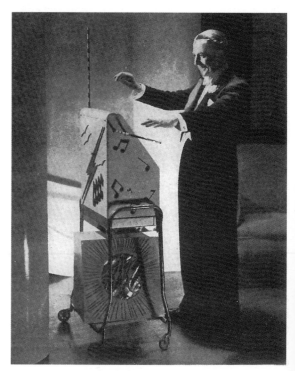

The Myrons

Balancing act. Arno Koehler born Germany, 1905, and Felix Slawinski born Poland, 1903, The Myrons, both naturalised Australians, first worked together in Poland in 1925. Before becoming an act they had both been boxers, wrestlers and gymnasts. They were a perch act, in which one partner would support an incredibly high pole on his feet, or on one foot, while the other would do foot juggling and hand balancing on the top. In 1948 they made a big impact in the UK, first at the London Palladium, then at all the top venues and finally in the Royal Variety Performance. They eventually returned to their adopted homeland, Australia, and from there toured the world as a number one speciality.

___ N ___

Valantyne Napier

The Human Spider

Contortionist, dancer. Born Joan Napier Valantyne in Melbourne, Australia, 1920. Val is the daughter of two well-known pros, HECTOR NAPIER and DOROTHY YVONNE who presented the act, The Spider and the Butterfly.

Val first came to the UK in 1948, with her partner TED WEEKS, as VYNE AND VALENTINE. Ted was a highly experienced acrobat who had done the lot in Australia with THE THREE MAYNARDS, THE FLYING WARTONS and, his own invention, PATILLO AND PESCO (with a small clown in a suitcase). He had been here in the late Thirties and stayed all through the war. He returned to Australia, played the Tivoli Theatres and toured Japan with the double act. They presented a unique combination of balancing, contortions and comedy until, like so many others in the Fifties, they went into revue. They did lots with DAVY KAYE. In these shows they presented their act and Val danced classical ballet as well as singing in the scenas. In 1951, Ted left to work on the Continent and Val became a single act, The Human Spider. In a huge, UV-lit web, she would perform contortions in a show-stopping act, dressed all in black with a hood. I remember the gasp from the audience as she took her call and removed the hood to release a cascade of blonde hair – a girl! And what a girl. She, alone, was responsible for her ton of props arriving at the theatre in time, finding digs, taking band rehearsals – the lot. No wonder variety pros were survivors. The spider routine was especially effective in panto and during the run of

Little Miss Muffet in Cheltenham she met and married the stage manager, JEFFREY JONES.

In 1961, the lack of Variety and the general state of theatre, forced Val and Jeff to sell up and move to Australia. They are still there and Val has written several excellent books on Variety. My favourite is *Act as Known*, a survey of Australian and worldwide vaudeville from 1900 to 1960.

Naughton and Gold

Comedy double act. Charles John Naughton born Glasgow, 1887, and James McGonigal (Gold) born Glasgow, 1886. My Gran used to take me on the train from East Croydon station to Victoria and then across the road to the Victoria Palace where the CRAZY GANG reigned supreme from 1947 to 1962. Charlie Naughton was the little, pot-bellied, bald-headed butt of all the sketches and of many of the Gang's evil offstage activities too. His appearances in the show were always eagerly awaited. He never had much to say but just walking on as Spartacus or Friar Tuck or Thisbe was enough. My Gran once said he looked like a piglet with a hat on. He, like all the lads, was a master of timing and he made every word count. JIMMY GOLD was in the sketches too but didn't make much impression on me. He was

fairly ill by the time I saw him. I wish I'd seen him at the height of his powers because he is always quoted as being the man who came up with so many of the gags.

As a young lad I thought they were just funny old men but, once I started to worry about how to get laughs, I realised just how good at the job they were. They should have been. Naughton and Gold had been a double act since, unbelievably, 1908 and their early years had been spent knocking it out around the British Isles, America, South Africa, Australia and the Continent, perfecting their routines. They were big panto-mime favourites and their spots were always broad slapstick. How we could do with a pair like them today.

They were top-rated double act in 1931. Their routine as workmen trying to set up for decorating, 'Turn It Round the Other Way' was a favourite. They weren't too sure about joining NERVO AND KNOX for an 'if it' idea of GEORGE BLACK's but took a chance on a 'Crazy Week' at the Palladium. The rest is history. Thirty-one years after that revolutionary week's Variety, after becoming the most loved team of comedians ever, after success in films, and after more Royal Variety Performances than anyone else in history, the Gang broke up.

JIMMY GOLD, too ill to work, retired and died in 1967. Charlie carried on, saying he had to: 'Jimmy had saved his money and I hadn't.' I was glad he hadn't because it gave me the dubious pleasure of doing *A Funny Thing Happened on the Way to the Forum* in Coventry with him and his 'minder' 'Monsewer' Eddie Gray. I say 'dubious' because neither of them had lost their sense of anarchy and from day one of the run I suffered from their 'helpfulness' on and offstage. I wouldn't have missed one red-faced moment. Charlie made about five fleeting appearances in the show and he scored on every entrance. He died in 1976.

Mary Naylor

Singer/pianist/accordionist/actress. Born Florence Mary Naylor, Nottingham, 1926. What a start to a career. Mary's stage début was at the Empire, Nottingham at just twelve years of age. JACK HYLTON was on the bill and within weeks she appeared in his radio show. That same year she did two TVs, when there were only five hundred sets in the entire country, and a season at the London Palladium in Hylton's show *Band Wagon*. She worked in a special section of the show called 'Youth Takes a Bow' with sixteen-year-old DICKIE HENDERSON and thirteen-year-old ERNIE WISE. The show went on the road with the addition of Eric

Bartholomew (ERIC MORECAMBE). The next two years were spent dodging bombs all over the British Isles and learning the trade.

Then came a West End revue, a film contract and the Palladium again, with TOMMY TRINDER and NAT JACKLEY. She did a radio series, *Shipmates Ashore*, and was voted 'Sweetheart of the Merchant Navy' and 'Pin Up Girl of the RAF'. Summer seasons, touring, and West End, revues and pantos followed. She was, at eighteen, then the youngest Principal Boy in the country. In 1946 she teamed up with the heart-throb crooner SAM BROWNE, and SAM BROWNE AND MARY NAYLOR became a top of the bill Variety act – and they opened at the Glasgow Empire!

In 1953 she met and married the American magician JACK KODELL* and from then on split her time between the UK and the States. At home she played in *Champagne on Ice*, topped in Variety, did several series of her own TV show and the forerunner of *The Black and White Minstrel Show*. Mary was the only white face in the cast! In America she starred in a revue, with Jack, written especially for her, *Maid in America*.

In 1962 Jack left the game and went into business. Mary joined him and, together, they changed the whole face of shipboard entertainment.* What a career. Mary has now retired and lives with Jack in Orlando. She says: 'We're both grateful for the wonderful, fulfilled life show business has given us.'

*See Jack Kodell.

Nazzaro

Impressionist. Born Ermino Nazzaro in Naples 1912. Another strange act. He would occupy the stage for up to fifty minutes demonstrating his talent for imitating animal and mechanical sounds. Where would he work today? Radio One? He was a success in his native Italy and headlined all over Europe. He came to the UK in 1949, did four weeks at the Palladium and worked all the number one Variety dates.

He described, in 1950, how he had the unique ability to control the flow of the bloodstream to his head and face and was thus able to perform his amazing and somewhat macabre 'Jekyll and Hyde' impressions. Urgh!

Bob Nelson

Aren't plums cheap?

Comedy speciality. Born Rupert Lambert, Burnley, 1893. Bob is a legend among the older pros. His phrase 'Aren't plums cheap?' is still used today – for no reason at all! He was originally a comedy balancing act known as RU LAMBERT and comedy balancing he did throughout his career. His great fan, Philip, says: 'He was a very funny man. Gormless and toothless with an off-beat nonsensical act. He would open by staggering on to the stage carrying a huge cannon ball. This he would drop on to the stage (and almost through it). Later he would spend time trying to catch it on the back of his neck. The rest of his turn was taken up with a futile attempt to climb up a pile of chairs. Just when he was in the most impossible situation he would climb down, shuffle to the footlights, deliver his homilies and then go back to the task in hand. It was a really droll act that, inexplicably, did not do as well as it ought.'

Nervo and Knox

Comedians. James Henry Holloway (Nervo) born 1897 and Albert Edward Cromwell Knox, 1896. It is, of course, as Crazy Gang members that I remember Nervo and Knox. The people who know, notably TOMMY TRINDER, say that Jimmy and Teddy were the real brains behind the Gang's success. Jimmy Nervo was the man who dealt with the management and came up with, and developed, most of the best ideas. Teddy Knox was, to me, the best performer of them all. His characterisations in the sketches were always totally his own, off-beat self. He looked funny, talked funny and walked funny. He was terrific in drag too. I missed Nervo and Knox as a Variety act and I'm sorry I did: people who saw them have described their, nearly always, wordless burlesques to me and there is nothing like them today. I have seen some badly shot video of their slow motion wrestling match and it is brilliant. Philip says: 'It would still be a sensation today – if anyone could do it.'

They were not the sort of performers who carried on doing the same old turn for years: they were always thinking, always updating their stuff. They did routines as foreign diplomats (they did speak in this sketch – a language totally of their own invention), gladiators, apache dancers, bullfighters, Don Juans, Merry Widow chorus boys and, most famously, as two ballet dancers handling a large balloon. You must have seen the remains of this routine in pantomime, usually done by the Dame and the comic.

They had a spot called 'Making a Talkie', very topical at the time. In this sketch one played a returning husband who, after discovering his wife's lover in the house, has a terrific punch-up with him. At the end of this the stage lights were dimmed. When they came up again the whole piece was played again in slow motion. Eye witnesses say it was a masterpiece of timing and acrobatic prowess. Totally unique.

JIMMY NERVO came from a circus family and spent his early years as a juggler/acrobat in the family act, THE FOUR HOLLOWAYS, and worked for FRED KARNO, the man who discovered CHARLIE CHAPLIN. Teddy Knox was an apprentice juggler and acrobat as well. He was originally CHINKO THE BOY JUGGLER, then, with his brothers, one of THE CROMWELLS. He and the trick cyclist MINNIE KAUFMANN appeared as CHINKO AND KAUFMANN, and he joined up with Jimmy in 1919. At this stage Teddy was a novice acrobat but, within a week, he had learned a complete tumbling routine. The lads established themselves as a bill topping duo, even playing with great success in New York.

It was their touring revue in the UK, *Young Bloods of Variety*, that was the inspiration for the Crazy Gang. In this show they made a feature of joining in everybody else's acts as well. GEORGE BLACK, in 1931, needing a shot in the arm for the Palladium, took a chance and had Jimmy and Teddy 'organise' a similar anarchic show for the great venue. It worked and the rest is history.*

Jimmy was married to Minna in 1939 and died in 1975. Teddy, first married to the music-hall star CLARICE MAYNE, died just one month after his second wife Betty Reeves (the daughter of the Gang's original agent Horace Reeves), in 1974.

*There is a fascinating look at the private lives of Jimmy, Teddy and the rest of the Gang in *The Crazy Gang* by Maureen Owen, Teddy Knox's niece.

Max and Harry Nesbitt

Comedy double act. Max born Cape Town, South Africa, 1903, Harry born Cape Town, 1905. Brothers MAX and HARRY came to the UK in 1927 and within four months were in a West End revue, *Blue Skies*, at the Vaudeville. Philip says: 'They both played banjos, did patter and usually finished on a ballad which they had written themselves. The zany, goofy comedy and facial contortions from the comic made them a vaudeville hit and they played all over the UK, America and the Continent.'

They were quite successful songwriters with over 200 published numbers to their credit including 'Georgia's Gotta Moon' and 'I Kiss Your Little Hand Madame'. Max died in 1966 and Harry in 1968.

Barbara Newman

The best goose in the business

Comedienne. Born Cardiff, 1914. From the 1940s on through to just a few years back, Barbara *was* the best goose in the business, as JOHN INMAN will tell you. She played opposite him in *Mother Goose* many a time. Philip remembers her before her avian histrionics came to the fore and says: 'Her other talents were rarely exposed which was a shame. She was a good soubrette in her younger days, a good feed for comedians and a genuine all round performer.'

Barbara with John Inman in Mother Goose

Pantomime and concert party were Barbara's forte. She started in a panto chorus and played Principal Boy, Principal Girl and Ugly Sister before the bird took over. She did concert party with TOMMY TRINDER, Variety as a comedienne and worked for ENSA during the war. She is now, alas, retired.

Nino the Wonder Dog

Speciality act. Another unique Variety act. Nino, as his progeny did later, would go through a routine of tricks, walking on a huge ball, etc, alone on the stage, all by himself. Not a trainer or presenter was in sight – though what he, or she, was shouting from the wings I'd like to have heard. At the end of his spot Nino would push his way through the tabs and take his call by throwing backward somersaults.

David Nixon

Magician. Born David Porter Nixon in North London 1919. Oddly, for someone who later became *the* television magician of his time, it wasn't magic that made him a household name. It was as a member of the panel of 'What's My Line?' that he achieved national fame. Yet he had done the lot before his naturally shy, avuncular personality caught the public imagination.

David Nixon with Basil Brush

From his childhood he had been magic mad. His dad, another magic fan, had taken him to see all the top men in the game in Variety and before the Second World War he had become a member of the Magic Circle. Once in the army he toured with ENSA and, on demob, spent four years with *The Fol de Rols* summer show. His charming, slightly posh approach would have suited that show perfectly. It was, however, in the summer show I started with, *Out of the Blue* that his big break came.* By the mid Fifties his magic had taken him to the top of the bill via his TV series,

It's Magic. Series after series followed including the unforgettable ones with the fox puppet, BASIL BRUSH. David was a lucky man, his magic associate, along with BILLY McCOMB was ALI BONGO and his script and ideas man was GEORGE MARTIN.

David was not a great magician but his affability and warm personality made him a most entertaining one. He was one of the very few performers to be elected King Rat of the GOWR two years running (1976 and 1977). Oddly enough the next Rat to achieve this was the man who took over as the top TV magician, PAUL DANIELS (1995 and 1996). David died in 1978.

*See Norman Wisdom.

Ossie Noble

The Clown Prince

Comedy drummer. Born Oswald William Noble, Treforest, South Wales, 1901. Ossie was a true clown whose brilliant comedy timing developed from having parents who were both deaf and dumb. He was initially a drummer who had quite a career as a straight musician with the bands of SYD SEYMOUR, JACK LEWIS, TEDDY JOYCE and JAN RALFINI. He spent two years as the highest paid drummer, xylophonist and vibraphone player in the country with IVOR MORETON and DAVE KAYE.

In 1938 he began a solo career as a stand-up comic but it was his transition to clowning that did the trick for him. I remember his two great spots. The 'putting up a deckchair' routine (TUBBY TURNER and LES WILSON also did it) and his speciality at the drums. He would open up with a drum solo then notice a lady's handbag lying on the stage, and go over to investigate the bag. Every time he went to pick it up a loud, off stage, noise would force him to drop it. It sounds childish but it was a very off-beat and beautifully timed bit of business. It was his agent, JOHNNIE RISCOE, who gave him this routine. Becoming bored with the handbag he would then spot a bust of a nude lady. This took him away from the drum kit and he carried on playing – on the bust. His big finish was a genuinely terrific drum solo. The business, invented by his agent JOHNNIE RISCOE, was beautifully timed interspersed with his own style of gibberish chat.

The mostly visual appeal of his spots led him to play successfully on the Continent in cabaret and circus. He featured an act in the stage version of the PETER BROUGH (with his dummy Archie Andrews) radio show, *Educating Archie*. He was with the show for ten years.

Ossie was married twice. His first wife, Margaret, died at thirty-five. He met his second wife, JO DAVISON, while she was working in a summer show for SANDY POWELL. He fell ill with cancer in 1972 but battled on until his death in 1975.

Noni

The clown to whom the Queen sent a flower

It was a Royal Variety Performance in 1928 that gave Noni his bill matter. At the end of his spot he took his call and wistfully complained to the musical director: 'What, no flowers?' Apparently Queen Mary *was* amused and gave the Secretary of the Variety Artistes Benevolent Fund (now the EABF) a flower from her posy to pass on to the clown.

Philip describes him so: 'He was one of the world's most famous clown acts. He was lauded as the successor to GROCK but I thought him greater. He did an acrobatic, juggling, musical mélange. He was an unusual clown in that he talked.'

I have seen a video of Grock and, despite the quality of the film and its German subtitles, he is, without doubt, the very best clown I have ever seen. If Philip thinks Noni was greater, what did I miss?

Noni at the piano

Bebe Norma

Dancing xylophonist. Born Norma Ellinger, Leeds, 1925. Bebe was a child prodigy, making her first broadcast at twelve and playing her first summer season (fourteen weeks in Blackpool) at thirteen. Originally she would play the xylophone and then dance but, by the time she arrived in our period, she would dance *and* play simultaneously. She did it at all the number one dates and number one summer seasons. She died in 1974.

Cavan O'Connor

The Strolling Vagabond

Singer. Born Nottingham, 1899. A man who sang for a living for seventy years. He was an old-fashioned straight tenor with that peculiarly nasal Irish tone. The Twenties and Thirties were his great periods. He made hundreds of records, lots under assumed names (one of his first was his signature tune 'I'm Only a Strolling Vagabond'). In 1935 he was featured on radio as the un-named 'Vagabond Lover'. When his identity was revealed he became one of the highest paid performers in radio. His 1946 series was listened to by a regular fourteen million. Of course he was a top of the bill Variety turn. I saw him late in life when DON ROSS, in the Sixties, toured him in Variety. He packed 'em out. His voice was quite stunning but his performance was very odd. He entered, dressed as a sort of smart tinker, stood centre stage, practically immobile, and simply sang song after song. The audience loved him.

His last appearance was at the Hackney Empire in 1985. He did an hour. He died in 1996.

Des O'Connor

Comedian. Born 1932. Although, sadly, we only see Des these days as a television host, his Variety background is impeccable. He knocked it out all round the country at every theatre you can think of. I first saw him as the opening spot comic and a good one he was too. His laid-back approach and cheeky charm were his main attributes then and age has not withered them, or him. Philip, always ready to give praise to the management, says: 'It was careful handling by his agent, CYRIL BERLIN that brought him to prominence. His "little boy" beguiling dimples and winning smile made his TV success certain.'

Des, by making everything he does look so easy, is the perfect example of how Variety was a great teacher.

Talbot O'Farrell

Singer. Born William Parrot, 1878. 'Talbot O'Farrell – the bloody great barrel' was how my Gran used to describe him. He certainly was a big bloke whom I saw in the touring revue *Thanks for the Memory* (see GERTIE GITANA). He was an Irish singer, even though he came from the North. Apparently he started as a Scottish singer, didn't do any good, swapped to Irish and never looked back. Nothing like the prototype Paddy, he wore check trousers, a black coat, a silk topper, white gloves – and spats! He was one of the handful of music-hall headliners who successfully went on into Variety. For all my Gran's colourful description, she liked him. He sang sentimental ballads like 'That Old Fashioned Mother of Mine,' and 'The Lisp of a Baby's Prayer'. He died in 1952.

Terry O'Neil

Comedian and dancer. Born Cork, Eire, 1922. Wait for this. His first London appearance was the *Windmill* Theatre at the age of twelve. He stayed there for three months – who would want to leave? When he met PEGGY HAIG, they married and became JOAN AND TERRY O'NEIL. Years later, Terry became very popular on Tyne Tees Television in a live lunchtime show, *The One O'Clock Show*, (five days a week).

Billy O'Sullivan

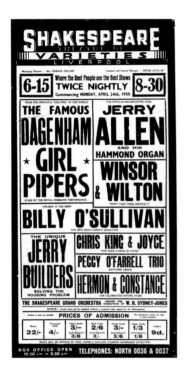

The rogue with the brogue

Comedian. Born in Dublin 1912. One of those names who never topped a bill but nevertheless worked in Variety steadily from end of the Second World War right through to its last knockings.

He began as an amateur singer in Dublin becoming a pro as a member of a vocal and comedy trio in the Thirties. They played the small dates all over Ireland. Worked with ENSA during the war as one half of THE SINGING SULLIVANS; his wife Renee was the other half. Sadly the double act finished in 1946 when a car accident forced Renee's retirement. Billy carried on as a single act till the early Seventies when he left the game and went to work at Harrods. Like most comics, particularly Irish ones, he was full of chat and charm and within twelve months was their Salesman of the Year. He died in 1987.

Tessie O'Shea

Two Ton Tessie

Comedienne. Born Cardiff 1914. Once seen never forgotten. The epitome of the 'full of fun' fat girl, she exuded jollity, friendliness and great style with lyrics and the ukulele banjo. She made her entrance in a Palladium revue on the back of an elephant. The elephant, objecting to the 'Two Ton' on his back, threw her off and she was out of the show for several weeks.

I'm not really sure exactly what she did in her act even though I worked with her. It was the

power of her personality that stays with me. She became a big attraction in Variety with her own turn and shared top billing with BILLY COTTON AND HIS BAND in a touring revue, *Tess and Bill.*

When Variety bit the dust she went to America and, after playing parts in musicals on Broadway (she got a Tony Award for one) she did films and television and became an even bigger star there than she had been here. She had one marriage (to David Rollo), sadly dissolved. She died, in Florida, in 1995.

Olivelli's

The celebrated show biz restaurant in Store Street WC1. It was the West End 'home' of overseas and London-based vaudevillians. It had an evening dining room in the basement where the pros would gather after their shows. Across the ceiling of this room was a trail of large (size 14) black footprints. Rumour has it that PRIMO CARNERA, the giant Italian heavyweight boxer, was eating there one night when a group of performers persuaded him to take off his shoes and socks. He did and the soles of his feet were painted. He was then held upside down while he 'walked' across the ceiling!

Ask anyone who knows Olivelli

OLIVELLI'S CONTINENTAL PENSION is known by all and recommended by everyone who has ever visited this Bohemian home of theatrical stars, whose names are household words.

Its food, its comfortable rooms completely modernised, make it an ideal rendezvous for the devotees of Thespis. "Mine Host" Olivelli is a past master of the culinary art ; his spouse, mother to all and sundry. Just ask anyone who knows them.

Believe it or not, all the bedrooms are tastefully furnished, and are equipped with central heating, hot and cold water, comfortable beds, reading lamps placed where they are genuinely useful and telephones within reach of every room. The cleanliness of the entire establishment is guaranteed because "Mother" Olivelli herself is responsible for this most particular item.

The Hotel Lounge is most comfortable, well furnished and equipped with a small but select library. The Dining-rooms are light and airy, and the service is all that could be desired.

It is interesting to know that "Mine Host" has had a very wide hotel experience, having

Ask anyone who knows Olivelli

studied every branch of the hotel business from the Managerial and Catering viewpoints. He is a linguist of no mean ability, which is very essential, because he comes into daily contact with so many Nationalities, each of whom he must satisfy, and satisfied they have always been.

Special facilities are available for storage of theatrical luggage.

A Garage adjoins the premises.

Luggage stored while you are out of Town

Trunks   ..   ..   **4d.** per week
Attaché cases and
        small parcels **2d.** per week

BURDEN & Co.
DISPENSING CHEMISTS
41, Store Street, BEDFORD SQUARE, W. C.

Telephone: 0211 MUSeum.

Vic Oliver

The Old Vic

Comedian. Born Viktor Oliver Samek, Vienna, 1898. Oddly enough I, who loved comedians, never liked him very much. He seemed too posh, too transatlantic, far too smooth and smutty for a lad who worshipped TED RAY and JIMMY WHEELER yet he

did the same sort of thing. Cracked gags in between playing the fiddle. I saw him in pantomime at the London Casino (now the Prince Edward) and liked him even less in that. Not his scene at all. Yet he seemed very popular with everyone else.

His long wartime association with BEN LYON AND BEBE DANIELS in their hit radio show *Hi Gang!* did the trick for him in Variety though he had had a fascinating early career as a musician on the Continent and in America. He went rather up-market as he got older and conducted big orchestras. Philip spotted an early review of his double act in America. *Variety* said: 'Mr Oliver looks more like a piano tuner than a comic. As for his fiddle playing, he is not half as funny as Kreisler.'

He married, believe it or not, Winston Churchill's daughter Sarah.

I apologise for these rather disparaging few words but it would be a boring world if we all laughed at the same things. Vic died in 1964.

Olsen and Johnson

Hellzapoppin

America comedians. John Siguard Olsen born Indiana, 1892, and Gilmore L. Johnson born Indianapolis, 1922. They came to the UK in the mid Forties with their smash hit American stage show *Hellzapoppin*. This was a sort of Crazy Gang-style show with lots of crossover-type gags and audience participation. (The man trying to deliver the potted plant that gets bigger throughout the show was one of theirs.) In fact BUD FLANAGAN and Ole Olsen used to send each other gags and ideas they thought would fit their respective shows. I didn't see them on-stage but *Hellapoppin* was filmed. Sadly, like any show that relies on an audience, it didn't quite come off. Olsen died in 1963 and Johnson in 1962.

Beryl Orde

Impressioniste. Born Marjorie Stapleton, Liverpool, 1914. Long experience, in every possible branch of the biz *before* she established herself on radio, meant Variety was meat and drink to her. She had a great range of impressions, vocal and visual. She was married to CYRIL STAPLETON of radio's *Show Band* fame. She died in 1966.

P

Freddie Parker

Accordionist. Born Middlesbrough, 1920. From show biz parents he formed FRANKIE PARKER AND HIS ACCORDION BAND for ENSA during the war. In the late Forties he got rid of the band and became a single act.

Ron Parry

Ventriloquist/comedian. Born Scarborough, 1922. Oddly enough I don't remember him as a vent but Philip tells me he was *and* made his own

dolls. I saw him in a revue with DES O'CONNOR and BILLY DAINTY when he was very good in the sketches.

Charlie Parsons

Comedian. Born Kirkham, Lancashire, 1906. The biography of him that I have certainly shows he had immaculate theatrical connections. He was the son of PAPA AND MADAME PARSONS (Madame-from Kirkham?), the brother of the SEVEN LANCASHIRE LASSIES, was married to MONA STANLEY of THE STANLEY TWINS AND MONA, and spent his early years working for the legendary DR WALFORD BODIE. He became a popular comic in Northern summer shows.

Gene Patton

Comedian/whistler/dancer. Born James Patton Elliott, Hetton-le-Hole, County Durham. Gene was the father of THE PATTON BROTHERS and those favourites on children's telly, THE CHUCKLE BROTHERS. He trained all four as dancers but, like him, they all veered towards comedy. Gene himself was a useful summer show performer where he would do black-faced EUGENE STRATTON and G.H.ELLIOTT songs and soft-shoe dancing. For many years he worked with, and understudied, the star revue comedian ERNIE LOTINGA.

Payne and Hilliard

Comedy double act. An act who all those in the know say was a very funny one. Tom Payne was the comedian, a little bloke who wore a long overcoat and a little hat, and Vera Hilliard was his missus. She was a large lady who sang as well as played opposite Tom.

In their most famous spot, Vera would enter as Josephine to be joined by Tom as Napoleon. Just before his entrance, the backcloth, of a mountain range, would be lowered so that he could step over it. As he did so, he would throw a handful of 'snow' up in the air and open with the line everyone remembers: 'I am, madam, Napoleon crossing the Alps.'

The rest of the sketch, says Philip, was very funny patter concluding with, naturally: 'Not tonight Josephine!' Oh, if only someone had written it all down.

Bob and Alf Pearson

My Brother and I

Entertainers at the piano. Real brothers they were, both born in Sunderland, Bob in 1907 and Alf in 1910. That unforgettable four-bar, sung phrase:

'We bring you melody from out of the sky
My brother and I'

was their signature tune. Big Bob at the piano and little Alf by his side. Their harmonies (as evidenced on their hundreds of recordings) and their clothes, were immaculate. Yet they gave us so much more. Good comedy songs like 'At the Baby Show' and a selection of funny voices that

were well featured in their pal TED RAY's radio show *Ray's a Laugh*. They were headliners in Variety and in their own shows. Their popularity remained undimmed until Bob's death in 1985. Alf retired then to concentrate on his golf and his beloved Grand Order of Water Rats. All us Rats cheered him to the rafters when he was elected our King in 1996.

Donald Peers

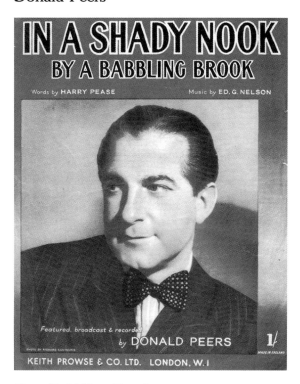

By a Babbling Brook

Vocalist. Born Ammanford, South Wales, 1910. Donald was the unlikeliest heart-throb of them all. He was a small, cuddly, friendly, avuncular middle-aged man when it all happened for him. After years of good honest graft around the theatres of the UK he suddenly became a teenagers' rave. Quite why it happened I don't know, but his recordings did something to the girls and it was during his radio show that, for the first time, I heard girls scream. He was the first 'pop' singer I know who filled the Royal Albert Hall. This nonsense did fade of course but Donald continued to be a most loved entertainer until he died in 1973.

Vic Perry

Entertainer. Born Woking, Surrey 1919. I've put 'Entertainer' at the top of this piece as, looking through his earlier biography, he announced himself as a 'radio artist, dramatic actor, vaudevillian, after-dinner speaker and television actor'. A fairly entertaining chap, I would have thought. I never saw him but Philip tells me he did do *everything* and all with great success. The son of a magician, THE GREAT NIXON (not David!) and the comedienne IRENE LEWIS, he began as a boy pickpocket magician. He was married to BEAU GOOMBER (the daughter of FARO the pantomimist and niece of THE LYONS TRIO, SOLO and THE DE VERE SISTERS). His all too short career embraced conjuring, pick-pocketing, producing, writing books on making cocktails, photography, straight acting (on stage and in films), after-dinner speaking and running a publicity agency. The rest of the time he just lazed about! He died, of exhaustion I should think, in 1974.

Bill Pertwee and Marion

Comedy cocktail

Bill and Marion (Macleod) met in summer show in Gorleston, in 1955. With encouragement from CHARLIE CHESTER they devised their comedy and musical spot and were spotted, and booked into Variety, by the agent, EVELYN TAYLOR. It was Evie who, enthusiastically, helped them work out their act, have musical arrangements written, photographs taken and new costumes made. They played most of the, by then, rapidly vanishing Variety dates. Bill claims they closed more theatres than anyone! I dispute this claim. I've always believed it was me and my partner Eddy Cunningham, HUDD AND KAY, who did the most damage. The mid Fifties of course heralded the birth of commercial television, the final blow to the old halls, to 'Comedy Cocktail' and to Hudd and Kay.

The teaming wasn't in vain, though, as Bill and Marion are still together as man and wife. They both went on to individual careers in theatre, radio and television. Bill found the perfect part to suit his personality – the irascible air-raid warden Hodges in TV's *Dad's Army*.

Jon Pertwee

Comedian/actor. Born Innsbruck, Austria 1919. What a pedigree. Jon's great-aunts were EVA, DECIMA, EMILY and BERTHA MOORE, his father was the novelist and playwright ROLAND PERTWEE and his brother was MICHAEL (another distinguished playwright and screenplay writer). He was a student at RADA, worked successfully in the 'legit' and eventually became a top-ranked voices man on radio in shows like ERIC BARKER's, *Merry Go Round* and *Waterlogged Spa*. With Eric he created a whole panoply of great characters like 'Wetherby Wett' the postman. Remember 'What does it matter what you do as long as you tear 'em up!' At the same time as his popularity grew on radio so did his drawing power in Variety. When the theatres closed Jon continued on the wireless as part of *The Navy Lark* team. (It was the longest running comedy show in the history of radio – until *The News Huddlines* came along!)

Jon scored even more heavily on television with his portrayal of 'Dr Who' and – can you ever imagine anyone else playing him? – 'Worzel Gummidge'. The return of 'Wetherby Wett'! Jon died in 1996.

The Peters Sisters

Singing trio. Three genuine sisters (Mattye, Anne and Virginia) born Santa Monica, California. I'll never forget seeing them at the Palladium for the first time. The roar that went up from the

audience as first one huge black girl walked on to the stage followed by a second, just as big, and then a third, even bigger, was tremendous. Then they started to sing and they really could. They stopped the show, both there and all over the country. Philip says, 'They were like three TESSIE O'SHEAS, blacked up!' The three girls retired and their equally large daughters, billed as 'The *Original* Peters Sisters,' took over.

The Petersen Brothers

Vocal duo. Real brothers from Cape Town. Wally born 1920 and Mervyn 1918. They came here in 1948 and scored heavily in Variety but from then on concentrated on radio.

Peiro Brothers

Jugglers. South American born, they played, and still do, with great success all over the UK. Their routines with hats and sticks are very novel and they introduce comedy into the act by featuring audience participation with the boladeros. You may have seen them, several times, with BRUCE FORSYTH and LARRY GRAYSON on TV's *The Generation Game*.

Wilfred Pickles

Give her the money Barney!

Actor/comedian. Born Halifax, 1904. Wilfred became a household name with his 'spot of homely fun' radio quiz show *Have a Go!* His warm, friendly approach and Yorkshire accent

broke the monopoly of the regular 'plum in the mouth' broadcasters. He toured all over the country with VIOLET CARSON, later to become famous as Ena Sharples in *Coronation Street*, his missus MABEL ('tell us what's on the table Mabel') and his producer, BARNEY COLEHAN (the deviser of TV's *The Good Old Days*). The shows were 'live' and good fun. Wilfred's sensitive, make yourself at home handling of the contestants was superb. The catchphrase '*Give* her the money Barney' was the one he used when he thought a contestant deserved the prize (usually a couple of quid) without being asked any questions. He successfully transferred his talents (though not *Have a Go!*) to television with series like *For the Love of Ada* with IRENE HANDL and to acting in films and in stage plays. He was Yorkshire through and through and a pal of mine, MICHAEL HARVEY, was thanked for playing a sketch with him for an entire summer season with – a glass of sherry! He died in 1978.

The Piddingtons

Mental telepathists. Husband and wife, Sydney and Lesley, born Sydney, Australia. The amazing Piddingtons were a sensation in the late Forties. Using a technique Sydney had devised while a prisoner-of war in Singapore, they gave incredible demonstrations of thought transference both on radio and in the theatre. Sydney could 'transfer' long passages from books, etc to Lesley who

would often be miles away, memorably once in a submarine and once in an aeroplane. They retired to Australia in 1954. Sydney died in 1990.

Channing Pollack

The Most Beautiful Man in the World

Magician. A devastatingly handsome, immaculately tail-suited, sophisticated, brilliant producer of exquisite white doves, from everywhere! He was a headline act both in the UK and abroad until he gave up the magic to become a leading man in Continental films. He left the act to his chauffeur who played the halls as FRANKLIN AND HIS DOVES.

Pop White and Stagger

Comedy knockabout act. Again an act I never saw so I rely on Philip's memories. 'They were a three-handed knockabout dancing act. Two blokes, one working in white face, dressed in tail coats and bowlers, playing old men and a girl. The two lads had a very funny face-smacking bit inside a dance routine. A standard act constantly in work around all the halls. They either opened or closed.'

Gillie Potter

Good evening England. This is Gillie Potter speaking to you in English

Comedian. Born Hugh Peel, Chipping Sodbury, 1888. The perfect place for Gillie Potter to have been born. I can hear him saying the words now.

Although he'd had a long career on the stage, in straight plays, concert party and musicals (he understudied GEORGE ROBEY in *The Bing Boys*) once again it was radio that made him a nationally known performer. He invented the English village of Hogsnorton and his monologues were a diary of the happenings there. Delivered in perfect English, his reports on the adventures of Lord and Lady Marshmallow, Canon Fodder, The Reverend Ezekiel Eggpedlar and General Sir Stimulant Maudlin-Tight were, to me, a lad from Croydon (where we played tennis with hammers!), a magic carpet into a wonderful surreal world.

Sorry to go on about this man but he was very special to me. He was very popular where audiences were on his wavelength but, at some of the rougher halls, he had a hard time. He would enter wearing a Harrow or Eton straw boater, tight blue blazer and enormously wide Oxford 'bags', carrying an umbrella. Once there he would address the congregation, says Philip, 'rather like a manager talking to his staff or a managing director at a board meeting. His total gravity and sincerity was his secret. He was a one-off.' He died in 1975.

Sandy Powell

Can you 'ear me Mother?

Comedian. Born Albert Arthur Powell, Rotherham, 1900. Yet another radio catchphrase that helped elevate a comedian to a better spot on the bill. Unlike so many who had became well known through the wireless, Sandy had years of experience on-stage to back up his radio fame. He was a brilliant visual comic, who will be remembered for a very long time as he was still working in his eighties. Happily for us, his two great routines, the dodgy ventriloquist and the even dodgier conjuror (in both he was assisted by his missus KAY WHITE, formerly DOWLER AND WHITE) are preserved on modern film. His wonderful 'send ups' were not always appreciated for their true worth and he used to recall playing clubs where people would advise him, 'Give it up. I could see your lips moving,' His standard reply was 'Ah yes, but only when the dummy's talking.'

Long before these masterpieces of burlesque were seen he had, incredibly, sold over seven million gramophone records. He had the foresight to plump for a royalty on each record rather than just take a flat fee. He was never a huge star name but his shows packed 'em out everywhere he played, be it for a week in Variety or for the season at the seaside. He did so many summers in Eastbourne that he became known as '*Mr Eastbourne.*'

He told his life story to HARRY STANLEY in the biography *Can You Hear Me Mother?* published in 1975. Sandy died in 1982 – the last of the great burlesque performers.

Arthur Prince

England's Premier Ventriloquist

Ventriloquist. Born Arthur James Prince, London, 1881. For nearly fifty years Arthur was a number one top of the bill, first in music hall and into our period, just, 1948. His dummy was a cheeky able seaman, Jim. It was said he was the very first to be able to smoke and drink while Jim was 'talking'. SANDY POWELL's unforgettable parody was based on him. He died, and was buried with Jim, in 1948.

The Two Pirates

Oh no there isn't!

Burlesque acrobats. Alfred 'Jock' Cochrane born Glasgow and Reg Mankin born London, 1917. A unique act who were featured many times on TV in *Sunday Night at the Palladium*. I'm sure you remember them. Little Reg would be suspended on a wire and perform the most amazing balancing feats with the big bearer, Jock. They actually did a finger-to-finger balancing trick. As the audience whispered, 'There's a wire!' Jock would assure them there wasn't. As they insisted he would walk downstage, leaving Reg hanging there, and assure them: 'Oh no there isn't!' to which, as if rehearsed, they would respond, 'Oh yes there is!' I wonder if they invented this bit of audience participation?

Jock's patter between the tricks was off-beat to say the least. At the Croydon Empire I heard him say: 'My wee partner will now ride around the stage, sidesaddle, on a cissy emu!' they were a wonderful act.

Eventually Reg married and emigrated to Australia while Jock retired to spend more time with his hobby – homing pigeons.

Alec Pleon

Funny face they call me – funny face that's me

Comedian. The son of a well-known music-hall act DAIMLER AND EDIE, born London, 1911. A popular featured act in West End and touring revue. His facial contortions earned him the title 'Mr Funny Face'. His extra talent was yodelling and, as a finish, it was a show stopper. I last saw Alec, with his funny face in the stocks, in a FRANKIE HOWERD film, *Up the Chastity Belt*.

Sid Plummer

The Zyli-Fool

Xylophonist/comedian. Born Balham, London, 1901. Originally a straight musician, xylophone and drums, with leading dance bands, MARIUS B. WINTER and BRAM MARTIN. He would often be featured as a solo xylophonist and this gave him the idea of a single act. In the mid Thirties, as a single, he played the West End, clubs, cabaret and theatres and all the number one dates. He played Dame in *Cinderella* at Her Majesty's. He continued with the act all through the war and after.

As the years went by his great prop, the xylophone* became a living, breathing thing. Sid devised, and built, all sorts of mechanical gadgets (he was originally apprenticed to an engineer) that made the instrument appear to spout smoke, have snakes running across it, almost fall to pieces and, unforgettably, sprout movable donkey's legs. At a given point a pair of hands would appear from nowhere and clap in rhythm. With clever use of ultraviolet light a tiny luminous soldier would appear to be dancing on the xylophone keys. No

wonder the kids loved him in panto. Philip, who knew him well, says: 'He was an original whose combination of comedy and brilliant musicianship has never been bettered.'

He died, after a thirty-two-year career in 1967 but his son TOMMY and his daughter-in law BERYL (THE PLUMMERS) are keeping the famous name alive.

* Sid's xylophone, donated by his son Tommy, is now on display in the Horniman Museum, South London.

___ R ___

Radcliffe and Ray

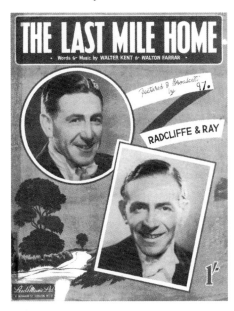

Singers. Dick Radcliffe born Swansea, 1914, and Ray Radcliffe, Swansea, 1910. Genuine Welsh brothers, they worked in a sort of LAYTON AND JOHNSTONE style. Again, through radio and records, they achieved popularity and toured the halls both as a featured act in Variety and as part of NORMAN EVAN's *Road Show*.

The Radio Revellers

Four-part vocal group. Freddie Holmes born Forest Hill, 1914. Stan Emeney born Tooting, 1911. Art Reed born, Camberwell and Al Fernhead. During the Second World War the four lads, who

had all been members of various vocal groups, kept in touch by letter and, on demob, they got together and formed The Radio Revellers.

'Four men, one song, it's the way the voices bleeeend that helps the tune along' was their signature tune. Remember them now? That tune was never off the air during the late Forties and Fifties. So much so that Freddie Holmes, the one surviving member of the group, told me the bandleader GERALDO once looked into one of their rehearsals and said 'I've just been reading your diary – the *Radio Times*.'

They were great-sounding with good comedy. So much so that Jack Hylton featured them in two CRAZY GANG revues at the Victoria Palace. They topped bills everywhere till, in 1958, they all decided they were too old for the music business. 'There were seventeen and eighteen year olds coming up and we wanted to finish at our peak,' says Freddie Holmes in his fascinating story of The Revellers in his book, *Four Men, One Song*. Freddie is still as bright as a button and living in Sidcup.

Mark Raffles

Magician/pickpocket. Born Taylor in Manchester, 1919, into a theatrical family and was interested in magic from the age of five. Luckily he had an uncle, a good semi-pro magician, who encouraged and instructed him. He began his professional career in 1938 as RAY ST CLAIR, a silent magician. His wartime service with ENSA took him to all corners of the UK and, having to supply a second spot, led him to devise his pickpocket routine. Post-war he played

virtually every Variety theatre with magic that was clever and fun, changing his name to MARK RAFFLES and becoming nationally known. He would stand in the foyer of the theatre looking, as he always still does, a distinguished and totally trustworthy toff. As the people filed into the theatre he would systematically 'dip' whichever ones took his fancy. Later, on stage, he would present his (unsuspecting) victims with whatever it was he had nicked. Sensational.

He, and his wife Joan, later presented THE WYCHWOODS, an act with disappearing and appearing live toy poodles, invented, with help from brother magicians, by JACK AND AUDREY SHAW. Mark and Joan's three children, Wendy, Tim and Jacqui, all followed them into the business, working together for twelve years as the vocal act GOLDEN BRANDY.

In 1997, he celebrated sixty years as a pro and, to mark it, produced a book called *Diamond Jubilee Memoirs*. I knew it would be a good 'un. A few years back I did a season in Margate when Mark was in the show next door. I spent more time with Mark and his pal NORMAN CALEY than I did in my own theatre. Their stories, friendship, advice and wit made my season and the book is like being in his company. It is a treasure house of good pro stories, gossip, and show-business secrets, capturing the unique atmosphere of a performer's life and work during the golden period of Variety better than any other book I've read. It's available from John Moore, 20 Woodend Road, Alloway, Ayr KA7 4QR. Do get it.

Ramoni Brothers and Detrina

Three-handed tap dancing act. A standard dancing act who played every date of consequence both in the UK and abroad.

Alan Randall

Musician. Born Bedworth, Warwickshire. A jazz musician and a brilliant multi-instrumentalist (piano/drums/trumpet/trombone/vibes and, of course, the ukulele banjo), who became known to a wider public through his uncanny impression of GEORGE FORMBY.

Alan began as a piano and vibes player in dance bands and had a solo career thrust upon him when he auditioned, and got a job, at the Windmill Theatre. He was a good solid musical speciality act all through the Fifties but never sang. He said: 'I never did because no matter what I sang I always sounded like George Formby.' Eventually, after months spent copying the Formby technique from records, he put a couple of George's songs into the act. Although his other musical talents are what gets audience to their feet, it is the ukulele banjo stuff that gets them into the theatre in the first place.

The Formby influence has been great on him. He has starred in his own stage version of the Lancashire Lad's life, provided the linking material for the best compilation of Formby's words and music *George Formby Complete* and, with Ray Seaton, has written a biography of his hero.

The Rao Brothers

Acrobats. Real brothers, Babu Shejawalker born Bombay, 1913 and Shanker born Bombay, 1923. They brought their balancing on a roller and perch act to the UK in the 1930s. When Shanker, after an accident, gave up performing he merely assisted his brother before returning to India in 1948. His elder brother remained here as a popular single turn, BABU RAO. Alone he featured routines on the slack wire. Shanker did return here in 1960 and they worked together again. Shanker died in 1979.

The Rastellis

Clowns. Their leader was Oreste Rastelli, born Bologna, Italy, 1900. A superb clown act (Oreste, his wife, son and a couple of others). Oreste had the usual complete training for a great clown: riding, acrobatics, balancing and trampolining. How I envy those circus folk. They are the best prepared, most reliable and flexible performers of all. I saw the Rastellis at the Palladium and there they did their clowning and a superb musical spot (for which they called themselves CHOCOLATE AND COMPANY). It is sad to see today's apologies for clowns.

Ravic and Renee

Roller skating speciality. Ravic born Berlin,

1925, and Renee London, 1926. They were really Mr and Mrs John and Eileen Lilley. I remember the act as RAVIC AND BABS – obviously a later partner. The act was quite something. Acrobatic roller skating performed at high speed on a small circular rostrum. Ravic was the fulcrum and Babs did the acrobatics. They were the forerunners of so many similar acts.

Rawicz and Landauer

Piano duettists. Marian Rawicz and Walter Landauer, both Austrian. Another act who became bill toppers through radio, they never sank to the music-hall level of sing-a-longs. They played 'highbrow' music but always managed to hit just the right level with what we would now call 'musical lollipops'. Pieces like 'The Warsaw Concerto' were their bag. They came to Britain to escape the Nazis and teamed up originally in a rather interesting way. Walter told me he was on holiday in the Alps when he heard someone playing the piano in a nearby house. He traced the source and there was Marian at his piano. Walter introduced himself and joined Mr Rawicz at the keyboard in a duet. They stayed together till Marian's death in 1970. Walter continued as a soloist till his death in 1983.

Ted Ray

Fiddling and fooling

Comedian. Born Charles Olden, Wigan, 1906. The comedians with the most recognisable voices on radio were Ted and TOMMY HANDLEY. I always thought they were very similar in style too. Fast-speaking, every line a quip, talkers. They were both the epitome of the never lost for a word, commercial traveller, barfly. The great difference was that Ted, unlike Handley, was a first-class stand-up 'live' comedian (Philip believes he was the first to come on-stage in an ordinary lounge suit). Ted was a well established Variety star well before the memorable radio show *Ray's a Laugh*, with its combination of sitcom, music (BOB AND ALF PEARSON) and ITMA-type characters (Jennifer, Mrs 'oskins and Ivy, Crystal Jollibottom, Sidney Mincing, etc). He was, till the end, popular on radio, the linchpin of the cod panel game *Does the Team Think?* 'Live' he would stand centre stage with just his fiddle and bombard the audience with a barrage of sharp gags, interspersed with good 'fiddling'. He played the Palladium more times than anyone (except JOE CHURCH), toured in Variety and revue and appeared in cabaret and, notably, in films. He was a first-class straight actor too. You'd think, 'a right clever dick', but he was such a lovely, clubbable sort of bloke that even the most jealous forgave him his talent. Ted died in 1977.

Rayanne

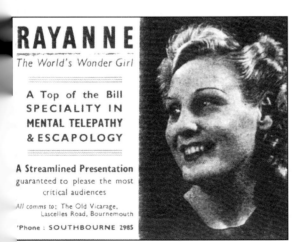

Mental telepathy act. 'Rayanne' was born Winifred L. Martens-Moore in Birmingham, 1918. Her partner was Jack Martens-Moore. (I wonder why they changed the name!) One of many 'Mind Over Matter' acts: the partner in the audience, collecting objects from the people, and the blind-folded lady identifying them.

Al Read

Comedian. Born Salford, 1909. Al was a great radio comic. He created, or rather caricatured, the characters we all meet in everyday life: the wife in the kitchen, the 'know-all' decorator/football fan/car park attendant, and the embarrassing small son. He achieved national institution fame via his Sunday lunchtime Al Read shows but, sad to say, he was a bit disappointing on-stage. As with The Goons, we all had our own ideas as to how the characters looked and, when I saw him 'live', they weren't mine. It was best to leave them in our imaginations. Happily, at the insistence of that loving chronicler of comedians and comedy, MIKE CRAIG*, the BBC have reissued a bunch of Al Read shows. Get them and relish a master of the medium. Al died in 1987.

*An ex BBC radio producer and comedy writer who has written, not only for most of our top funny men, but, for us, two terrific books about great comedians, *Looking Back with Laughter*, Volumes One and Two.

Ralph Reader

Producer/choreographer/writer of songs and sketches. Born Crewkerne, Somerset, 1902. So very few people know that the man whose name will forever be associated with the Scouts' *Gang Show* had the most amazing career of any performer I know. So many have forgotten that he choreographed and staged hit after hit show on Broadway and in the West End, turned down an enormous offer from MGM to stage their musicals and created that unforgettable moment in the Royal Albert Hall's Festival of Remembrance. The moment when those thousands of poppies descend. It is unfair that this born showman should only be remembered for those arm-waving, woggle-wearing lads singing 'I'm Riding Along on the Crest of a Wave'. It is a good song, though, but then so were most of those he wrote, perfectly tailored, for the Boy Scout movement shows. BUD FLANAGAN begged Ralph to let him have one of them. He did: its title 'Strollin''. For many years he contributed songs and sketches to the Victoria Palace CRAZY GANG shows.

He was first asked to put a Scout show together in 1936 and, much to the chagrin of the top people who wanted his services (IVOR NOVELLO, whose early musicals Ralph staged, advised him, 'Get rid of it, or you'll become known as the Gang Show Man'), he stuck with the show, and his lads, till 1974 when he retired. He wrote his life story in *Ralph Reader Remembers* (1974). The great man of entertainment (will we ever know just how far he *could* have gone) died in 1982.

Joan Regan

Singer. Born in Plaistow, London. One of the most popular vocalists of the Fifties, Joan has had a fascinating life which really should be written in its entirety. Great success, great problems, much happiness and much heartbreak, the lot.

Her large family were all good amateur performers and Joan, before she was ten, was winning talent competitions with her impressions. It was her 'discovery' by BRYAN MICHIE that led to her first variety work proper and she toured with his show.

Joan was married at 17 to an American paratrooper and, after the birth of her two sons in the United States, she returned home when the marriage broke up. She made a private recording which inspired the agent KEITH DEVON to take her on. Cabaret work followed and then commercial records. She had a string of hits including one which became her signature tune, 'May You Always'. She had success on TV. Not surprising as at this time, 1956, the photographer, Baron, declared her one of the ten most beautiful women in Britain. He wasn't a bad judge. Her second marriage, in 1957, again an aborted one (they divorced in 1963), was to HARRY CLAFF, the son of a well-known music-hall performer of the same name. Harry, the son, was the manager of the London Palladium. They certainly must have seen a lot of each other at work as Joan starred in several revues and pantos at the famous theatre. Summer seasons in all the top resorts followed and, of course, headline status in Variety.

Joan's third marriage, in 1966, led to living in Florida and we did not see her again till the late Eighties. She returned home to be welcomed with open arms, after a horrendous accident in which her life was saved by her husband, Dr Martin Cowan. Since then her constant appearances in theatre, on radio and television, have proved she should never have gone away.

Reggie Redcliffe

Novelty xylophonist. Born Cardiff, 1918. A Variety act, as a dancing xylophone player, from the age of fifteen. He began our period with a 1946 Royal Variety Performance where his inclusion of ultra violet (UV) lighting and the gimmick of changing costumes while he was playing, earned him a great reception. Those were the days when a successful RVP appearance could 'make' you. He played all the number one dates from that moment on.

As Variety began to die that wise old bird of an agent, BILLY MARSH, advised him to put on skates and do the act on ice! He did, very successfully.

Beryl Reid

Comedienne/actress. Born Hereford, 1919. *Educating Archie* was the radio show that introduced us to her first two great creations: the schoolgirl 'Monica' and the Brummie, 'Marlene'. Beryl was a rare creature in those Variety days, a really funny lady who was just as good, visually, as she sounded. She was a number one heroine of mine. A lady who did the lot: concert party, summer shows, musicals, revue, Variety, straight plays and films. For a full and frank life story please read her autobiography, *So Much Love.* She remembers *everything!*

Like all the really good Variety performers, she was an excellent actress and had the chance to prove it. Her Sister George in *The Killing of Sister George* was just the start of a cornucopia of brilliantly observed characters, funny and sad, that we had the pleasure of enjoying.

Philip remembers: 'Beryl, in her early days, went to see JACK GILLAM (a producer who never paid more than he had to – there's a surprise!). Jack asked her what she did. 'The lot,' said Beryl, 'sing, dance, comic, feed. I can do everything.' 'How much do you want?' enquired Mr Gillam. 'Three pounds,' replied Miss Reid. 'You're booked,' he said, 'I've always wanted someone who could do *everything* for three pounds!' Beryl died in 1996.

The Reid Twins
Britain's Ace Twin Act

Dancers/acrobats and balancers. Twins Marjorie and Constance born Eccles, Lancashire, 1923. Philip says: 'They did their mirror routine around all the halls.'

Eddie Reindeer

Comedian. Born Eddie Reinhardt, Cardiff. I knew Eddie very well. He was godfather to my son. I wish I knew a bit more about his career. By the time I met him and his missus, Flo, Variety was on its last legs. We played the odd dates that were left together especially the rather peculiar 'Continentals'. These were a last resort for the crumbling Variety halls. They took out the stalls seats, put in tables and chairs, served chicken and chips in a basket and hoped this, supposedly, sophisticated cabaret style entertainment would save the game. It didn't.

Eddie was an old-fashioned, JIMMY WHEELER type, patter comic. He wasn't right for fostering a 'Continental' type atmosphere – but then, who was? My happiest memories of him are travelling back from the 'Continental' Chatham on the train. These journeys were pure joy to me. He would regale me with tales of music hall, Variety, digs, stars, eccentrics, has-beens and never-was-es.

We did panto together at the Opera House, Belfast. He played Dame – the butchest there ever was. He really came into the biz too late. He was loud, boisterous, unsubtle and totally lovable. He died in 1983.

Dick and Dot Remy

Comedy acrobatic act. Brother and sister, Dick

born Alabama, 1920, and Dot born Alabama, 1922. After appearing together in American vaudeville, cabaret and musicals from, respectively, five and three years of age, they played all the top variety and summer seasons in the UK. Dot is a big girl and this is the basis of their comedy.

Renaldi

Comedy acrobatic act. Born Reginald Edward Smith, South Molton, Devon, 1909. Half of RENALDI AND KARIN. As British as roast beef but a Continental name seemed to be essential in our period. This act played mainly in circus but certainly found a place, as a standard act, in Variety.

Revell and Fields

Comedy double act. William Revell born Clapham, London, 1903, and Pat Fields born Salford, Lancs, 1916. Billy began as an eccentric dancer in cabaret and Variety and played musical comedy till he became part, in turn, of the Variety acts BUCHEL AND REVELL and THE THREE SPARKES BROTHERS. In 1949 he teamed up with Pat as REVELL AND FIELDS. Pat was first a member of the famous PENDER TROUPE of stiltwalkers. She, poor devil, was also the worse end of a pantomime horse. She became a solo singer and eventually joined Billy. They played all the number one dates and pantomimes, Pat as Principal Boy and Billy as Dame.

Revnell and West

The long and short of It

Double comedy act. Ethel Revnell born 1895, Gracie West born 1894. I never saw this most popular female double act. Gracie retired in 1953 but Ethel carried on and I saw her as one of the few lady Dames in panto (her timing and attack was that of a bloke). She made me laugh a lot. Ethel was six foot one, and skinny with it, while Gracie was just over four feet. Their two most successful characters were Ethel and Gracie, two evil schoolgirls. They did play *Babes* in pantomime with little Gracie as the boy. Nowadays you never have comics playing the children. With the

right pair it would add a lot. Ethel died in 1978 and Gracie in 1989.

The Rexanos

Comedy acrobats. They worked in clown style with tumbling and tricks on, and off, a table. Philip remembers they were sometimes called BOBO AND REXANO.

Billy Rhodes and Chika Lane

Comedy double act. Husband and wife Billy, born Manchester, and Chika (Ellen Rachel Timperley) born London. Before the war Billy, after a career that encompassed the flying trapeze, rep and bandleading, produced the comedy adagio act with his wife. Their most famous routine, 'Romeo and Juliet' was born in the Forties and was featured in ISSY BONN's touring revue and their own shows. Sadly Billy was forced to retire with arthritic problems in the early Fifties. He died in 1963. Chika, a long-time resident of Brinsworth House, died in 1996.

Joan Rhodes

The Mighty Mannequin

Strongwoman. Born London. Now we're talking speciality acts. Joan was a beautiful five feet seven inches tall, 36″-22″-37″, 140 pound – strongwoman. This gorgeous-looking, spectacularly costumed, lady would tear London telephone directories into quarters, break six-inch nails and bend half-inch steel bars in her teeth, sing, recite monologues and then invite blokes on to the stage to attempt tug-o'-war with her. Such was her impact that, while performing in Rome, King Farouk sent her tiger-lilies every night and asked if she would like to break one of his beds!

Joan left home at fourteen and became a street performer (this is where today's speciality acts are coming from), working with strong men and escapologists. She toured Spain as a dancer and, in 1949 joined the famous PETE COLLINS show, *Would You Believe It*. This led to her being a featured act on all the Moss Empire number one dates. She played everywhere else too, on TV, in Variety and cabaret in no fewer than fifty different countries. She was never out of work for twenty-five years.

Today Joan confesses she is 'twice the lady I was – well nearly!' She has made a new career for herself as an actress, painter and poet.

The Three Rhythm Rascals

Musical act. Multi-instrumentalists, they played guitars, banjos and saxophones. They were originally members of RALPH READER's *Gang Shows* during and after the war. Their combination of music and comedy made them a popular attraction in summer show and Variety.

Johnnie and Vi Riscoe

Comedy double act. Johnnie born Leeds, 1910. I only know Johnnie as an agent and Past King Rat of The Grand Order of Water Rats, and Vi as a prominent, and popular, Past Queen Ratling of the Grand Order of Lady Ratlings, but Philip has filled me in as to their performing heritage.

Johnnie began as an eccentric dancer and stiltwalker (he worked alongside ARCHIE LEACH who later became CARY GRANT). In the early 1930s he went to Holland and stayed for five years, the last three as principal comic with the Dutch Nationale Revue. He came home in 1937 and played Variety and revue.

After the war he teamed with Vi and they played, for a short time, as a double act on radio and in Variety. In one memorable gag Johnnie, with chair and whip, would open Vi's mouth and try to put his head in. Vi's début was pretty impressive, at the Palladium: she was one of the famous TERRY JUVENILES. She borrowed the name and formed a double act with PEGGY DESMONDE as THE TERRY SISTERS. They played the Palladium too. The act split and Vi became a well-known soubrette in revue. She met and married Johnnie and their double act was born. When the Riscoe agency was formed Vi retired and her great legs can now only be seen, by the public, at Lady Ratlings affairs.

Ken Roberts

Comedian. Born Henry Tydfil Roberts in the Rhondda, South Wales, 1916. Ken was a natural entertainer and started as a lad, encouraged by his brother Tom and his sisters, Ceridwen and Gretta. With Tom he emigrated – to England and, together, as LEWIS AND ROBERTS, they played Variety and summer seasons everywhere. Ken

did the lot: singing, dancing, playing drums and, of course, comicking.

Before the Second World War, he and Tom created THE FOUR BROWNIE BOYS (Tom, Ken, LAURIE HALLETT and NICK NISSEN) an act that topped all over the country, including the Palladium. During hostilities he was with ENSA and, I'm told, was just as entertaining in his 'proper' Army job as a regimental sergeant-major.

Out of uniform he climbed the ladder to become a popular principal comedian in summer shows, among them *The Fol-de-Rols* and SANDY POWELL's productions. He played pantomime at all the number ones and, on television, did *Kindly Leave the Stage*. He played parts in sitcoms notably with SIDNEY JAMES. He was a kind, gentle and extremely clubbable chap (he was Captain of the Vaudeville Golfing Society in 1979), who created fun wherever he went, especially in the Water Rats Lodge Room, where his wild Welsh tenor version of 'The Sound of Music' was greatly enjoyed. He was voted Rat of the Year in 1994, and died the following year.

Chic Robini

Accordionist. Philip says: 'Chic was a good opening act. He played the same numbers every time but he got an audience singing. Just what was needed.'

Cardew Robinson

Cardew the Cad of St Fanny's

Comedian. Born Douglas Robinson, Goodmayes, Essex, 1917. Tall, thin to the point of emaciation, wearing his old school cap and long scarf, he became a household name with his character 'Cardew the Cad'. He invented the Cad while in the RAF *Gang Shows* and, via radio, became a top of the bill. He made a film featuring the evil ageing schoolboy and (the ultimate accolade for a performer on the wireless) was the star of a cartoon series in the comic paper *Radio Fun*.

When his peak as a 'name' passed he did well with his scriptwriting and short-story writing. I worked with him in farce and, let me tell you, despite his incongruous looks, he could pull birds like no one I've ever met! He had wit, enthusiasm and, for the ladies, deadly charm. He died in 1993, greatly missed by his Brother Water Rats, the charities he worked so hard for and – girls from Land's End to John O'Groats.

Anna Rogers

Impressioniste. I'm afraid I know nothing about Miss Rogers but Philip says: 'She played all the number one dates constantly. She finished her act by blacking up on stage and doing Jolson which usually stopped the show. She was a riot – and a very difficult lady. She would come off and start rucking immediately. The spot was too large, the tabs were closed too soon (or too late), the band were too loud or not bright enough etc, etc. She became such a nuisance the number one tours dropped her. A shame. She was a fine performer with outstanding talent if only it could have been harnessed.'

Rhoda Rogers

Acrobatic dancer. Well that's what Philip said! remember Rhoda as a beautiful redhead making my spotty schoolboy palms sweat. But, before she was billed, by PAUL RAYMOND, as the British Brigitte Bardot (in his last knockings of Variety nude shows) Rhoda had been a good dancer and half of a double act with her husband CYRI

A whistler and bird impressionist from childhood, though he was all set to become an accountant, it was show business he really wanted to be part of. He joined STEFFANI'S SILVER SONGSTERS (a choir of 22 golden-voiced lads) at 18 via broadcasts on Radio Luxemburg and the BBC's *Children's Hour*. After wartime service he toured with a JACK TAYLOR revue, *Stardust* before joining up again with Steffani. It was that gentleman, eventually to become his manager, who encouraged Ronnie to study singing in London and yodelling in Switzerland. Now, as RONALDE, he began to work his way up the bill in variety as a solo act.

Ronnie Ronalde started recording and became

DOWLER. He played an old man and she his stage-struck daughter. On retirement she became a successful producer of shows. She died in 1996.

Sunny Rogers

Accompanist? Born Jessie Mary Rogerson, Ashton under Lyne. I'm wrong to write 'Accompanist' because, although I know Sunny best as FRANKIE HOWERD's much abused piano player 'Madame Rogers', it will, I'm sure, amaze you as much as it did me to discover just what she has done. Originally a child performer, she has been a Tiller girl, half of a Western rope-spinning act (with BUCK WARREN), a leading lady in revue and a producer of stage and floor shows. All this, of course, is why she was such a superb timer of the comedy she did with Frankie. She never was, and never will be, a 'poor old soul'. Sunny is happily retired in Brighton.

Ronnie Ronalde

The Voice of Variety

Singer/siffleur. Born Ronald Charles Waldron in London 1923. Ronnie was much more than a voice. His act was a combination of vocalising, whistling, yodelling, bird impressions and a terrific personality. He was one of the biggest draws of the Fifties.

a million-selling artiste with songs like: 'If I Were a Blackbird', 'In a Monastery Garden', 'Bells across the Meadow' and lots of others. He was soon a headliner, breaking box-office records everywhere, here and all over the world. He made regular visits to the United States and filled Radio City (with a capacity of over six thousand) every night for ten weeks. In Canada he topped that: he filled a Toronto venue with 25,000 souls for a fortnight.

In the late Fifties he did a concert in Guernsey. He liked the island so much he bought a hotel and stayed, meeting his wife Rosemarie there. They raised five children and, when they were grown up, he moved on to New Zealand, where he lives today. A happy man who made millions of people happy and scores of theatre owners even happier, he still broadcasts and does live concerts. So many people write to me asking where they can get Ronnie's records and I'm happy to say they are now available again.

Rondart and (various) Jeans

Dart-blowing speciality. Born Ronald Romlinson, West Auckland, Co. Durham, 1929. We had 'em all in Variety! Rondart (now how did he think of that name?) was originally a BEN JENKINS discovery. He, of course, did a novelty act with darts. His big finished was blowing the darts from his mouth into the board. Where is he now? CHRIS EVANS needs you.

Rex Roper

Western act. Born Charles Victor Knight, Bristol, 1919. Rex is probably the last in a long line of Variety cowboy acts like TEX MCLEOD, CAL MCCORD, CLAY KEYES, BUCK WARREN and PHIL DARBAN AND WENDY. His story is that of a real pro, one whose vast experience in every sort of venue, in every part of the world, has enabled him to adapt and be still working at nearly eighty years of age.

Rex was inspired to perform rope-spinning by seeing WILL ROGERS in *The Ziegfeld Follies* in America. Rex's father was a Texas Ranger and champion sharpshooter (TWO GUN RIX) who started a Wild West show in England. His son was

featured in the show and in variety as BOY REX. At fourteen he became REX ROPER and at seventeen he toured America with his sister Enid as REX ROPER AND MAISIE.

He spent the war years with the RAF in RALPH READER's *Gang Shows*. Back home he toured the halls with the revues *Canada Calling* and *Hello Canada* as a 'Canadian' cowboy. His wife joined the act and they became REX ROPER AND BILLIE THE KID. They did long stints in Germany and France in cabaret, theatre and circus and eventually returned to England. They did TV and toured the Bailey Club circuit, supporting all the top liners. From 1986 to 1991 Rex played host, and did his routines as Sheriff of The Silver City American Adventure Park in Derbyshire. A dream come true for him was a visit to the Will Rogers Ranch in Hollywood in 1992. There he won the Gold Award for roping and showmanship, Senior Division.

As Rex himself said when I asked him to give me some details of his career: 'I never gained great material wealth through being a variety performer but my life has been made richer by all the wonderful people I have worked with.' So many of *our* lives have been made richer by the dedication and unquenchable desire to perform exemplified by true pros like Rex.

Tommy Rose

Female impersonator. Born 1916. Originally a straight actor, Tommy turned to 'drag' after war service in the Navy. Well, well, well. I saw him at the Croydon Empire in the revue *This Was the Army*. He used to team up with SONNY DAWKES (a popular member of the Somerset and West Music Hall Society) to play Ugly Sisters in panto. They toured the halls as DAWKES AND ROSE.

Ron Rowlands

Light comedian. Born Ronald Beadle, London, 1927. Both his mum and dad were in the biz: he WALLY BEADLE, a well-known comedian and she NORMA DARE. Ronald, as so many performers did, joined their double act and it became BEADLE, DARE AND ROWLANDS. He became a successful second spot comic but never, Philip says, 'achieved the success TV would have brought him'.

Harry Rowson

Comedian. Born Liverpool, 1921. He started as a ventriloquist and, wisely, to gain experience, spent time as a straight man and stooge. He was a starring comic for Philip (in HINDIN, RICHARD AND HICK's *Hello From SEAC*).

Derek Roy

The Fun Doctor

After an apprenticeship as a singer and comic, with the GERALDO orchestra, Derek's big break came with the radio show *Variety Bandbox*. He and FRANKIE HOWERD alternated as resident comics and, borrowing the CROSBY and HOPE idea, started slagging each other off. This did both of them a world of good and led to them both having their own shows. While the temperamental Frankie went on to become a comedy icon, the more workmanlike Derek settled for regular work in Variety and panto. He was a good old-fashioned, value for money, pro. He died in 1981.

Billy Russell

On behalf of the working classes

Character comedian. Born Albert George Brown, Birmingham, 1893. A multi-talented chap if ever there was one. His dad was a scenic artist

and Billy inherited his gift. As I sit here writing I'm faced by a beautiful huge display board of him as his famous character (based on BRUCE BAIRNSFATHER's First World War cartoon), 'Old Bill'. Billy painted the board himself to advertise his Parlophone records. We exchanged letters quite a bit and he always came up with clever topical gags for me. His letters were beautifully illustrated too.

He became very popular on early radio with his topical tirades against the Government, the Establishment and the Mother-in-Law! As Variety died he created all sorts of characters in the legit. Easy for him whose make-up and attention to detail (down to transfers on his arms as 'tattoos' when he was Old Bill) had always been perfect. The actor TONY SELBY appeared with him in a play about a group of blokes who put up tents for a living (*The Contractor* by David Storey) and, on the opening night, Billy went round every dressing room and rubbed dirt under all the actors' fingernails. 'For authenticity', he said. He died (in 1972) as he sat in a television rehearsal room waiting for his call. He had spent an amazing seventy-two years in the biz.

Duo Russmar

LEW LANE, the floor show producer, remembers them as 'One of the most stylish of all hand to hand balancing acts'. Philip remembers them as

'two well muscled *men*'. I remember them as a husband and wife team as per the photograph. What happened?

___ S ___

Bunty St Clare

Speciality dancer. Born Valerie St Clare Bell, Birmingham, 1928. Bunty was one of the first, when she was just thirteen, to produce an act lit by fluorescent lights. I remember her at the Croydon Empire dancing on a staircase. She did the staircase routine (which so many have claimed they invented) and a tap routine on pointe. Her big finish was a Russian dance.

St Denis and Beryl

Acrobatic tumblers. Tommy St Denis born Edinburgh, 1916. A great background of five years with THE SEVEN ROYAL HINDUSTANIS led to his pre-war double act with the legendary JOHNNY HUTCH and his post-war duo, PRESCO AND CAMPO. The act we all saw was with his wife, BERYL MELVILLE.

Freddie Sales

Comedian. Born Frederick Harry Walker, Hull, 1920. A highly underrated character comedian whom I got to know, far too late, when he returned to England from America in the early 1990s.

Freddie, from three generations of a show biz family, had a tough apprenticeship. He went into revue when he was sixteen, played in drama and spent time with the fit-up shows in Ireland. Like all good comics, he spent time as straight man and second comedian. He did this at the Empire, Belfast for three years.

He worked in Australia, Hong Kong, for the American forces in Okinawa and in summer revue at Butlin's. He did a season in the Bahamas and returned to an, almost, Varietyless UK. His agent booked him a tour of the North-East clubs and he hated them. He was all prepared to give up the game when he got a surprise offer from America to appear, as an English comic, in a big revue. He did it and from then on was hardly out of the top US venues. He even received the ultimate accolade – his name above the title of the show in Las Vegas. After years of service to the business here he had finally cracked it in the Colonies.

I first saw him in Variety dressed in a royal blue suit with a yellow cap and socks, cracking gags and playing the soprano sax. But his big spot was his brilliant characterisation of a baby in a play-pen. He spoke, moved and thought like a baby. How many still remember that big, nappy-wearing infant, banging his 'poon'?

He retired in 1991 and returned home. I was delighted to be able to spend time in his company. He was a witty, observant commentator on life, in and out of show business, and a brilliant writer. His description of the opening night of a big Australian circus and revue is a masterpiece (it's in my anecdote book), very reminiscent of GERARD HOFFNUNG's essay on the barrel of bricks.

Freddie died, hardly having had time to enjoy his retirement, in 1995.

Leslie Sarony

Comedian/songwriter/singer/dancer. Born Leslie Legge Sarony-Frye, Surbiton, Surrey, 1897. You'll have to forgive me going on about Leslie. He was very special to me. I consider him to be one of the most interesting contributors to light entertainment over the last seventy-five years.

Let's get the facts over first, before I start eulogising. He started as a pro directly he left school, joining the famous juvenile troupe, PARK'S ETON BOYS. When the First World War happened he lied about his age, joined the army and was one of the few to survive the campaigns on the Somme. At least that terrible war started Leslie writing songs.

On demob he resumed his career in Variety, pantomime, revue and musical comedy. He was a terrific dancer (he did his hornpipe by a wooden-legged sailor all through his career) and, in 1926 he played the juvenile lead, Frank, in the original production of *Showboat* with PAUL ROBESON. In that same year his song-writing, singing and recording careers began. Between 1926 and 1939 he worked for every recording company in the country. During his long career he made more than 350 records (including his last, an LP I produced, of his most famous songs in 1980). Well, 350 under his own name: he made dozens more under assumed ones! He recorded lots with JACK HYLTON and his band. Those were done in the days when there was no editing and he told me: 'You had to get it right first time. Any mistakes and you were very popular. You had to go back and do the whole thing all over again.'

In 1935 he formed, with LESLIE HOLMES, THE TWO LESLIES. They topped Variety bills for eleven years and did a Royal Variety Performance in 1938. Holmes, with infectious smile and jolly person-ality, played the piano and sang, while the effervescent Sarony danced around the piano and sang too. They wrote most of their own material though one of their biggest hits, 'The Old Sow' (with Sarony's juicy raspberries) was their adaptation of an old folk song.

The act split in 1946 and Sarony carried on with a new partner, MICHAEL COLE. They lasted three years but the magic of the original combination wasn't there and, in 1950, he became a single turn.

As happened to so many of the good 'uns, by the 1970s he was much in demand as a character actor, playing everything from Samuel Beckett's *Endgame* to film roles in *Chitty Chitty Bang Bang* and *Yanks*. He had quite a success on television, as a senile delinquent, in *I Didn't Know You Cared*. He still played Variety, though, mostly in veteran revival shows.

To many people he seemed to be a miserable old so-and-so but not to me. He didn't suffer fools gladly and, consequently, could come out with very cruel, but very funny, one-liners. He was a tiny, old-fashioned, dynamic, forthright and hard-working dyed-in-the-wool pro. To him enter-taining was a job of work, yet his songs were special. Just read these titles and a long-vanished world comes flooding back: 'I Lift Up My Finger and I Say Tweet Tweet', 'Jollity Farm', 'Ain't It Grand to Be Bloomin' Well Dead' and 'I Like Riding on a Choo Choo Choo'. If you ever attend the Changing of the Guard you'll still hear his 'When the Guards Are On Parade' being played.

I could fill the rest of this entry with the titles (and you'd know most of them), of the 150-odd songs he had published. Alas, I can't tell you even the titles of the songs and parodies he wrote for the all-male Vaudeville Golfing Society 'dos'. They are masterpieces of Rabelaisian doggerel.

Leslie, quite rightly, was awarded the gold badge of merit by the Songwriters' Guild of Great Britain. He deserved a peerage – but he'd have told 'em! He died in 1985.

Don Saunders

Musical clown. Circus clowns today in this country, seem, to me, a pretty shabby lot, mostly confined to running around the audience distracting the punters while equipment is being assembled in the ring. I always want them to be something special. Where are the CHARLIE CAIROLIS, the POPOVS, the RASTELLIS? Where are the Don Saunders?

I saw Don in circus and he was a true clown. He had all the best visual and musical gags in his spot. His last bit I remember so well. With one tug at his costume he would, in a split second, change the tail suit he was wearing into full Highland regalia complete with kilt! He'd pick up a set of bagpipes and exit playing, 'Scotland the Brave'. What a finish.

Saveen

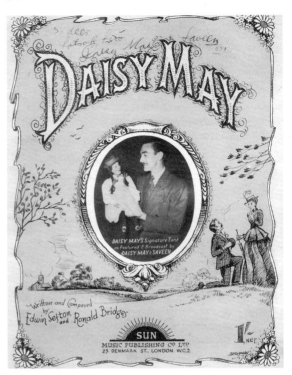

Ventriloquist. Born Albert Saveen, Southwark, London, 1914. They say that all 'vents' are a bit peculiar. Thinking about Albert I'm inclined to agree. He was the man who created 'Daisy May', a tiny schoolgirl dummy. Remember the song he always finished his act with:

'Daisy May, people say she'll marry me some day,
And from the way she sighs, and looks into my eyes,
I somehow think that Daisy may.'

'Daisy May' had her own bank account and her own listed telephone number. I rang Albert one day and 'she' answered the phone. I couldn't get him to speak as himself. Finally I had to be satisfied with 'Daisy May' saying: 'I'll ask Mister Saveen to phone you back.' He did and, after telling me she had given him my message, he carried on as if nothing had happened! Oo er!

He was originally a printer and it was during the Second World War that he developed his gift for ventriloquism. He had been wounded and it was his entertaining the lads in his ward that made him determined to do it for a living. On demob he rapidly became a featured act in Variety. It was radio and the promotion of 'Daisy May' that cracked it for him. He later added a wonderful parrot to the act and, most spectacularly, a live dog that spoke; it usually said about three words at the end of the act but it always brought the house down. Before he took his call he would exit with the dog and lock it away in a special box. I never found out how he did it – and I hope I never will.

He finished his days not as a performer but as an agent, and died in 1994.

Scott and Foster

Comedy patter act. Scott born Arthur Simpson, Leamington Spa, 1901, and Foster, born Betty Fielding, Great Yarmouth. Arthur and Betty met, and married while they were both in concert party at Dovercourt. They played revue and musical comedy and, eventually went into 'rep'. 'Their rep work,' says Philip, 'helped them greatly as their historical burlesque acts were all dialogue with no visual business.' They went into Variety in 1935 and stayed with it till they retired for Arthur to take over the running of the then, Variety Artistes Benevolent Fund*. They were the very popular hosts at Brinsworth House till Arthur died in 1968. Betty died just two years later.

*Now the Entertainment Artistes Benevolent Fund.

Billy 'Uke' Scott

Singer/composer and ukulele player. Born Sunderland, 1923. On radio Billy always finished his spot by saying: 'And finally, to prove that melody can be played on the ukulele…' He would then go into an intricate 'uke' solo where he did *indeed* prove that melody could be played on that much abused instrument. He was just superb. I especially loved his playing of the original wooden ukulele, not the more strident 'Formby' instrument.

He began at the Empire, Newcastle in 1936 and, from then on his boyish, full-of-fun personality and brilliant musicianship enlived Variety bills everywhere. He always featured his own songs

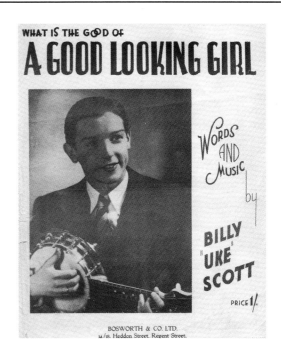

WHAT IS THE GOOD OF
A GOOD LOOKING GIRL
WORDS AND MUSIC by
BILLY 'UKE' SCOTT
PRICE 1/-
BOSWORTH & CO. LTD.
14/18. Heddon Street. Regent Street.

and some good 'uns he had too. My son's god-father, the comic EDDIE REINDEER, always used a song of Bill's which I think sums up the life of a Variety pro perfectly. Here's just a snatch of 'You Go On With Your Show':

'Trav'ling round in a small Revue
Learn the game like the troopers do
'Til you've caught every train from Crewe
You go on with your show.
Once it's over you're feeling grand,
Had them eating out of your hand
If you didn't you blame the band –
and go on with your show.'

When Variety finished Bill became an agent for a few years. He packed that in and, discreetly, put it about that he would like to work on-stage again. To his amazement, he wasn't forgotten. He played summer seasons, pantos, one-night stands, the lot. A few years back we had a Water Rats Lodge near Manchester. Bill turned up and took the Lodge by storm. He did his show biz parodies of famous songs. All updated and just brilliant. MIKE CRAIG recorded them, just for the Rats.

Bill is now retired and living on a narrow boat. It's a crying shame that, in the words of his signature tune, 'He's only singing for one.'

Victor Seaforth

The Man with a Thousand Voices

Impressionist. Born 1918. Victor is another Variety legend who this year celebrates fifty-four years in the business. His amazing character studies, rather than impressions, include JOSE FERRER as Toulouse-Lautrec and CHARLES LAUGHTON as The Hunchback of Notre Dame.

His first professional work, in 1943, was as part of the MORRIS AND COWLEY touring show, *The Squire's Party*. He was then a vocalist, so naturally his first impression was of a singer, MAURICE CHEVALIER. He did summer seasons, a stint supplying the skaters' voices in a Wembley Ice Show, played the London Casino with VIC OLIVER and toured in Variety supporting in star revues. It was in *The Norman Evans Show* where he met his wife, SUMA LAMONTE. Their best man was REG DIXON. He was a great favourite of HAROLD FIELDING who used him often on his *Music for the Millions* shows. He became a popular featured act in Variety and supported every top of the bill from THE INK SPOTS to JIMMY YOUNG.

When Variety finished, Victor developed his compering skills and carried on with cabaret and clubs. Now he is as busy as ever, not only performing but booking dozens of acts through his successful agency.

Harry Secombe

Comedian. Born Swansea, 1921. The great 'Hairy Seagoon' autobiography has only recently been published (*Arias and Raspberries, Strawberries and Cheam*). Harry, who originally wanted to be a journalist, is an excellent writer and, like all his other stuff, it is good. That said *I* won't say too much here. I can tell you that he began entertaining his brother soldiers in the Second World War and that on demob he auditioned, and got into the game, professionally, at the Windmill Theatre.

Just post-war was an exciting time for comedy. The new wave of ex-servicemen performers brought a totally different sort of humour with them. None more than Harry. He met, while at the Windmill, MICHAEL BENTINE and renewed his friendship with SPIKE MILLIGAN, whom he had met during the war. Rather like my generation of comics did at Butlin's and the United Dairy teashop in Charing Cross Road, they would meet and pour out their ideas and ambitions. PETER SELLERS joined the trio through a radio Variety show. Harry always seemed the most obvious Variety performer of them all, having had some success on the halls after he left the Windmill.

1951 was the year *The Goon Show* started and comedy, in this country, was changed for good. It was anarchic, irreverent and totally uncosy. Just what we were all looking for. The show, against all odds, made its four mainstays, Spike, Michael, Harry and Peter, stars.

Harry became the most popular simply because he was the most up-front, jolliest and least dangerous of the team, and he could sing, gorgeously. He headlined everywhere and in every possible medium: radio, television, pantomime, Variety, films and musicals. Although he has just been touring with his old musical vehicle, *Pickwick*, we mostly see him now as the somewhat (compared to his rollicking past) subdued host of the religious sing-song TV show, *Highway*. He is now a 'Sir' and a highly respected show biz elder statesman.

Peter Sellers

Comedian/actor. Born Southsea, 1925. An impressionist in Variety who became an international film star. So many books have been written about Peter all I can tell you about is his

Variety background.

He came from a famous theatrical family, THE RAY BROTHERS. They were responsible, in the 1910s, for staging more then thirty revues. His father was BILL SELLERS, the pianist. Peter was well established as a Variety turn and a voices man on radio – *Variety Bandbox, Henry Hall's Guest Night* and *Ray's Laugh* – when, in 1951, he joined *The Goon Show*. His contribution to this mould-breaking comedy show is well remembered and documented. HARRY SECOMBE said in his book, *Goon to Lunch*: 'Standing next to him on *The Goon Show*, I could never get over the way he would shrink himself for Bluebottle and then seconds later, puff himself out for Bloodnok. It was almost frightening to see it happen.' It was his uncanny gift of being able, vocally and physically, to become the character he was playing that led to his international stardom. Harry remembers when Peter was asked to speak in his own voice he said he couldn't: 'I don't know what I sound like.'

He became a Water Rat and when I asked him about his work he said: 'I'm nothing, just a blank blackboard waiting to have a face drawn on it.' A fascinating, brilliant mass of confusion. He died in 1980.

Harry Seltzer

Comedian. Born Hull. One of my favourite people in show business. I know Harry well through the Water Rats. He was our King Rat in 1969. I can do no better than quote from his own potted biography, which he wrote for *The Performer – Who's Who in Variety*, 1950. It's lovely stuff.

'I began my professional career as a boy ventriloquist in WILL MURRAY's *Casey's Court*. It was Will Murray who taught me to walk and talk and I tried to copy everyone who was part of the show. I even practised tap dancing until two or three o'clock in the morning in the digs. I practised in stockinged feet. I left the game for a while till FRANK E. FRANKS offered me a job as comedian in one of his touring shows. I played Jewish parts in the sketches and even went on for the midget whenever he was off.

'I took up eccentric dancing [something he still does today, he did it on *Barrymore* just last year] and joined ARCHIE JEREZ in a double act, RENO AND ANDY. We toured the UK and the Continent for eight years till the act grew into THE THREE STORRS. We stayed together for three years till I reverted to a single act and went on the road with BUD FLANAGAN. Next, why I'll never know, I gave up the game and became a bookmaker. It was an expensive lesson so, in 1950, I returned to the business I knew. I am, at present, touring as the comedian with PETE COLLINS's *Jungle Fantasy*.'

When I was King Rat, in 1989, I christened the diminutive, gentle Harry 'My Minder'. His running gag now is looking for trouble with everybody, including, at his initiation, FRANK BRUNO. Harry has, at last, retired to Brinsworth House where he is, as always, the driving force behind all their social activities.

Semprini

Old ones, new ones, loved ones, neglected ones

Pianist. Born Bath, 1908. How well I remember that gentle signature tune, interrupted by the equally gentle voice of Albert Semprini, telling us that tonight we would hear 'Old ones, new ones, etc.' He did have a style of piano playing that, like RUSS CONWAY's, JOE HENDERSON's and CHARLIE KUNZ's, was immediately recognisable. His, however, was a more classical style. So it should be. Born of an English mother and an Italian father, he studied, from the age of eight, piano and cello. At ten he was in Milan, being taught at the Verid Conservatoire. At eighteen he held diplomas in piano, composition and conducting and he became the deputy conductor at several of Italy's leading opera houses, including La Scala.

After refusing to work with the enemy during the war he was eventually accepted into ENSA where he played piano for forward units and in depots and hospitals. He became a huge star recorder and broadcaster in Italy and Spain, not only as a soloist but as the conductor of his own forty-five-piece orchestra.

He returned to the UK in 1949 where, as a soloist, he scored in cabaret and on radio and became a big draw in Variety. At one time he seemed never to be off the air and his 'Semprini Serenade' (with the BBC Revue Orchestra) notched up its hundredth programme in 1959. He died in 1990.

Leslie Shannon

Comedian/impressionist/drummer. Born Whitechapel, London, 1920. Almost Leslie's first job, after demob, was as the drummer and vocalist with THE JERRY ALLEN TRIO in *Strike a New Note* at the Prince of Wales. He stayed with Jerry for five years and in 1949 became a single act with E.J. HINGE's touring revue, *Fanny Get Your Fun* (see DAVY KAYE). He stayed with the revue for a year and then joined TOMMY TRINDER's road show. He always said Trinder had taught him all he knew.

Lester Sharpe and Iris

Sleight-of-hand magician. Born Leslie Partick Molloy, Southport, 1918. I'm indebted to Lester's wife Iris for these notes on their career.

Lester, during the war, entertained not only as a member of the famous *Stars in Battledress* but with two other groups I'd not heard of, *The Muddle Easters* and *The Nomads of the Nile*. He

became a pro on demob and one of his first dates was His Majesty's Theatre, Barrow-in-Furness. It was here he met Iris who was doing a juggling and balancing act with her father, JACK ENGELEN AND IRIS. They were married within six weeks. One of their first jobs together was a six-month season in India where they had to provide twenty-four changes of programme. Iris says: 'We did much the same thing but wore different costumes for each different programme!'

They were a constantly busy Variety speciality and, in later years, played cabaret and children's shows. Their partnership, on and offstage, lasted over forty-five years. Lester died in 1994.

Sydney Shaw

Harmonica player. Born London, 1921. Sydney, whom I worked with on Sunday Concerts, was an excellent player and a good solid act. He told me he started, in 1934, with a shilling mouth organ and began playing amateur shows, The birthday present of a chromatic harmonica led to him turning pro with THE FIVE TEARAWAYS. As part of the act he worked in Variety and revue with HUGHIE GREEN's GANG and LEON CORTEZ's COSTER BAND. He went solo in 1940 and has remained so to this day.

Ann Shelton

Singer. Born Patricia Sibley, Dulwich, London, 1923. Ann became 'The Forces' Sweetheart' Mark Two through her singing of sentimental ballads during the war. Saucy devil that she was, she even

LAY DOWN YOUR ARMS
(AND SURRENDER TO MINE)

2/-

Recorded by
ANNE SHELTON
on PHILIPS PB.616.

FRANCIS, DAY & HUNTER LTD. 138-140, CHARING CROSS RD. LONDON W.C.2

took the German song, 'Lily Marlene' as her signature tune. Her biggest big hit, however, was a post-war song, 'Lay Down Your Arms'.

She was 'discovered' at the age of sixteen by LEN URRY, who ran a BBC discoveries show. She was heard by AMBROSE and joined his band at London's Mayfair Hotel. During her five years with Bert Ambrose, she recorded and, with the band, played anywhere an audience of service personnel could be found. She became so popular that a career as a single act had to be and she topped bills in Variety from the Palladium on. For a year, in 1950, she toured all over the States. In 1944 she sang in the UK with the GLENN MILLER band and was invited to go to Paris with him. Ambrose wouldn't let her go, fortunately, as the flight he wanted her to share with him was his last.

As happened to so many when rock and roll arrived, she faded from the scene but still worked regularly. If no paid work came along Ann would fill in with charity shows and military reunion concerts. She was a great one for getting people along to entertain the Not Forgotten Association and, for all her efforts here she was awarded the OBE.

In the late 1980s, her voice was as good as, if not better than, it was when she was at her most popular and her nationwide tour with THE NEW SQUADRONAIRES drew packed houses everywhere. Ann was a great girl to work with. She had the most beautiful face and was full of fun. Her talent for wringing every ounce out of a ballad was legendary. I still think her version of 'My Yiddisher Momma' was the best I've ever heard – and she was a Catholic!

Her husband and manager, DAVID REID, died in 1990 and Ann in 1994.

Cecil Sheridan

Comedian. Born Dublin, 1910. I remember him as the principal comedian in an Irish revue at The Met, Edgware Road, *Glocca-Morra-Begorra*, where he featured his self-penned parodies. There were lots of Irish shows at the Met during its last years. He was a well-known Dame comedian in Ireland and Scotland where his early days were spent as a script and song writer. He must have been good; his clients included SCOTT SANDERS and GEORGE LACY. He was the business partner of the Scottish impresario, PETE DAVIS.

Elva Sheridan

Comedienne. Born Thornton, near Bradford. A lady who seems to have had more changes of name than a serial bigamist. She started in concert party at the age of twelve and then on to the halls as a single turn. She met and married MARK SHERIDAN (son of the famous music-hall singer of 'I Do Like to be Beside the Seaside') and they formed the double act, LEDSON AND SHERIDAN. They spent three years with BIG BILL CAMPBELL's Western show, *Rocky Mountain Rhythm*. They changed their name to ELVA AND MARK SHERIDAN. Mark died in 1946 and she became ELVA SHERIDAN AND JACK FORD. She saw in the Fifties, on radio, in *Happidrome* with HARRY KORRIS, he being 'Mr Lovejoy' and she (replacing 'Enoch') 'She-noch'. They appeared on Variety bills together along with yet another double act of hers, SHERIDAN AND BEE (Bee Thorburn). What she eventually called herself, I wish I knew.

The Sherry Brothers

Acrobatic dancers/musicians. Born Costock, Notts, Peter Sherry 1910, Sam Sherry 1912. The incredible Sherry family were the nine children of the music-hall performer DAN CONROY. The old man taught all his children to dance and the result was THE FIVE SHERRY brothers who were a top of the bill show-stopping act who sang, played fiddles and did acrobatics, often all at the same time. Three of the girls did a musical act, THE SHERINA SISTERS. After the war the two youngest lads, Peter and Sam, formed a double act and earned a good living in Variety and as 'Captain and Mate' or the horse or cow in panto. As Variety bookings got fewer, they retired, in 1956, Peter to the Isle of Wight and Sam to Galgate, Leicester, where he ran a boat-hiring business. In 1980 Sam's autobiography appeared in the BMHS magazine, *The Call Boy*. It is fascinating and he tells just what he and Peter did in their double act. If only all the acts had done that.

They would open with an up-beat popular song then go into a light comedy number, sung in harmony while Sam played the guitar. They then both played the fiddle while dancing, and would finish with a fast dance showing off their acrobatic tricks.

Peter died in 1979. Sam was, just a few years ago, making something of a come-back, teaching interested parties the step dancing that his father had taught him seventy years before.

Ella Shields

Male impersonator. Born Baltimore, USA, 1879. Yet another music-hall star who gained a new lease of life through DON ROSS's *Thanks for the Memory* revue. I saw her in that show in the Forties.

She had, believe it or not, first appeared in London in 1904, having previously played musicals in America. By 1910 she was working in 'drag', after a producer saw her impersonate an old soldier at a party. She married WILLIAM HARGREAVES, the man who wrote the song for which she will always be remembered, 'Burlington Bertie from Bow'. He wrote it as a reply to an earlier VESTA TILLEY song about a toff called 'Burlington Bertie'. Vesta's 'chap' was an elegant 'swell' whereas Ella's was a broken-down, fallen on hard times, trying to keep up appearances, tramp.

It was a very strange experience watching this rather scary woman/man prowling around the stage half singing, half speaking, still with an American accent, those wonderful lyrics: 'I've just had a banana with Lady Diana.'

She actually returned to the States in 1929 and,

after years away, was brought back to the UK from Australia by Don Ross in 1948. She spent her last years with *Thanks for the Memory* and even did a Royal Variety Performance in 1948. She died in 1952.

Harry Shiels

Comedian. Born Thomas Dowell, Edgbaston, Birmingham, 1906. Harry was the son of a comedian, HARRY SHIELS, and carried his name on. His first shows were with his dad in the late 1920s. He was a dance band drummer before he formed the act, THE BROWNIE BOYS. The 'Boys' were STAN KEWLEY, TOMMY LEWIS and TYD LEWIS (who later became the well-known comedian KEN ROBERTS). He worked as a double act with Stan, SHIELS AND KEWLEY and eventually, after the war, became a solo turn. For many years he played Dame in number one pantos but never achieved high billing in Variety.

Mrs Shufflewick

Shuff

Female impersonator. Born Rex Coster. I'm not sure about Rex's date of birth as he was left on a doorstep as a baby and brought up by a foster mother in Southend-on-Sea. Patrick Newley tells me he changed his name to Rex Jameson (after the whisky!)

Once again we are talking legends. 'Mrs Shufflewick' was a truly unforgettable creation. Just as NORMAN EVANS was the typical old Northern boiler and ARTHUR LUCAN the mad Irish mother, Rex was the archetype Cockney auntie to a tee. She was the woman down the pub (in her case 'The Cock and Comfort') who, outwardly, fairly prim, would suddenly spill out tales of sexual adventures ('I've always been weak willed and easily led') that would make your hair curl. Then, just as quickly, her bottom lip would quiver and she'd go all sentimental and assure you, half spoken, half sung: 'I'm an ordinary Cockney mum.'

He/she was a tiny, bedraggled figure with a little bit of moth-eaten fur round her neck ('untouched

pussy – practically unobtainable in the West End of London'), always clutching her handbag, handy for keeping souvenirs of past romances in. Rex became a cult figure in the London 'camp' pubs but he'd had a hell of career before then.

He started in 'rep', was with RALPH READER'S *Gang Show* during the war, and, on demob, graduated to doing a single (as a vicar!) at the Windmill. He was spotted for radio but, as they thought the vicar routine was too strong, he invented Mrs Shufflewick and got away with it.

Soon he was topping bills everywhere in Variety, pantomime and radio. On television he was one of the first performers to be voted 'Personality of the Year.' The world was his oyster. What went wrong I do not know. LEW LANE, Past President of The British Music Hall Society, says: 'Fame did not turn its back on Rex – Rex turned his back on fame.' He was a notorious boozer (Guinness and barley wine), so perhaps that was it. He seemed to disappear off the circuit and fell on hard times. But, ever the survivor, he came back to be a star again in clubs and pubs. Audiences adored him.

Off stage he was a flat-capped, watery blue-eyed, quiet little chap with a wicked sense of fun who, like so many other great artistes, would give his last shilling away to anyone whom he thought needed it.

I did Variety with him and remember him going into a pub full of dour, hard-drinking Carlisle blokes and shouting, 'Finish your drinks, we're going to have an orgy!' One of the shortest train journeys I've ever had was from Penzance (we'd been doing a *Workers' Playtime*) to London, overnight. Rex got out the booze and myself, Rex and ANITA HARRIS didn't stop laughing till the train pulled into London.

When he died, in 1983, his funeral was attended by hundreds of the great and good of show business. What a pity they didn't show their affection in more tangible forms while he was still with us.

Reub Silver and Marion Day

Double piano act. Reub and Marion were husband and wife piano duettists à la RAWICZ and LANDAUER who played all the independent number one theatres* and the better number twos.

*Most of the number one theatres were Moss Empires. The booker for these was the formidable CISSIE WILLIAMS. If she didn't like what you did you didn't play the best theatres. Reub Silver was a fine musician but had a slightly malformed back. Because of this the sensitive Ms Williams, says Philip, would not use the act if it was avoidable.

Peter Sinclair

The Cock of the North

Comedian. Born Kirkintolloch, Scotland, 1901. My own memories of Peter are as JIMMY CLITHEROE's Grandfather in radio's *The Clitheroe Kid*, where his beautiful, resonant voice was forever haranguing the errant Jimmy.

His pedigree was immaculate. He'd worked not only Variety but, before that, music hall. The general opinion of him as a solo Variety turn is that he should have been a much bigger star than he was. I suppose with greats like HARRY LAUDER and WILL FYFFE around there wasn't room for another Scots comedian. He was, however, kept busy all through his long career (something we

all wish for) with radio and in films. He died in 1995.

Sirdani

Don't be fright

Comedy magician. Born Sydney Daniels, South Africa, 1900. Sirdani, the brother of the drummer and bandleader, JOE DANIELS (Joe Daniels and His Hot Shots), was the first magician to become a success through radio! Well, if PETER BROUGH, as a ventriloquist on radio, could do it – why not?

I can remember, as a small boy, crouching on the stairs outside the living room desperately trying to write down his explanations as to how he did the tricks. His catchphrase, 'don't be fright', was his encouragement to a volunteer from the audience.

Rather like THE PIDDINGTONS years after he did things like naming cards held up by members of the audience in a studio miles away from where he was.

We couldn't wait to see him in the flesh, hence his featured spot in Variety. He died in 1982.

The Skylons

Acrobatic novelty. Philip says: 'Their feats of strength on a bar and other equipment made them a spectacular speciality in the number ones.

The Smeddle Brothers

Comedy double act. Well known as Ugly Sister in EMILE LITTLER pantos Arthur Smeddle and his brother Jimmy began, like so many, as dancers. They were in the chorus of C.B. COCHRAN's show, *Evergreen* at London's Adelphi Theatre in 1937.

They formed a dancing duo for variety and, later, added miming to records. Rumour says they were sent, by an impresario, to Paris to see those masters of mime, THE BERNARD BROTHERS and bring back their act, which they did very successfully.

The Five Smith Brothers

Mr and Mrs Smith's Five Little Boys

Harmony singers. Five brothers Alfred, Harold, Martin, Stanley and Roy from Newcastle-on-Tyne. Remember their opening: 'Hello! Hello! Hello! Hello! Hell-oo-oo!' The five Geordie lads, whom I first remember featuring slightly up-beat versions of all the good old North-east songs – 'Blaydon Races', 'Keep Your Feet Still Geordie Hinny', 'The Lambton Worm', etc – made a very different and pleasant sound. Gentle, but butch, harmonising, backed with guitar and clarinet. Records and radio (notably as regulars in the JEWEL AND WARRISS vehicle *Up The Pole!*) made them Variety top of the bills.

All five were destined for careers as professional footballers. Alfred played for Liverpool, Preston North End and Southport, Harold for Glasgow Rangers and Roy for Birmingham. They sang together at local concerts and their first professional week, at the Empire, Gateshead, sealed their fate. Martin, sadly killed in a car accident, was replaced in the act by the clarinettist, RONNIE CULBERTSON.

Inevitably the demise of Variety led to them all going their separate ways – mostly to running pubs in the North-east. An LP of theirs was reissued a little while back and it is good.

Don Smoothey

I'm having a bit tonight

Comedian. Born Fulham, 1919. One of my very

Smoothey and Layton

favourite comedians. A man who never fails to score with his combination of great music-hall technique and warm Cockney personality. He is show business through and through.

He began, at the age of twelve, at the famous Italia Conti school where his brother LEN LOWE was a star pupil. His first job was in the show where so many kids from the school started, *Where the Rainbow Ends* at the Holborn Empire. He followed this with a spell in *Cavalcade* at Drury Lane. The legit, however, was not for Don. He entered talent competitions and TONY GERRARD, who more or less started the talent type shows, took him under his wing. Don won competitions everywhere and was now really a pro.

On joining the army in 1939, he started entertaining as half of a double act with LEN MARTEN and in 1942 became a member of the official army organisation, *Stars in Battledress*. In 1946 came demob and Don started his Variety career at the Grand, Clapham Junction (the theatre that Corin and Vanessa Redgrave are now trying to save). Summer season followed and more Variety as DON MAXWELL. He changed his name to CHESTER LADD when DICKIE VALENTINE's father, a comedian named DICKIE MAXWELL, complained that Don was getting all his work! A long tour with a stage version of a radio show, *The Old Town Hall* (remember 'Penny on the Drum'?) followed. A tour with RALPH READER's *The Gang's All Here* was another high spot. In 1950 his brother BILL, half of the act LEN AND BILL LOWE, married the beautiful JEANNIE CARSON, moved to America and Don joined his other brother, Len, as half of a new act LOWE AND LADD.

In England, the brothers had had great success; in Australia and New Zealand, they became stalwarts of Variety especially on bills with Dickie Valentine (Dickie Maxwell's son!) In 1955 they, and Dickie, realized a life-long ambition – they played the Palladium. Dickie's manager was TOMMY LAYTON and, when Len decided that he wanted to go into television, Lowe and Ladd called it a day. Don, now DON SMOOTHEY, carried on as a solo comic until Dickie Valentine persuaded him that Tommy Layton, who had watched Lowe and Ladd so often and knew their act very well, would be quite capable of doing a spot with Don. He was and SMOOTHEY AND LAYTON were born. The two lads were together until 1960, where our story finishes.

Don, whom I had the great joy of being with in *Underneath the Arches*, has, since then, played numerous weeks in what is left of Variety, countless summer season and pantos. He is, thank Gawd, still at it.

Professor Sparks and Thelmina

The Electric Lady

Comedy speciality act. CHARLIE CHESTER, that cherisher of strange acts, described it to me: 'He would enter as a mad professor and switch on his machine, which generated electricity. He would then pick up two swords, put one on the machine and the other on his wife, Thelmina. She was holding, by a pair of tongs in each hand, a six-inch nail. The audience would see the nail go white hot until she finally snapped it in two. He would give all sorts of demonstrations of how Thelmina, and their son, could conduct electricity.

The best bit of the act was audience participation. He would get a bunch of volunteers on stage to 'bath' the Electric Baby. The more they dipped the flannel into the water to wash the

metal baby the more the electricity would be amplified. Their contortions were very funny. Nowadays he'd be locked up.'

Spence and Davies

Comedy musical act. John Richard Spence from South Shields and William Charles Davies from Hackney East, London. You always know when performers are getting on a bit, when they never publish their birth dates! Spence and Davies must have been because they were a double act before the First World War. Indeed Bill Davies first performed during the war. I saw them later in one of JACK TAYLOR's revues. They were a popular, standard act playing mostly cabaret and Variety during the summer.

Dorothy Squires

Singer. Born Edna May Squires, Pontyberem near Llanelli, Wales. You always have to be careful writing about the immortal 'Dot' – in case you get sued! – but I have only good things to say about this real trooper and superlative show woman.

She began as the vocalist with a local dance band, coming to London, now as Dorothy Squires, at eighteen. She became the singer with CHARLIE KUNZ. It was a one-night gig with BILLY REID's Accordion Band that changed her life. Billy could write songs and Dot could sing 'em. Throughout the Forties and early Fifties the pair of them topped Variety bills everywhere and sold

Ernest Staig

Motor cycle acrobat. Born Watford, 1906. Ernest, an ex-high wire walker and wall of death rider put together the act, THE AUSTRALIAN AIR ACES, in Australia in the late 1920s. He adapted the, usually alfresco, wall of death routines for the Variety stage. They were a rather specialised act as their setting – a globe of death and a huge revolving table – took a long time to assemble. Everything had to be done just so to compensate for the rake (slope) of the music-hall stages.

Stanelli

Musician and comedian. Born Edward Stanley de Groot, Dublin. Originally a serious musician (he was a scholarship student at the Royal Academy of Music and the Royal College of Music studying violin), he graduated, via conducting his own composition with the Bournemouth Symphony, the London Symphony and the Hallé, to Variety. He was, firstly, half of the act STANELLI AND EDGAR – they were two excellent classical and popular violinists who danced, tap/soft shoe while they played in unison and then became a solo turn in his own touring show, *Stanelli's Stag Party*. He died in 1961.

One of Stanelli's big features was his Horn Orchestra. This was a huge iron bedstead sort of contraption that he would wheel on stage. Attached to the 'bedstead' were dozens of horns all of a different note, on which he would play tunes.

thousands of records. Everything was lovely till she met an unknown actor, ROGER MOORE; she parted from Billy and she and Roger married in 1953. Far be it from me to comment but many people tell me Dorothy neglected her own career to promote Roger. She succeeded, he became a film star and they parted in 1961.

The indestructible Dot battled on. She consistently made the charts, all without the help of TV exposure or airplay on radio. She didn't know why the powers that be were ignoring her so, in 1970, in a fit of pique she hired the London Palladium to show 'em all. Her Sunday night concert was a sensation. She packed the place and all those who had dismissed her as a has-been had to eat their words. Her version of 'My Way' made the charts and her concerts all over the British Isles were triumphs. Her annual London concerts became a regular event and her audiences, those who remembered, those who saw her as our own tragic JUDY GARLAND figure and those, like me, who just love a great theatrical performer, adored her. I've just heard that CDs of her 1970 and 1971 concerts have been released on Sterndale Records. Demand them from your record shop.

Clifford Stanton

Personalities on parade

Impressionist. Born Wimborne, Dorset, 1909. He began as a chorus boy and super in West End musicals and plays and then became assistant to the legendary ventriloquist, ARTHUR PRINCE. It was Arthur who spotted his potential as an impressionist and encouraged him to devise *Personalities on Parade*. The act took him to all the number one halls and cabaret in the West End.

Tommy Steele

Entertainer. Born Thomas Hicks, Bermondsey, London, 1936. Tommy just makes it into our period but what he did during the last four years of it is, even by show business standards, fantastic. After his early years as a merchant seaman he and his guitar appeared at a trendy youth-orientated venue in Soho, The Two Eyes coffee bar. Here, in 1956, he was 'discovered'. Within a few weeks he made his first record, a hit, written, as so many of his early ones were, by LIONEL BART. Before the end of that year he'd done his first TV and made his début in Variety. He was top of the bill at the Empire, Sunderland. Next year he made his first movie, The *Tommy Steele Story*, toured Europe and Scandinavia, did an hour-long TV Special and his first Royal Variety Performance.

It does make him sound like a typically hyped-up pop act of today but he was different. He was genuinely talented. As the years went by he proved he could handle everything he attempted: pantomime, musicals, classical acting and more films. He became a great favourite both in the UK and in America. These days he is content to produce, when he feels like it, highly popular song and dance shows centred round the Steele personality. His, truly, is *the* show business Cinderella story.

Steffani

Producer and boys' choir presenter. Born Frederick William Wisker, Beccles, Suffolk, 1904. I've met so many blokes who were, at one time, members of Steffani's well-known boys' choir,

GREETINGS FROM STEFFANI'S SILVER SONGSTERS.

STEFFANI'S SILVER SONGSTERS. They toured all the number ones with great success but, usually, once their voices broke, they went into other trades. One who didn't was Steffani's greatest discovery, RONNIE RONALDE. He knew he had an ace in the hole with Ronnie. He disbanded the Silver Songsters and became Ronnie's personal manger. Together they toured everywhere here and all over the world. He died in 1974.

Joe Stein

Comedian. Born Joseph Shipper, Manchester, 1904. Joe was an instant hit when he played London for the first time (the Met, Edgware Road in 1928). During his long career he played every number one theatre in the country, except the Palladium. He was the principal comedian with the infamous 'drag' show, *Soldiers In Skirts*, for close on ten years. Surely a record. Philip says: 'One record I know he held. All the time I knew him he wore the same suit and hat that he wore when he first came into the business! And I'm not sure it wasn't the same shirt too!'

Stan Stennett

Certified insanely funny

Comedian. Born Cardiff, 1925. Stan, after a wartime stint with *Stars in Battledress*, became a member of THE HARMANIACS comedy vocal trio. As a solo comedian he featured often on Welsh-based radio shows like *Welsh Rarebit*. We always looked forward to Stan coming to our local: his combination of excellent guitar playing, interspersed with strange vocal effects and Robert Orben one-

liners was just up the street of my young, thirsting for something a bit off-beat, pals.

He went on to become almost a permanent fixture with *The Black and White Minstrel Show* and, when he could escape them, he starred in panto everywhere. Happily, the inventive Stan in still successfully working and producing, mostly in his home country, Wales.

Stainless Stephen

Comedian. Born Arthur Clifford Baynes Sheffield, 1892. Alas, I never saw him 'live', but I heard him often on radio where he made a name for himself with a sort of early VICTOR BORGE routine. Whereas Borge punctuated his stories with noises to represent full stops, commas, exclamation marks, 'Stainless' actually said the punctuation marks: 'This is Stainless Stephen comma comedian question-mark.'

He knew radio very well, his first broadcast being in 1923 as an amateur. He became a pro three years later and the 'Stainless' bit was a sort of promotional gimmick for his home town. He had a local firm make a steel waistcoat for him and later added a steel hat band. His final sophisticated outfit included these, plus waistcoat buttons that lit up and a luminous, revolving bow tie!

He remained a great radio favourite all through,

and after, the Second World War. This led, naturally, to a good position on the bill in Variety, always tailoring his material to the town where he was playing.

Although he was a bit too old-fashioned for my taste when I first heard him, I now relish the occasional recordings that come to light. I enjoy *his* enjoyment of language. I'm indebted to Geoff Mellor (whose book *They Made Us Laugh* is a treasure trove for lovers of comedy) for this letter to the *Daily Mirror* when they jumped the gun by announcing his death eleven years before it happened. He wrote: 'You must excuse the writing but as I have been dead for six years you can't expect much! I retired from the stage in 1952 and since 1954 have been living in Kent – a Gentleman Farmer – raising nothing but my hat!' Stainless Stephen (semi-solvent). He did die in 1972.

Doreen Stephens

Singer. Born Stockton-on-Tees, 1922. Another voice that became familiar to me, via radio, in the Sunday *Billy Cotton Bandshow*. Doreen, on the back of her success with Bill, went solo and was a featured act at the number one venues.

She was 'discovered' by her fellow townsman, JIMMY JAMES, and really did serve her apprentice-ship as the lady who did the 'vocal refrain' with the bands of JACK HYLTON, MAURICE WINNICK and THE SQUADRONAIRES.

Renee Strange

Puppeteer. Born Newcastle-upon-Tyne, 1923. Renee's father was LESLIE STRANGE (formerly WILFRED ST CLAIR). Leslie, I've recently found out, did an act similar to that of BRANSBY WILLIAMS (the music-hall actor who specialised in Dickensian characterisations).

Renee started, just before the war, as a singing cartoonist but we knew her better as a puppeteer. She played for ENSA and received the Africa Star for her services. She narrowly avoided death after the ship she was returning home in was torpedoed. She spent thirty-six hours in an open boat only to arrive here and be sent on tour with a series of TOM ARNOLD ice shows! Philip says: 'She had first class puppets and an excellent presentation. A featured speciality act at all the number ones.' She played a Royal Variety Performance in 1946, later retired and was last heard of as the matron of a London hospital.

Donald B. Stuart

Variety's longest laugh

Burlesque magician. Born London, 1894. Donald, a forerunner of TOMMY COOPER, discovered early on, unlike so many, that magic should be entertaining and so turned to burlesque while he was still cutting his teeth in Australia. He returned home in 1929.

He was six foot seven inches tall and, Philip says: 'His entrance was a good one. He would walk on, take off his hat and hang it on a nail nine feet six inches from the floor of the stage. There it would stay until he exited.' He played all the number ones here and was, as you can imagine, an excellent and much sought-after Abanazer in *Aladdin*.

Billy Stutt

Missus woman

Comedian. Born Belfast. Never a star but an excellent front-cloth comic who supported all the big top of the bill singers, mostly up North. It's very important for a star singer to have someone precede them who can really put the crowd in a good frame of mind. Billy was terrific at this. He had a stack of good stories and one-liners and established a rapport with an audience by playing one side off against the other and always finding a 'missus woman' somewhere in the stalls whom he could confide in. When Variety finished he worked in summer seasons, mostly in the Morecambe area, where he died in 1996.

Jill Summers

The Porteress

Comedienne. Born Honor Margaret Rozelle Santoi Simpson Smith, Moncton Green, Lancashire 1910. Would you believe that the 'Percy' chasing 'Phylis' in *Coronation Street* had an impeccable Variety background? Well probably you would. You

don't get a voice like that at RADA. Jill was born practically in a dressing room. Her mother was a musical comedy star, MARIE SANTOI, and her dad a tight-rope walker, ALF FULLER.

She began as half of a double act with her brother, TOM F. MOSS. He was a terrific tenor and Jill, who could also sing, was the comedy content. Tom's unreliability caused them to split and, in 1949, Jill went solo. She invented a 'Tart' routine which was very similar to HYLDA BAKER's act with 'Cynthia'. Jill did it first. Her standard Variety act, which I saw, was 'The Porteress' a 'lairy' lady porter. She first worked with BILL WADDINGTON (later to become the object of her *Coronation Street* lust as 'Percy') in a JIMMY BRENNAN revue in 1955.

After an appearance in TV's *The Good Old Days* she did her first TV series in 1957. It disappeared without trace so back to Variety she went. She played the number ones, twos and threes, holiday camps, clubs and was one of the few successful female Dames in panto. She was part of a later tour of DON ROSS's *Thanks for the Memory* show.

She started to get parts on the telly but couldn't resist a live audience and devised, and played in her own production show especially for the working-men's clubs (something that had never been done before). In 1982 she began played 'Phylis Pearce' in *Coronation Street*. She created an unforgettable character full of all the things she'd learned in Variety. At the end of her career (the right way round) she was a nationally known star at last. She died in 1997.

Randolph Sutton

On Mother Kelly's Doorstep

Light comedian. Born Bristol, 1889. The last surviving member of the DON ROSS touring revue, *Thanks for the Memory*. Ran, like all the other members of that never to be forgotten trip down Memory Lane, was recruited for the show in 1948, but he had done a bit before then.

He began in the 1910s as a juvenile in dramas such as *Uncle Tom's Cabin* and played in that forcing ground of the light comedian, concert party. He didn't really crack it until after the First World War when he became very popular on gramophone records with songs like 'My Girl's Mother', 'When Are You Going to Lead Me to the Altar Walter?' and, of course, 'On Mother Kelly's Doorstep' (a song that had been rejected by an earlier light comedian, FRED BARNES).

His cheeky, Bristolian, innuendo-loaded voice, was perfect for recording. His career in the studios started in 1915 and he made his last in 1969. He was the original recorder of so many songs that have since become standards: 'My Blue Heaven', 'Bye Bye Blackbird' and 'Give Me the Moonlight'.

He didn't need the recordings to score in Variety. He was a handsome, always immaculately dressed, wonderful teller of the story in the song. He acted every word and you *knew* he meant every word he sang. I saw him lots of times: he was my Gran's favourite and, whenever he was in the area, there we were. He was one of the first, before the influx of pop stars, to play Principal Boy in pantomime. He was a bit of a hearthrob, with that elusive and much maligned gift from the gods – charm.

He died in 1969 at the end of a week where he'd done two concerts and spent a day in the recording studios.

Hal Swain

Musician. Born Halifax, 1894. Originally apprenticed to an engineer, he was sent to Canada where he became involved in music. He formed, with himself on saxophone, his own band and, in the 1920s, brought then to London where they had a five-year residency at the Princes Restaurant. He was musical director at the famous Kit Kat and the Café Royal. His band here included LES ALLEN as the vocalist. He led orchestras in Scarborough, Harrogate and Blackpool and was the musical director for the stage version of the radio show *Happidrome*.

His band did their own act in Variety and, when the Second World War began and musicians were called up, he formed the act I remember from radio. With three girl accordionists and himself on sax, they were HAL SWAIN AND HIS SWING SISTERS. The last job I can find he did (thanks to the Northern music-hall historian GEOFF MELLOR) was as musical director at the Bearwood Windsor Theatre. He died in 1966.

Swan and Leigh

A standard comedy duo on the isometric bars. It proves how far gymnastics has advanced when you realise that Swan and Leigh's big closing trick, in the 1950s, is today used by athletes as a warm-up exercise before competitions.

— T —

Tambo and Tambo

Musical clowns. I never saw them but Philip tells me: 'They were an old-fashioned duo who did a bit of knockabout stuff, a bit of hand to hand

balancing and marched up and down playing tambourines. They were usually last on the bill following the star which meant, because of the strict time allocation essential to twice nightly shows, the length of their act varied according to how long everyone had done before them. Sometimes their act would consist of sixteen bars of their opening number followed immediately by the National Anthem!'

Suzette Tarri

Comedienne. Born Islington, London. 'Red Sails in the Sunset' heralded Suzette's appearances on radio, and in Variety as well, I assume. I never saw her live though I remember her quavery, sing-song voice, bemoaning her domestic tragedies on the air. She was voted 'top radio comedienne' at the beginning of our period (1945).

Amazingly she was, originally, an oratorio contralto. Philip says: 'Her radio name ensured her popularity as a single act at all the number one halls.' She died in 1955.

Tattersall

Jerry and Company

Ventriloquist. Born James Tattersall, Manchester, 1914. Like so many 'vents' Jim was hooked at a very early age. He made his first doll at eight, from a rubber ball and a shawl. Then his creations became a bit more sophisticated – and how. His star dummy, 'Jerry', headed a company that included a life-sized old man, a dog and a baby. The act featured thirty different mechanical effects, all of which, like the dolls, Jim built himself.

Harold Taylor

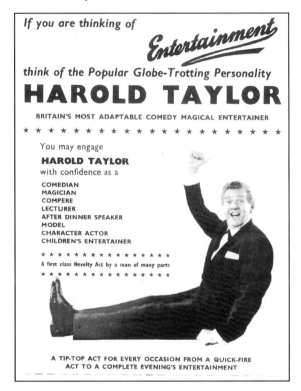

The Witty Wizard

Magician/entertainer. Born in Didcot, Berkshire, Harold was one of my favourite magicians. Whereas so many, with po faces, try to make you believe they are genuine mystics, he made the whole thing fun. From his self-deprecating introduction: 'I'm one of the better cheaper acts' to his, again self-invented, nickname, Three Tricks Taylor, Harold entertained.

After becoming hooked on magic as a boy, he honed his talents during the Second World War and, directly after, started his career proper at the Windmill. Variety followed. The addition of songs and cornet playing to his magic meant he was a valuable host in summer season shows too. He was certainly the most adaptable of performers, keeping a foot in every camp: Variety, summer shows, cabaret, private parties, after-dinner

speaking, writing, lecturing – you name it – he worked successfully worldwide.

The nickname, Three Tricks, was unfair. He could do the lot from big tricks to close-up magic. Above all he made me laugh. I remember him doing the curtain speech at one of his summer seasons when he said: 'I mean this sincerely – well, I'm always sincere but tonight I'm even more sincere than usual.' He died, to leave the world of magic taking itself a bit too seriously, in 1993.

Terry-Thomas

Comedian/actor. Born Thomas Hoar-Stevens, London, 1914. Terry became, through his highly successful film roles, the typical American idea of the silly arse. Well, perhaps not quite the silly arse, more the comical, caddish British rotter. People do forget that, before his illustrious movie career, he had been a good Variety turn.

He was originally a dancer who, pre-war, with his first wife Ida, played cabaret at most of the top West End clubs. The war saw him touring all over the Continent with *Stars in Battledress*. Contemporaries said he sounded more like an officer than the real ones. He did make sergeant.

His big break came with the SID FIELD vehicle at the Prince of Wales in 1946, *Piccadilly Hayride*. He had a featured spot in the show. It was billed as 'Technical Hitch'. In this Terry was a radio disc jockey who, just before he went on the air, broke all the records he was about to play. With the aid of a pianist he impersonated all the artistes on the records. This was the spot he did when I saw him in Variety. I still cherish his INKSPOTS.

With his cut-glass accent, gap-toothed grin and gimmicky cigarette holders he went on to fame on TV (JOHN FISHER found lots of terrific clips of his performances when he made Terry the star of one of his *Heroes of Comedy* TV shows) and then, of course, in films. First British films and then internationally. Alas, poor Terry suffered with Parkinson's Disease. This put paid, far too early, to his career. He died in 1990.

Billy Thorburn

Pianist. Born William Arthur Belmont Thorburn, London, 1900. A child prodigy on piano and

church organ, he played in concert party after the First World War. He graduated to playing with the top bands of the Thirties: JACK HYLTON, JACK PAYNE and THE SAVOY ORPHEANS. He formed his own band in 1936 and they were the dance band in the radio series, *The Organ, the Dance Band and Me*. The loss of so many musicians to the Second World War effort forced him to go solo and he toured, and broadcast, extensively well into our period.

The Tiller Girls

The most famous name connected with dancers in Variety. None of us who saw them will ever forget that long line of gorgeous legs, high kicking in perfect unison. What a spectacular and superb opening they were to any stage show.

Unbelievably, they began in 1890, the inspiration of JOHN TILLER. He was a wealthy Lancastrian cotton magnate fascinated by amateur theatricals. The collapse of the cotton industry forced John to find another way of earning a living. He had noticed that the chorus dancers in the professional shows he saw never really had a striking effect. They, more or less, were allowed to do their own thing. His idea was to drill a quartet of girls to dance, in perfect unison, rather like a corps de ballet. He worked them into the ground to achieve what he wanted and it was worth all the hassle. The girls, THE FOUR LITTLE SUNBEAMS,

opened in a show in Manchester and, for the first time, an audience encored a team of chorus dancers.

He opened Tiller Schools in Manchester and London where young girls were trained and groomed to join his troupes. By the 1920s they were appearing all over the world. John, who died in 1926, had created a unique style.

Throughout our period the girls were featured in all the top shows, in the UK and worldwide. Their standards were never allowed to drop due to the iron control of, variously, ROBERT SMITH, DORIS ALLOWAY and BARBARA AITKEN. The man who put *The Black and White Minstrel Show* on stage, ROBERT LUFF, took over the organisation in 1973. Barbara Aitken remained as director and choreographer until there was no longer anywhere for them to work.

Many of the girls stayed friends and if you get the chance to catch the 'age cannot wither them' troupe, THE ORIGINAL TILLER GIRLS, please do. More good news is that DOUGIE SQUIRES ('The Young Generation') is anxious to re-form the Tillers. It will be a joy if we are able to see those beautiful, untouchable, showstoppers once again.

Togare

The Valentino of the Sawdust Ring

Lion and tiger trainer. Born Georg Kulovits, 1900. (I've managed to slip one or two circus acts into the book because, like almost every pro I know, my original ambition was to run away and join one.) Togare was a showman, made the whole thing look easy yet dangerous and had a great confident presentation. For starters he dressed like Douglas Fairbanks senior and had the same flashing smile. The famous circus man CYRIL MILLS said: 'I always felt the public, especially the female section, was far more interested in the man than the lions.' He had a dramatic opening. His assistants would open two gold doors through which Togare, escorted by a bevy of girls, would enter. His animals would join him by jumping down into the ring through a huge Chinese dragon's mouth.

He began in the 1920s as a beast boy – cleaning out the cages and assisting the trainer, then graduated to training, and showing lions, tigers

pumas and bears. He worked all over the world but I saw him with Bertram Mills Circus at Olympia. He retired in 1958 and taught his second wife, who until then had been a medical student, to show the lions. I've heard of sending the wife out to work, but really!

Arthur Tolcher

One inch long – eight notes

Harmonica player. Born Arthur John Stone-Tolcher, Bloxwich, Staffs, 1922. Younger people remember Arthur as the man, in tails, who came on at the very end of the MORECAMBE AND WISE TV shows, put his harmonica up to his lips, only to be told, by Eric: 'Not now Arthur.'

Arthur was a great pal, a real old-fashioned, enthusiastic, dyed-in-the-wool pro. We met in BRANDON AND POUNDS's summer show, *Out of the Blue* in the early Sixties. Arthur was the musical speciality act and, as everyone had to in the little summer shows, played sketches too.

His mum and dad were old music-hall performers and he was on the boards at eleven. He toured the country in a 'discovery' show with the equally unknown Eric and Ernie. They never forgot him. He played the Palladium and all the principal halls and was a member of the RAF *Gang Show* during the war. He was a pantomime stalwart doing season after season for the SALBERGS in his native Black Country. He was an ever reliable small part player. One Christmas he even accompanied FRANK IFIELD in his big hit, 'I Remember You'. He was dressed as Friar Tuck at the time!

He was a funny man offstage. The spot he hated doing most was a medley of Irish tunes. He would play the ukulele *and* his tiny, 'one inch long – eight notes' mouth organ at the same time. If the

audience, for the rest of the show, weren't too responsive he would say: 'Right. Rotten are they? Then I'll definitely give them the Irish!'

He could turn his hand to anything required and his last shows were as small part and chorus in Cameron Mackintosh's productions of *My Fair Lady* and *Oliver!* He died in 1987.

Jack Train

Colonel Chinstrap

Impressionist and comedian. Born Plymouth 1902. Jack was an actor who drifted into Variety via West End plays. He stooged for NERVO AND KNOX for five years, did crowd work in films and radio as a voices man. Of course it was TOMMY

HANDLEY's mould-breaking show ITMA that made Jack a household name. He created 'Colonel Chinstrap', a bibulous old army man who would drink anything and bum a gargle from anyone: 'He landed on the shores.' 'What shores?' 'A large gin and tonic – I don't mind if I do!'

He dabbled in Variety and when that was over became a popular, 'comedy relief' panellist on radio with *Twenty Questions* and TV with *What's My Line?*

Tommy Trinder

You lucky people

Comedian. Born Streatham, London, 1909. 'Tommy Trinder,' said Philip, 'a whole book could be written about him.' As far as I know there never has been a book about the man whose almost permanent address in the 1940s was c/o the London Palladium. There should be.

Without doubt he was the comic of his day. He worked like a Cockney, spoke like a Cockney, had a Cockney's eye for the topical and the Cockney's natural talent for answering back and pricking pomposity. His ad libs are legendary. A favourite of the Royal Family at a charity show, he reminded King George VI that the last time he had performed before him was when Tommy was second on the bill and the King was still Duke of York. 'You've climbed very high since then,' said the King. 'You haven't done so bad yourself sir,' was Trinder's reply. He was good in sketches too and had a fistful of speciality spots, notably his CARMEN MIRANDA spoof.

Like so many Variety comics, Tommy got his first break through a talent competition and, discovered by WILL MURRAY, became a pro at twelve in the 'Casey's Court' company. From boy soprano he graduated to stand-up comic working cine-variety and music hall. He did a stint in South Africa and, back home, toured with an ARCHIE PITT revue. By the 1930s he was principal comic in concert party and in more number two touring revues. He took a chance and relinquished his top billing at the number two halls to become bottom of the bill in the number ones. It worked and he steadily climbed up the posters until he reached the Mecca, the London Palladium. He opened there with ARTHUR ASKEY. Two months later the show was off. War had been declared.

He continued to top in the provinces and began his incredible tours entertaining the forces. Suddenly he was back at the Palladium. This time the show ran just four nights – the air raids on London were just too much. In Manchester for panto he, and his fellow pros, found themselves incarcerated in their hotel all night while the bombs rained down outside. 'Tommy,' recalls WEBSTER BOOTH, 'spent from 6.30 in the evening till 7.30 the next morning entertaining us and all the other guests.' It was the start of many marathon performances he gave, on and offstage.

In 1941, at last, he got a *long* run at the Palladium with the revue *Gangway,* and was resident, in his own shows and pantomime, at the famous theatre till the end of the decade. He was a great self-promoter and during his Palladium reign, inspired by an advertising hoarding that announced, 'Your name could be here for a penny a week', he hired more than twenty sites around London. They all said: 'If it's laughter you're after – Trinder's the name!' He had several successful films to his credit too, especially *Champagne Charlie*, where he played GEORGE LEYBOURNE opposite STANLEY HOLLOWAY'S THE GREAT VANCE.

Sadly, I think, he spent more and more time abroad. Seasons in Australia, South Africa, Canada, New Zealand and America meant that he became an unfamiliar face to new young audiences. He was the first compere of TV's *Sunday Night at the Palladium* but somehow never recaptured his total domination of the light entertainment scene.

He was still a star on radio, however, and the many times he crossed wits with TED RAY and JIMMY EDWARDS in *Does the Team Think?* showed he had lost none of his quick-witted edge.

In 1971 he celebrated an incredible fifty years in the biz but he carried on in summer season and panto till sheer exhaustion confined him just to the occasional appearances on chat shows and nostalgia programmes. He was a gem for anyone to interview. He had an encyclopaedic memory for names, dates and places and, unless inter-rupted, would happily do an entire programme on his own.

He was King Rat of the Grand Order of Water Rats four times and his stentorian ad-libs are missed to this day. He died in 1989.

Troise and His Mandoliers

6·30 TWICE NIGHTLY 8·50
SPECIAL MATINEE WHIT-MONDAY at 2·30

THE MOST NOVEL BAND OF ALL
The B.B.C.'s Most Popular Broadcasting Band
All New Numbers—Played and Sung the way you like them best

PERSONAL APPEARANCE OF

GREAT RADIO WEEK!

TROISE
AND HIS
MANDOLIERS
WITH THE WONDER TENOR
DON CARLOS

Bandleader. Born Pasquale Troise, Naples 1893. Yet another band who made top of the bill status through broadcasting. Troise was a naturalised Italian who, after learning clarinet and mandolin before he was twelve, came here to the UK to be part of SIDNEY FIRMAN's Radio Dance Band. They

were the top broadcasting orchestra in the days of 2LO.

He formed the Mandoliers and a second group, the Banjoliers, in the early Thirties and was a regular broadcaster from then on. He claimed to be the first to form a band of mandolin players. (I'd have kept quiet about it!) Like so many others, both bands disappeared with the coming of rock and roll.

Sophie Tucker

The Last of the Red Hot Mommas

Entertainer. Born Sophie Abuza, of Russian Jewish parentage, in Boston, USA, 1884. Not too many America vaudeville stars have made it into this book but Sophie couldn't be ignored. She was one of our very favourite entertainers – and a Lady Ratling.

She first sang in her father's kosher restaurant in Greenwich Village in New York. She went into vaudeville as a black-faced act billed as 'The World Renowned Coon Shouter'. Her long career is detailed in her autobiography, *Some of These Days*. She did everything in America: vaudeville, musical comedy, revue and night clubs, slowly but surely climbing the bill.

Sophie first scored here in 1922, at the Stratford Empire, toured all the number ones and did a revue at the London Hippodrome. In 1925 she came here for cabaret at the Kit Kat Club at the same time doubling in Variety at the leading London halls. In 1925 she first sang a number specially written for her, 'My Yiddisher Momma.' Like 'My Way', everybody, Jew, Catholic, Methodist, even agnostic, sang it. I saw her do it and she was simply the best. Her recording sold a million copies, even though Hitler banned it. She had success here again in the 1930s, and, in 1934, topped at the Holborn Empire and did the first of her Royal Variety Performances. After the war, accompanied by TED SHAPIRO (a brother Water Rat), her visits here were almost annual events.

When you read the lyrics of her point numbers they are totally innocuous but, boy, did she get every single innuendo out of them. She was short and fat yet on-stage she appeared tall and elegant. It's almost impossible to work out how this change could happen but Philip says DON ROSS gave the best answer he ever heard: 'You see,' said Don, 'she has built-in footlights.' Pretty good eh? The great lady died in 1966.

Joan Turner

The voice of an angel – the wit of a devil

Comedienne/singer. Born Joan Teresa Page, Belfast, 1922. Surely one of Variety's most talented ladies. She was, almost, another GRACIE FIELDS. She did indeed have the voice of an angel with an incredible range. Her operatic arias would stop the show and she was, at times an inspired, first-class visual and vocal comedienne.

She began in revues and road shows for ERNIE LOTINGA. He, generously, released her from her contract with him to enable her to pursue a career as a single act. She was a hit everywhere she played and was all set for star status. Alas, she was too erratic and undisciplined to allow herself to be channelled in that direction. She has tackled most things, including musicals and straight plays. I saw her play the lead in *The Killing of Sister George*, and she was terrific. Happily, the great survivor, despite all her tribulations, is still at it. Believe me, *An Evening with Joan Turner* is an adventure not to be missed.

Tubby Turner

Hif hit's ho kay with you hit's ho kay with me

Comedian. Born Clarence Turner, Great Harwood, Lancashire, 1882. Yet another of the good, solid Variety comics who never really made the number ones but is still remembered with great affection by many people.

Tubby Turner began in concert party in Blackpool and later toured the country in TOM CONVERY's revue, 'On the Panel'. As he said in his biographical notes in 1950: 'I played everywhere from Hetton-le-Hole to the London Palladium.' Indeed it was at the Palladium where he first introduced a routine so often copied since. The pot-bellied Turner would walk on in short trousers, a too-small blazer and wearing a tiny boater. He would carry a deckchair which he would then attempt to put up. After several minutes of business he would, in total frustration, hurl the chair across the stage. It would land miraculously, in perfect, ready-to-sit-in, position.

A great fan of Tubby's, Bryan Hay from Chesterfield, has told me some of his gags – 'perfect for his stuttering delivery'. On a train an old lady asks him if the train stops at Kings Cross. 'If it d-d-doesn't,' he stammers, 'th-th-there'll be a h-h-hellova bump!'

Tubby worked with his wife, FLORENCE REVILL in sketches for forty-six years. She would appear in the deckchair saga where she would advise him: 'There's no bottom in this deckchair.' Tubby would point to his large backside and reply, 'What the 'ell's this then?' She would assist in his routines where he tried to play the harp and the organ and be constantly thwarted in her attempts to recite by the interruptions of her old man. Unusually, then, for a music-hall comic, Tubby also wrote. Geoff Mellor, (author of *Northern Music Hall*) tells me he had a play, *Summat for Nowt*, produced by the Oldham Repertory Company. I wonder if there is a copy anywhere – I'd love to read it. Alas Tubby died, just before his play was performed, in 1952.

___ U ___

Stanley Unwin

ndescribable. Born Pretoria, South Africa, 911. The amazing Stanley, inventor of the anguage that sounds almost like a real one but sn't, just made it into our period. He became a full me pro in 1960. He worked for the BBC from 940, first maintaining transmitters, joining the War Reporting Unit for two years, and then ecoming a mobile engineer working on outside roadcasts all over the world.

His invented language, 'Unwinese', began with is fascination for languages and his spicing up of edtime stories for his children. It was in 1948 at his unique talents were first heard on the air the total bemusement, but amusement, of all ho heard him.

He did loads of broadcasts, tellys, voice-overs on commercials and brilliant after-dinner speeches. These days he just does what he feels like.

He has written several books including his fascinating life story, *Deep Joy* published by Caedmon of Whitby in 1984. Caedmon also published a smashing collection of 'Unwinised' children's tales, *Fairly Stories*.

___ V ___

Henri Vadden and His Girls

Juggler, balancer and dancer. Born Henry John Vadden, Islington, London, 1907. He started as a page in his father's act THE LOWELL BROTHERS. From 1934 the act with 'the girls' (originally his wife and sister) was his spectacular speciality. His sensational closing trick is still talked about with humour and affection. He balanced, via a stick on his chin, a huge, spinning, iron-clad cartwheel. At the given moment one of the girls would knock the stick away and the mighty wheel would come crashing down, still spinning, to be caught on the spike of the old-fashioned Prussian helmet he was wearing. Philip swears his neck shortened by about three inches over the years he knew him. I remember saying to him one night as he came off: 'Doesn't that hurt?' With a pitying glance he replied: 'Course it bloody hurts!'

Dickie Valentine

Singer. Born Richard Brice, 1930. Dickie was, before rock and roll, a top pop attraction in the 1950s. He was once a member of the backstage staff at the London Palladium before he joined the TED HEATH BAND as a featured vocalist alongside LITA ROZA and DENNIS LOTIS. I saw him many times in concert with Ted Heath at the Davis Theatre, Croydon when Big Band Sunday Concerts were regular events. He would score with his own songs and give us a bonus with his impressions. He had a series of successful records and, on leaving Ted Heath, his boyish good looks, lovable personality and great voice catapulted him to top of the bill in Variety and pantomime.

His early death, in 1971, was through a car accident on his way home from playing cabaret at Caerphilly, South Wales.

Vera Valentine Lovelies Royalty Girls

Dancers. One of the best lines of girls of the post-war years. The beautifully gowned dancers were a featured speciality on many Variety bills. Their sensational cancan routine never failed to stop the show. They were choreographed by VERA VALENTINE.

Reg Varney

Comedian. Born Reginald Alfred Varney, Canning Town, London, 1916. Another Variety pro whose success in TV has proved the value of his apprenticeship.

Reg began as a solo straight pianist and developed his gift for comedy during his army days with *Stars in Battledress*. After demob he toured in the revue *Tokyo Express* and did summer season with HEDLEY CLAXTON's famous training ground for stars, *Gaytime*.

He became an established top comedian in Variety, pantomime and production, but of course it was television that made him nationally known. *The Rag Trade* and *On the Buses* were the series that did the trick. Reg's wonderfully naturalistic acting and inventing of all sorts of comedy

'business' added so much to these shows. Whenever he can be persuaded back on stage from his West Country home, he paralyses audiences who only know him from the telly. His Variety act, a combination of piano playing and comicking, is as effective as ever. The true pros never lose it!

Olga Varona

Aerialiste. Born Queensland, Australia, 1920. She came to London in the mid Forties with her husband and partner ARCHIE COLLINS. A lady aerial act was a big novelty then and she played, with great success, all over the UK. Mr and Mrs Collins returned to Australia and regularly contributed an excellent series of Variety days reminiscences, via Eddie Trigg, to The British Music Hall Society magazine *The Call Boy*.

Frankie Vaughan

Mr Moonlight

Singer. Born Frank Abelson, Liverpool, 1928. Frank's career began with a trial week (for nothing!) at the Kingston Empire. The very next week he topped the bill in Manchester at a hundred pounds. His powerful personality and attacking style of singing was just what Variety of the Fifties wanted.

It was the music-hall star, male impersonator HETTY KING, who advised him to use a silver knobbed cane and wear the top hat which became his trademark. His signature tune, 'Give me the Moonlight,' has links with music hall too. It was originally featured by an earlier 'heart-throb' FRED BARNES.

He made films, even one in America with Marilyn Monroe, and remains a genuinely popular top of the bill star.

Norman Vaughan

Comedian. Born Liverpool 1923. A gentle light comedian whose compering of TV's *Sunday Night at the Palladium* and catchphrases, 'Swinging' and 'Dodgy!', made him a star. Not exactly overnight. Norman began as a boy with THE ETON BOYS and DUDLEY DALE's GANG. He was part of a three handed dancing act with WYN TAYLOR AND BEBE. It was during the war that he developed his comedic talent and, in the mid Forties, was a regular in concert party and Variety. His big break came when he took over from BRUCE FORSYTH at the Palladium. I'll always remember him for the marvellous 'marching to music' routine (with HARRY SECOMBE and ERIC SYKES) and that classic 'Roses Grow on You' television commercial.

Verdini

Comedy magician. Born Frank Hladik, Czechoslovakia, 1909. Performed all over the Continent and the Middle East until he came to the UK in 1948. He quickly established himself and, via a season at the notorious 'nudie' Windmill Theatre, played all the leading halls as a featured speciality. I got to know Frank very well when he became a resident of Brinsworth House. There, on open days and at garden fêtes, he would take charge of the children's entertainment. His friendly personality, clever tricks, balloon modelling and impression of CHARLIE CHAPLIN enchanted the kids, and me. Frank died in 1994.

Vesta and Ashton

Xylophone playing/dancing speciality. Vesta was born Audrey Austin, Guiseley, Yorks, 1917. Ashton was born John Kenneth Austin, Leeds, 1911. They were both seasoned pros (she as a dancer and xylophonist, he as a musical clown) before they formed the double act in 1939. They were a constantly employed standard musical speciality.

Edward Victor

Magician/shadowgraphist. Born London, 1897. Edward Victor is one of the reasons Variety, when it was good, was the very best sort of light entertainment. Suddenly, in the middle of a (hopefully) first-class parade of comedians, singers, dancers, jugglers and performing animals, a really different act would add spice to the mixture. Edward presented the simplest of ideas. The cavemen probably were the first to do

it. Working behind an illuminated sheet, he would throw on to this screen, shadows: silhouettes of animals, birds and, most importantly, famous personalities. They were all, with the help of the simplest props, created by the manipulation of his hands. His animals lived and breathed, and got laughs, and his personalities, from Queen Victoria to Winston Churchill, gained admiring applause. I can still remember the impact this silent show, with commentary by Edward from behind the screen, made on me.

He was also a superb sleight of hand magician, and an important member, indeed a vice president, of the Inner Magic Circle. Many of the classic close-up routines used by magicians today were invented by him.

The son of a Swiss hotelier, he began his career as a seventeen-year-old magic-struck member of J.N. MASKELYNE'S company at St George's Hall in London. He played Variety everywhere both pre- and post-war. I saw him, in the Fifties, with the touring revue, *Educating Archie* alongside its star, the ventriloquist PETER BROUGH and his charge, ARCHIE ANDREWS.

I would really love to have seen Edward in panto. He played Abanazer in *Aladdin* nearly every Christmas from 1937 on, where his shadows were presented on a sheet hanging from Widow Twankey's laundry line. Now that *is* the way to work in a speciality act. His last appearance was at the Liverpool Pavilion in 1960. He died in 1964.

The Two Virginians

Comedy jugglers. A Danish husband-and-wife team. The missus, MINA SAHLSTROM, was born in Copenhagen in 1920 and was a dancer until she teamed up with her husband in 1944. As jugglers they played in circus and Variety all over the world and all the number ones in the UK.

Vogelbein's Bears

Hans Vogelbein was the trainer and exhibitor of these highly dangerous, always muzzled, bears. BOBBY ROBERTS, of the famous Robert Brothers Circus, told me that bears were the most untrustworthy of all animals. 'Their eyes are always blank. You can't tell what they're thinking.'

Hans did love his charges, though, and when he was confined to hospital for a long period, they wouldn't eat. When he got back home they were in such poor health that he was advised to have them destroyed. With tears streaming down his face, he shot them himself.

Unable to face the thought of more bears, he trained a chimpanzee, GILBERT. They played all the number one dates as GILBERT AND PARTNER. The pair would enter hand in hand and Gilbert would receive his cues by Hans squeezing his paw. Their running gag was Gilbert returning time after time to look through a hole in the stage. 'Down there,' Hans told us, 'is the chorus girls' dressing room.'

I worked with them and Gilbert would sit in their dressing room, feet on the dressing table, smoking a fag. Hans gave up the act, he said, 'when Gilbert started giving *me* the cues by squeezing *my* hand!'

The Seven Volants

Acrobats. Their boss was JOHNNY HUTCH born Middlesbrough, 1913. Johnny is still the driving force behind so many different acrobatic troupes. He served his apprenticeship, ten years of it, with THE SEVEN ROYAL HINDUSTANIS. He appeared as part of all sorts of acts: THE FOUR MANUELS, CORNELLA AND EDDIE, PRESCO AND CAMPO and THE RAPID FOUR. THE FIVE VOLANTS were formed in 1947 and, by the Fifties, had become the seven.

In recent years Johnny has fronted the comedy team, THE VETERANS, and is a highly regarded teacher of acrobatics.

Voltaire

Electrical illusionist. Born Bobby Arrendoff, London, 1910. As an ordinary conjuror, with an extremely silver tongue, he persuaded Sir Oswald Stoll to let him have the Shepherd's Bush Empire for a fortnight so that he could perfect the, never-been-done, Indian Rope Trick. He couldn't do it either, and fled, in shame, to Canada. He vowed he would return and did. Twelve years later, in

Voltaire with Jack Paine

1946, he played the Bush with his new electrical illusions act. This time everything went well and he played all the number one dates from then on. His creativity earned him an award from the Magic Circle and a medal for 'chutzpah' from me and Phil.

Bill Waddington

Witty Willie

Comedian. Born in Oldham. Long before he

became the irascible Percy Sugden in *Coronation Street*, Bill was a popular supporting act in variety.

Once again it was the Second World War that convinced Bill, the son of a farmer, that the quick-witted approach he used when he was a car salesman could be put to better use. He started entertaining with *Stars in Battledress* and, on being invalided out in 1945, became a pro.

Bill had a good career in Variety and pantomime till the early Sixties when he retired to his farm in Higher Disley to breed beef cows. Returning to the business for just two episodes of *Coronation Street*, such was his impact that Percy was invented for him. The *Street* made him a household name as it did with those other, ever adaptable, Variety pros, JILL SUMMERS, BETTY DRIVER and TOM MENNARD.

Dougie Wakefield

Dougie Wakefield and his gang

Comedian. Born Sheffield, 1901. Began as a child performer and became a light comedian till he discovered his gift for low comedy. Didn't he have the face for it? He developed his comedy in a series of revues staged by ARCHIE PITT, GRACIE FIELDS's first husband. He met and married Gracie's sister Edie. He, and his gang, JACK BUTLER, BILLY NELSON and CHUCK O'NEIL, starred in what is described as 'a classic of modern Variety', a piece called *Four Boys from Manchester*. The gang created all sorts of burlesques on things like, *Spectre de la Rose*. I never saw Dougie Wakefield 'live' but I have seen him and the lads on film. I remember particularly them doing a routine where they were handcuffed to each other yet passed a jacket from one end of the line to the other. LILIAN AZA, Gracie's agent, told me Dougie was one of the very best comedians she had ever seen. Sadly, I must take her word for it. He died in 1951.

Roy Walker

Singer. Born Roy Francis Walker, London, 1929. Radio, as it did so often, made him a Variety name. He was touring from the age of fourteen till the agent STANLEY DALE got him an audition with the BBC. His first broadcast was in 1947 and he even did early television. He became a regular on radio and on the Variety circuit.

Oswald Waller

Character comedian. He seems to have been more of an actor than a turn with an impressive list of parts played in drama, musicals and farces, both in the UK and in America. He played the title role in *The Windmill Man* which played *twelve* seasons at the Victoria Palace (almost as many as THE CRAZY GANG). He is in this book because of the people who he worked with as a part of a double act: CHICK FARR, HARRY ANGERS, BILLY BENNETT and CHARLIE CLAPHAM. He must have been a good 'un and I'd love to know more about him.

Max Wall

Comedian. Born Maxwell George Lorimer, Brixton, London, 1908. Forgive me for waxing eloquent about a truly funny man. He was, like all the very greatest, something from another world. Everything about him was funny: his face, his movements, his voice. When he was on song he was just brilliant. When he wasn't, not so good.

Fair enough. As someone once said, 'Only the mediocre can be consistently acceptable.' He was a highly temperamental instinctive comic genius. The complete Max was a product of knocking it out around the halls (first as a dancer in Variety and revue) and a turbulent private life.

His unforgettable creation was Professor Wallofsky, a lunatic, surreal, pianist who lives on (sort of) in FREDDIE STARR's impression.

After leaving his wife and children for a beauty queen he was, in effect, banned from the number one theatres (things were very different then). He went into the working-men's clubs, where lesser artistes would have sunk without trace, but not the indestructible Max. His comeback began with his show-saving contribution to a West End musical, *Cockie*. In 1974 he appeared on a Palladium bill with ETHEL MERMAN and the critics hailed him as 'a real authentic music-hall great'. Well, those of us who loved Variety had known that all along. Suddenly Max was the flavour of the month. Happily, unlike some others, his adoration by the Yuppie set did nothing to reform him. His one-man show was a unique combination of wit, corn, aggressive audience control and couldn't-care-less flouting of all the rules. Brilliant.

The last days of his career were crowned with a plethora of funny and moving straight parts on stage, television and in films. What he would have achieved if the powers-that-be hadn't so hypocritically ostracised him, at the height of this powers, we can only imagine. His fascinating biography is aptly titled *The Fool on the Hill*. He died, recognised at last, in 1990.

The Wallabies

Acrobats. A spectacular acrobatic act mostly featured in big production shows. The act consisted of eight girls, all fast tumblers and pyramid balancers. They were managed by the legendary Australian, DIGGER PUGH, whose agency supplied speciality acts all over the world.

Nellie Wallace

Left to right *Billy Merson, Nellie Wallace, Teddy Knox and Jimmy Nervo*

The Essence of Eccentricity

Comedienne. Born Glasgow, 1870. There has to be a book written about one of the greatest grotesques of music hall whose career extended into Variety days. I just managed to see her in DON ROSS's music hall veterans' show, *Thanks for the Memory*. She sang one of her most famous songs, 'Under the Bed, – It's Never Been my Luck to Find a Man There Yet'.

She really was a most eccentric-looking lady, 'like a worried hen', someone described her. Her comedy often featured her being chased by every man she ever met. Have a look at her photograph and you'll see the joke.

She was a great heroine of SIR ALEC GUINNESS. In his autobiography he tells us of his admiration of her and her 'perfect theatrical timing.' She died in 1948.

Tommy Wallis and Beryl

Multi-instrumentalists. Tom, the son of SID PLUMMER the comedy xylophonist, started playing xylophone and drums while still at school. His first experience on the boards was with his dad, playing duets together in Sid's act. Tommy made his solo début in 1949 at the Palace Theatre Bath and Variety and pantomime followed. He did his xylophone act and accompanied the rest of the show on drums, on CSE tours and in revues.

In 1951, he played his first London date, Collin's Music Hall, with SAM KERN the composer of *Mary from the Dairy*. In 1954, while playing a resident season at Butlin's, Tommy developed a musical clown act and a drum speciality with spectacular UV effects and met his future wife, Beryl, one of the SHERMAN FISHER GIRLS. They became a double act and married in 1959. Bigger and better dates followed and their TV début. Tom says the six months they spent in summer season in Scotland was a great experience. The constant changes of programme meant lots of new routines to be devised and many more instruments added (they play more than ten between them).

In 1960, Beryl gave birth to their son, Tim, a fitting curtain to the period we are concentrating on. While so many Variety acts bit the dust in the Sixties, Tom and Beryl went from strength to strength. They fitted into the pop concert scene perfectly and, in 1963, did a tour with FRANK IFIELD, on which the smallest names on the bill were THE BEATLES. Adapting their talents to cabaret and, most importantly, to cruise liner shows, in 1974 they changed their name to THE PLUMMERS. After 25 years of not cashing in on his dad's fame, Tom decided it would be nice to keep the family name alive.

Tom tells me he and Beryl are now semi-retired. Don't you believe it. Whenever the call comes, try and stop 'em. Whether in summer season, cabaret or on the cruise ships, it is always a joy to see two dedicated and highly talented pros showing the rest how it should be done.

Albert and Les Ward

Musical novelty act. Albert born 1917 and Les 1925, both in Cardiff. The two brothers really pre-dated LONNIE DONEGAN with their own version of skiffle. They played guitars, bicycle pumps, washboards – anything that would provide an accompaniment to their country and western-type comedy songs. Their popularity on all sorts of radio Variety shows, *Welsh Rarebit, Variety Bandbox, Ignorance is Bliss* and *Workers' Playtime* led to them becoming a popular middle of the bill act in Variety, summer show and pantomime.

Warren, Latona and Sparks

Warren, Daveen and Sparks

Comedy acrobats. Leslie Warren and Joseph Latona born Sydney, Australia, 1920, Maisie Sparks (Mrs Leslie Warren) born Sydney, 1922.

An Australian trio who played all over the world. Their sensational opening was performed by Leslie; he would 'fall' from the highest stage box available on to the stage itself. In 1955 Latona left the act and it became WARREN, DAVEEN AND SPARKS. They were always based in Oz but often returned to the UK, always as a featured act in the number one halls. Leslie died in 1995.

Francis Watts

Conjuror. Born F. Barrie Watts, Willsbridge, Glos. A standard Variety act that scored with the gimmick that Francis would 'conjure' with any object handed up from the audience.

The Wazzan Troupe

Acrobatic ensemble. Philip says: 'They were usually a collection of seven to ten Arabs, Moroccans and Tunisians – all doing the same act. They formed pyramids and finished with a fast routine of tzinsikas, flips, etc. They always accompanied their tricks with bags of noise and were a first-class act for any bill.'

Dorothy 'Dottie' Wayne

Comedienne/siffleur. Born in Harrogate 1936. Dottie says: 'Variety was on its last legs by the time I entered the business.' Not quite, she became a pro in 1956. It was BARNEY COLEHAN who gave her her first break. She auditioned for him, singing songs to her own guitar accompaniment. The very next day the Musicians Union pulled all the BBC orchestras out on strike and her first TV appearance happened – a spot in a Variety show

with BILL MAYNARD, JOAN REGAN and STAN STENNET.

A summer show in Filey, as a real professional, followed and her debut as a turn was at the Hull Continental in 1957. More summer seasons with JOHN AND ADELE BERRYMAN's *Evening Stars* company came next and a six-week stint at the naughty nudie showplace, London's Windmill Theatre. She stopped the show – with her clothes on.

Like so many others, Dottie served her apprenticeship with the famous *Fol-de-Rols* before embarking on the solo career which has served her, and us, so well. From being a featured act with *The Black and White Minstrel Show*, she has played Variety, pantomime, cabaret, radio and TV all over the world. Her mix of comedy, songs, audience participation and show-stopping whistling make her a unique act today.

Bert Weedon

(Back row left to right) *Bruce Welch, George Harrison, Mike Reid, Lonnie Donegan, Bert Weedon, Con Claskey, Brian May, Dec Claskey.* (Front row) *Joe Brown and Chas McDevitt at a tribute when Bert was King Rat*

Mr Guitar

Guitarist. Born in London, 1920. Believe it or not Bert was playing Variety as a solo act in the early Fifties. He began, self taught, at the age of twelve before working in London dance bands. The Second World War found him working with the likes of DJANGO REINHARDT and STEPHAN GRAPPELLI.

After the war he was a featured soloist with all the top British bands including MANTOVANI, TED HEATH and CYRIL STAPLETON. In 1956, he formed his own quartet but it wasn't until 1959 that he hit the jackpot on record with a cover version of 'Guitar Boogie Shuffle'. Bert was the guitar player on so many hit records, by people who were voted top guitarists. But often, on their recordings, it was Bert doing the playing.

His classic instruction book, *Play In a Day* sold two million copies and inspired players like ERIC CLAPTON, JOHN LENNON, BRIAN MAY, PAUL MCCARTNEY, MIKE OLDFIELD and GEORGE HARRISON, to take up the instrument. He is still the most respected and loved of all guitarists. The greatest tribute I've seen to him was at a Water Rats Ball when he was King Rat. A jam session at the end of the cabaret, led by Bert, included GEORGE HARRISON, LONNIE DONEGAN, BRUCE WALSH, PHIL COLLINS, BRIAN MAY, DEC AND CON CLUSKEY (THE BACHELORS), JOE BROWN and CHAS MCDEVITT.

Happily he is still playing and it's a sobering sight when, while so many young groups fill the stage with gigantic blocks of equipment, Bert plugs his guitar into a speaker no bigger than an attaché case and fills the place with glorious sound. His one-man show not only attracts guitar buffs but everyone who enjoys the company of a superb and totally professional entertainer.

Señor Wences

Ventriloquist. Born Wenceslao Moreno, Penaranda, Spain. A great vent who played the West End and all the UK's number one theatres. He was, says Philip, one of the first to create a doll by putting a tiny wig on his hand and using his thumb as the mouth. His patter was done in broken English with muttered asides including, my favourite bit, him opening a cabinet to disclose a disembodied head that shouted, 'Sssaright!'

Billy West and His Harmony Boys

Pianist/comedian. Born William Fretwell, Sheffield, 1903. Originally a song 'plugger', then a musical director. He produced and arranged all the music for his act, THE HARMONY BOYS, in 1938. Again success in radio ensured that they were a popular speciality on the halls throughout the Forties and Fifties.

The Western Brothers

Topical songs at the piano. Kenneth and George were cousins who teamed up in 1925. Again it was radio that brought their act popular fame. They played the characters of two silly arses. They always wore tails when I saw them, and monocles of course. Their laconic, laid-back 'remember the old school tie', and, 'play the game you cads' delivery belied their topical, and often very sharp, satirical monologues to music. Variety audiences always enjoyed someone 'sending up' the nobs and they were masters of this. When there were no nobs left to send up, they retired. Kenneth had a tobacco kiosk on Weybridge Station for many years. He died in 1963 and his partner in 1969.

'Checker' Wheel

The Man with the Educated Feet

Roller skating act. I worked with Checker once, at the Met, Edgware Road. I was half of a double act, HUDD AND KAY, and the date at the Met was our first week's Variety. Top of the bill was a lad with whom we'd just finished a season at Butlin's – CLIFF RICHARD. Of course the audience only wanted to know about Cliff but Checker's unusual solo act was warmly received, especially his big finish, where he tap-danced on roller skates!

I last saw Checker in Sunderland at a TV recording. Like so many other good speciality acts, he gave up the game when venues dried up.

Jimmy Wheeler

Wheeler and Wilson

Ay Ay – that's yer lot!

Comedian. Born Ernest Remnant, Battersea, London, 1910. Would you believe that the epitome of the boozy, four-ale bar story teller was, before he became one of our very greatest front-cloth comics, an assistant in a science lab, a ballroom dancer, a straight actor, a bandleader and a film bit player and extra. He joined his dad and formed the act WHEELER AND WILSON, 'The Sailor and the Porter' in 1929. The act, so the reference books say, was filmed. I'd love to see it.

After twenty years of the double act he became a single turn and was an instant hit with his aggressive, BILLY BENNETT style of comedy. He

became a sure-fire hit on any bill from the Palladium to Bilston. I have an old 'manager's comments' book in front of me and on his page it says, 'actual salary £200 – estimated value £1000!'. He was an accomplished fiddle player and would constantly interrupt his playing of 'Mistakes' with one-liners, such as 'My father said beer never hurt anyone – then a barrel fell on his head!' à la MOREY AMSTERDAM.

He did like a drink and stories about him are legion (see *Roy Hudd's Book of Music Hall, Variety and Show Biz Anecdotes*). As his old friend Philip says, 'He stopped a lot of gin going bad!' Jimmy died, greatly mourned by us, his Brother Water Rats, in 1971.

Billy Whitaker

Billy Whitaker

Minni Law

Comedian. Born in Streatham, London, 1914. Billy was the son of the great music-hall ventriloquist, CORAM but carved his own niche as a variety, revue and pantomime comedian. Though he did work alone he is best known for his on, and off stage, partnership with the comedienne MIMI LAW (the sister of JERRY JEROME). They were together from the Forties when they were the stars of the touring revue, *Hi Diddle Diddle*.

Billy was the sort of comic I really enjoy. He had great warmth, a slightly off-beat sense of fun and was inventive and original in sketches. BILL PERTWEE and I often enthuse about Billy's sketch with a collection of life-size, rubber-headed dummies. At one stage of the plot, Billy, infuriated by the lack of response, would punch one of the dummy's heads. We can never forget the sight of the rubber face slowly resuming its proper shape. His post office clerk behind a portable grille was a favourite too.

I love him as Dame in pantomime too. So did NORMAN WISDOM and KEN DODD. They both employed him for many a Christmas season. He was that, so hard to capture, combination of genuine harridan and bloke in a skirt. His NORMAN-EVANS-type face helped as well.

Billy and the effervescent Mimi never stopped working (he even learned to play the piano in his sixties). They were for ever devising revues and shows which they both appeared in, especially for the Esplanade Pavilion on the Isle of Wight. Billy was the entertainments manager there till shortly before he died, in his eighties, in 1995. Mimi is as bright and enthusiastic as ever and living on the Isle of Wight.

Albert Whelan

The Australian Entertainer

Entertainer. Born Albert Waxman, Melbourne, 1875. Another music-hall star who carried on into Variety in veteran shows. He was credited with being the first man to have a signature tune. He would walk on, dressed like a 'toff', whistling a tune ('The Three Brothers' waltz), remove his hat and gloves and park his stick. This business took an eternity and once, when given an eight-minute spot, he just had time to get on, remove the props, put them on again and exit. He joined up with BILLY BENNETT as half of a blacked-up patter act. They called themselves ALEXANDER AND MOSE. They took out their own Variety shows with top of the bills Bennett and Whelan *and* (nobody knew it was them) Alexander and Mose. Four stars for the price of two!

Albert made dozens of records and my memory of him is broadcasting, on John Sharman's *Music Hall*, where 'The Three Trees' (a monologue with music) is the piece I remember best. He died in 1962.

The Whiteley Brothers

Tom, Dick and Harry – (actually Ben Whiteley, born 1901, his brother Harold, born 1903 and his son Derek, born 1920). Originally the FIVE WHITELEYS (the act of Ben and Harold's parents). A musical clown, acrobatic, knockabout act from a family who had been involved with circus and Variety from the early 1800s.

Dawn White and Her Glamazons

Dancers. Philip remembers the act well: 'They were the forerunners of the ROLY-POLYS. Six enormous ladies who tap-danced. Dawn White was a singer and her pièce de resistancé was the splits at the end of a number. The tabs closed on this. If they hadn't, what followed would have been the highspot of the act. Six enormous girls trying to haul the biggest one of the lot to her feet. Not an easy, or particularly attractive, piece of business.'

David Whitfield

Singer. Born Hull, 1926. A sort of latter day CAVAN O'CONNOR. A handsome, hugely popular, singer of dramatic ballads whose recordings made him a star. He had a totally un-show biz background. He'd been a delivery boy, a cement humper, a coalman and a sailor in the Royal Navy. It was HUGHIE GREEN's stage version of *Opportunity Knocks* that gave him his first break. He toured with the show for eight months. He got a regular gig at a hotel in London and it was there that a rep from Decca spotted him. His first record, 'Marta', was successful but his second, 'I Believe', was a hit. He began his Variety career in 1953 and headlined everywhere. He played pantomime too. I remember him as Robinson Crusoe at the Palladium. His biggest record, 'Cara Mia', made it to America's top ten and resulted in him playing, with great success, over there.

As popular music changed and groups became the thing, David's star faded, although he, and his all too rarely played records, are still remembered with great affection. He made a good living till the end in the clubs. He died while working on a cruise ship around Australia in 1980.

Leslie Whittaker

Pianist. Born Liverpool, 1926. He appeared with several well-known bands starting as a boy with Archie's Juvenile Swing Band. He played keyboard with the Al Podesta and Younkman Orchestra and did a two-piano act in Variety, BUNTY HOUSTON AND HER MELODY THREE. He was ISSY BONN's accompanist.

Claud Williams

The Great Claud

Comedy magician. A comedy magic solo act who worked in an Eton suit! One unforgettable gag: he would successfully perform a trick and unveil a notice on an easel which read 'Claud'. A second success would reveal the words 'The Great Claud' and a third would show 'Claud Almighty'. He was never a star but a good, solid, sure-fire act who played all the number ones and twos.

George Williams

I'm not well

Born 1913. He was a white-faced patter comedian of the old school. He told clean, and very funny stories with immaculate timing and an endearing personality. He was a regular broadcaster in *Workers' Playtime* and *Variety Bandbox*. He was working up to his death in 1995.

Denny Willis

Comedy. Born Williams, 1920. An excellent

Scottish comedian, son of the legendary DAVE WILLIS. He toured in Variety, fed by JOHNNY MACK, the son of another famous comedian, but never really got the recognition he deserved. Philip says he was badly handled by the powers-that-be and, by his sheer versatility, lacked that definite personality a top comic must have. He was a brilliant visual comic and his 'Quorn Quartette' routine (where he desperately tried to keep up with his three fellow huntsmen in their unison singing and choreography) was a real classic. He did the routine many times, by public demand, on *The Good Old Days* and in the Royal Variety Performance of 1960.

At one time he was the principal comic with *Out of the Blue* (the summer show I started with) and the boss of the show, DICKIE POUNDS, said: 'Denny was not good a learning lines. He preferred to fall over. Whenever I handed him a sketch he would shake his head and say 'Words! Words! I hate 'em.' He died in 1995.

Ernie Wilson

The father of JIMMY WHEELER. They did a double act, WHEELER AND WILSON. 'The Sailor and the Porter' was their bill matter and they worked together around all the number two theatres until Jimmy decided on a solo career. Then Ernie retired.

Wilson, Keppel and Betty

Eccentric dancers. Jack Wilson, Joe Keppel and, originally, Betty Knox. Two white night-shirts, containing two pencil-thin, fez-wearing, doleful, ancient, dancing-in-perfect-unison, 'Egyptians'. Add a glamorous, veiled 'Cleopatra', a couple of Grecian urns containing sand (which the two lads scattered across the stage to dance on) and you have one of the great speciality acts – Wilson, Keppel and Betty. 'Cleopatra's Nightmare' was their bill matter. They were a permanent and much loved part of Variety. Their famous music, 'Ballet Egyptien', was originally arranged for them by a bar-room pianist, HOAGY CARMICHAEL. They used those band parts for three decades.

Jack Keppel was a Liverpudlian and Joe Wilson came from Cork. They met in the USA where they teamed up as a double tap dancing act. They played all the small theatres and even appeared as an act preceding the very popular Jewish melodramas.

They teamed up with BETTY KNOX (she had originally been the partner, in vaudeville, of JACK BENNY) and created the act that everyone remembers. They returned to the UK and were an instant success both there and in Europe, playing all the number one theatres, the West End and three Royal Variety Performances. Betty retired in 1941 to go into journalism and her daughter Patsy took her place. Many people have claimed to be 'the original Betty' or 'the one who took over from Betty' but Phil remembers just two, the mother and daughter.

Jack and Joe were totally different blokes. Joe, reputedly, went home each night to count his money while Jack, whenever they played in London, repaired to OLIVELLI'S (see entry). Here, in the company of all the other 'Jack the Lad' performers, he would lead, from the piano, the entire room in libellous songs and parodies of his own composition.

They played Las Vegas and, it's rumoured, caused chaos in American Customs when they brought in several bags of their own sand!

Eventually Joe retired to Cork (with his money!) while Jack spent his last days as a popular resident of Brinsworth House. Their unique act is preserved on film in The National Film Archive.

Mike and Bernie Winters

Comedy double act. Real brothers born Weinstein in London's East End, Mike in 1927 and Bernie in 1930. In their excellent autobiography, *Shake a Pagoda Tree*, Mike and Bernie tell, in the most colourful detail, of their early years and adventures in the roughest district of London. Mike was a clarinet student at the Royal Academy of Music while Bernie's education was picked up in the London dance halls. He did learn to play the drums though and it was as a musical act that they went into the business. In the beginning Mike did the bits of comedy in the act. One night, Mike tired of the lack of laughs, put the 'funny' hat on Bernie and said: 'You be the comic'. A good move. They battled away sometimes in the business and sometimes out of it. Mike was a street trader and Bernie a steward on a liner. Mike did well with the selling, and even opened a couple of proper shops. Bernie played all the number threes as a solo act.

In 1952, they joined up again, they thought, for good. Almost immediately they became two of an old-established act THE THREE LOOSE SCREWS (JACK PARR was the third). Two years later they were a double act again. Tours for the American forces in Germany followed and then summer seasons and Variety back home. They had a very hard time till they found themselves on the bill with the new teenage rave TOMMY STEELE. The kids in the audience liked them and their big break, as resident comics on TV's *6–5 Special* happened. They split the partnership when Bernie was offered a contract as an actor in films. It didn't work out so, in 1960, they were together again – the end of our period, of course, but a great restart for Mike and Bernie, who got a week at the Palladium with SHIRLEY BASSEY and scored. Lots of TV work followed and they remained a popular top-of-the-bill act till they parted company for good. Mike went to America where, among all sorts of enterprises, he became Angelo Dundee's manager (the man who *managed* MUHAMMAD ALI). Bernie had a pretty good career as a solo performer but died, far too young, of cancer.

Ken Wilson

Eccentric dancer and comedian. Kenneth George Wilson born Dagenham, Essex, 1926. At one time he was the featured speciality act with the LEON CORTEZ COSTER BAND. He devised a very funny, 'putting up a deckchair' routine which served him well in Variety as a solo act and still does.

Marie Wilson

Trick cyclist. Born Marie Van Dooren, Middlesbrough. A cyclist who began her career with a combination cycle act, THE SIX DAIMLERS and later was a member of THE WONDER WHEELERS. She became a single act and produced a cycle number for a line of girls at the London Palladium. The spot had great novelty in that the whole routine was performed on one bike!

The Wilton Brothers
Introducing their mother

Multi-instrumentalists and vocal harmony act. The family name was Goulding and they came from Bradford. The lads would sing and play (between them, six instruments) before they did indeed introduce their mother, MONICA

WILTON, who would give, according to their own publicity material, 'descriptive song and popular chorus'. They played all the number twos but Scotland was their main stamping ground.

Robb Wilton

Robb Wilton with his wife Florence toast their golden wedding in 1954

Comedian. Born Robert Smith, Liverpool, 1881. One of my great heroes. A classic comedian who would have been a top situation comedy actor had he been alive today. His early career in drama must have sowed the seeds for his masterly characterisations, superb 'slow burn' timing and 'real' acting. We all know him for 'The Day War Broke Out' – 'How will you know which one is Hitler?' (Wilton pause) 'I've got a tongue in me head haven't I?' but, thankfully, his great earlier sketches (partnered by his wife FLORENCE PALMER) – 'The Fire Station' ('Can you keep it going until we get there?'), 'The Police Station' and 'Mr Muddlecombe JP' are now available on cassette too. Robb died, greatly mourned, in 1957.

Paul Wingrave/Rajputana

Juggler. Born Frederick W. Priest. A standard feature speciality act who seems to have had more changes of name than a politician has changes of mind. He was originally MOZZETTO, then RUPERT INGALESE in a 'flash' act, RUPERT INGALESE AND HIS FLUNKEYS. At the outbreak of the Second World War he became PAUL WINGRAVE then, in the Forties, was RAJPUTANA. I wonder which one I saw?

Anona Winn

Singer/actress. Born Anona Lamport, Sydney, Australia, 1907. After a classical music education she did chorus work in musical comedy and came to England in 1927. She recorded and toured with her own Variety act, ANONA WINN AND HER FOUR WINNERS. She played Principal Boy in panto and the title role in *Peter Pan*. I remember her best as a panellist on radio in *Twenty Questions*, and as the host of a favourite, all-girl, chat show, *The Petticoat Line*. She died in 1994.

Joan Winters and Guy Fielding

Comedy double act. Joan is the eldest daughter of the late, much loved musical director, CHARLES SHADWELL. (Fans of radio's music-hall shows will remember Charlie's infectious laugh. The comics loved him!) It was radio that made Joan a household name too. She played the part of JACK WARNER's upper crust 'little gel' in *Garrison Theatre*. She played the London Palladium with Jack in the stage version of the show in 1940.

Guy Fielding began as half of a double dancing act, with his sister Heather, before moving into IVOR NOVELLO musicals and light comicking. Their start as an act together is a real show biz special. They had seen a double act, who they were assured were retiring, in Variety and thought, 'We could do that'. They paid an unnameable pro £500 for a script, had parodies and band parts written and costumes made. They opened at the Met, Edgware Road and were horrified when one of the 'retired' double act turned up and accused them of stealing the act! Apparently the unmentionable one had sold the script without his partner's knowledge. All was well as the 'retired' one said he *had* split with his partner and he was now in the 'legit'. Who was he?

In the mid Fifties, apart from the Variety act, Joan did several advertising magazines on TV and played parts in drama. In 1961 they went to America, tried various theatrical ventures and appeared in musicals including *The Boy Friend*. Alas, the American Equity situation, which meant an almost closed shop for English artistes, rapidly cooled their enthusiasm and they retired to live in San Diego. They were divorced and Guy returned to England where he married the widow of PETER CAVANAGH. He died some years ago but Joan remained in the States and now lives in California.

Eileen Winterton Trio

Dancers. Eileen born Purley, Surrey. Eileen began as a solo dancer in ballet and opera companies, in cabaret, concert party and pantomime. She formed her trio in 1939. Phil says: 'The girls not only did the usual tap routines but interpolated excellent classical ballet too.' Most girl dancing acts used to open the first and second halves of a bill but not Eileen's girls. They were always a featured speciality. I see Eileen often and, until recently, she was still working, playing small parts on television.

Norman Wisdom

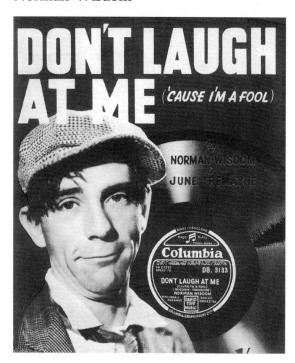

Comedian. Born London, 1919. One of the few British comedians to become, through his highly successful films, an international star. Incredibly Norman is still at it. Still doing the act I first saw him do at the Palladium umpteen years ago and still packing 'em out wherever he plays. Apart from being a great admirer, I have a special interest in Norman as he (a few years before!) had been in the summer show that was so special to me, BRANDON AND POUNDS' *Out of the Blue*. Ronnie Brandon and Dickie Pounds always claimed that it was while working for them that Norman found his 'gump' character. He invented him as a 'volunteer from the audience' to assist the speciality act in the show, DAVID NIXON. Norman is the natural successor to the legendary visual comics. So much has been written about the great man I can add nothing. Suffice to say he is, rightly, a legend.

Vic Wise

Comedian. Born David Victor Bloom, Southampton, 1900. Vic started his career in South

Africa as 'The World's Youngest Magician' at the age of thirteen. He learned his comedy first as a straight man then as a comic in Australia and America. He acquired an American accent which was very fashionable in the Variety theatres here during the Forties. He was half of two double acts, BLOOM AND ASHER and ALDA CAMPBELL AND VIC WISE before he became a solo comedian. I remember him mostly on radio and as an excellent character actor on television and in films. He died in 1976.

David Wolfe

The hypnotist with a sense of humour

Hypnotist. Born London, 1909. One of the rash of hypnotists who appeared in Variety in the Fifties. Just as with hypnotists today, his act, to quote the man himself, 'can be thirty minutes or two full hours. It is designed to provide the maximum amount of humorous entertainment.'

Eva May Wong

China's sweetest personality

Plate spinner, acrobat and contortionist. We do not mention her age. Petite, charming and ageless, she is the female Peter Pan of Variety. She was trained by her parents and, at a very early age, toured all the leading European circus routes. Whisper it, but her first London date was before the war! She became a standard act on every number one bill and at the Palladium. She still looks seventeen on stage and it is her winsome personality that sells the tricks so well. 'Age cannot wither her…'

Charly Wood

Unicyclist and pedestal juggler. Born Charles Vandenhouten, Brussels, Belgium, 1919. A standard, excellent juggler, another graduate from Continental circus (CIRCUS TONDEURS) to the halls.

Georgie Wood

Wee Georgie Wood

Comedian. Born George Balmer, Wearside, 1897. One of the most famous names in the history of music hall and Variety. He was a midget (four feet, nine inches) who, like JIMMY CLITHEROE later, specialised in little boy characters. He hated the prefix 'Wee'. He was an outspoken, well-read, amazingly self-educated bloke whose books (notably *I Had to Be Wee* and *Royalty, Religion and Rats*) and columns (in trade papers like *The Stage* and *The Performer*) were a fascinating mixture of sharp insight, gossip and prickly comment. At Lodge meetings of The GOWR (He was King Rat in 1936) he and I had several 'run-ins' over everything from the words of songs to the worth of LARRY GRAYSON. He was a fund of self-opinionated knowledge about the business. I liked him very much.

His career was an amazing one. He was a music-hall star, both here, in South African and America, before the First World War with impressions of MARIE LLOYD and VESTA TILLEY. He was assisted in those early days by ETHEL BURNS who would also do a spot on the bill as half of COSGROVE AND BURNS, 'Comedy duettists'. Ethel was with George for eight years.

In 1916 he met the lady who was to play his stage mother till their joint retirement, in 1953, DOLLY HARMER. George produced more than forty different sketches during his long career, starred in fifty pantomimes and appeared in straight plays. He did a film based on one of his sketches. A sort of 'Just William' thing called *The Black Hand Gang*. The sketch and the screenplay were both written by those doyens of song and script writers, R.P. WESTON and BERT LEE.

In 1933 he married, in the States, an American vaudeville performer, who was two inches taller than him, EWING EATON. She came back here with George and they even appeared on-stage together but, alas, two years later, the marriage was dissolved. He never, ever talked about her again.

At the start of our period he was still at it though he was seriously considering James Agate's advice to him: 'You began as a juvenile prodigy – don't go on to be a senile prodigy.' At the age of fifty-one he told audiences that he had no intention of retiring but would be dropping the 'Mother and Son' sketches. Eventually he did and he and Dolly Harmer worked on with George playing a character created by J.J. Bell – 'Wee Macgreggor'.

In 1953 they both retired from performing. Dolly died in 1956. George spent the rest of his days writing, arguing with his Brother Rats and extolling the virtues of Catholicism. (He was a fanatical convert and the story goes that when he met the Pope, a cardinal who was outside the door became worried about the length of time George had been with the pontiff. He opened the door a crack to hear His Excellency interrupt George's fervent monologue with: 'But Mister Wood, I *am* a Catholic!') As you can imagine, he was a stalwart and vociferous member of The British Music Hall Society. The great, not 'Wee', performer died in 1979.

Woodrow

Hat juggler. Peter Woodrow born London, 1930. He followed in the footsteps of his father, STETSON. He was a well-featured act in Variety and ice shows and appeared in the Royal Variety Performance of 1946.

Charlie Woods (Woods and Jarrett)

Double songs at the piano/dancing act. A first-class teaming of two large black guys. BERTIE JARRETT would sing songs at the piano, à la FATS WALLER. They had good patter and a sensational dancing finale where Charlie would dance on a staircase built up to, and on, the piano. They played all the UK's number one theatres.

Arthur Worsley

Ventriloquist. Born Failsworth, 1920. At the age of eleven his bill matter was 'The World's Youngest Ventriloquist'. He was certainly the best vent I ever saw. You *really* couldn't see his lips move. The fact that Arthur himself never spoke may have helped. His dummy, Johnny Green, was the personality plus governor who spent the entire act criticising and giving instructions to Arthur, 'turn me round son!' He did radio from 1934 and the classic story is of a sound engineer saying to him, 'Can you put the dummy nearer the mike?' Sadly, Arthur packed it in far too early and now lives in retirement in Blackpool.

Harry Worth

Comedian. Born Tankersley, Yorkshire, 1919. We all remember Harry as the character that made him such a favourite on television but Variety buffs knew him first as a ventriloquist. He was, even then, the lovable, apologetic bumbler. He had a line that I've never forgotten, to justify his being on-stage at all. He would plead: 'Last week, when I came out of the stage door, a huge crowd picked me up and put me on their shoulders. I said, "Are you taking me to the Town Hall?" They said "No. You're for the river!"' Harry died in 1989.

Chris Wortman

Character singer/dancer. Born Wood Green, London, 1920. A good all-rounder in concert party, musical comedy, revue and as Dame in pantomime. His quick-change Negro characterisations, à la G.H. ELLIOTT and GENE PATTON, are how he is best remembered. He toured in the Forties with the *Stars We'll Remember* show where he impersonated EUGENE STRATTON. He repeated this stunning impression in several TV documentaries. He worked up until his death in 1989.

Bobby Wotherspoon

Xylophone/vibraphone player. Born Bolton 1919. From a classical music training at Trinity College he began as a pianist with a boys' band. He formed a double xylophone act with his brother, THE WOTHERSPOON BROTHERS, and continued this with another partner JACKIE ALLAN, who in turn became JACKIE ALLAN AND BARBARA. In the Forties he started a single act and, through regular broadcasts, became a popular addition to Variety.

Bert Wright

The Agile Ancient

Acrobat and dancer. Born Alexander Stanley Wright, Bow, London 1903. A very versatile performer whom we remember in the make-up of a decrepit old man, as half of BERT WRIGHT AND ZENA (his wife). He had a long apprenticeship with THE MONGADORS (the famous French juggling family), as a 'perch man' in American circus and as half of the act TWO AMERICAN RUBES until he, and Zena, became the popular act that played all over the country. Eventually the stresses of such a hard life took their toll and blindness forced Bert to retire.

Bobby Wright

Comedy double act. BOBBY WRIGHT AND MARION. Bobby born Stepney, London, 1891, and Marion born Detroit, Michigan, 1902. A popular Anglo-American-style patter act. Bobby learned his trade in American burlesque where he met Marion. Their first visit to the UK in the 1920s was not a success, probably ahead of their time, but when they returned, just in time for the Second World War, they were an instant hit. By then we were, via films and radio, more in tune with American humour. In 1949 they emigrated to Australia where Bobby died in 1971.

Freda Wyn

Speciality act. Freda was a contortionist who performed her tricks on a large web which filled the stage. She played the part of a glamorous spider.

___ Y ___

Carl and Roger Yale

Two genuine brothers who came to the UK from their South African home in the 1940s. They played their comedy act at the piano in Variety, pantomime and revue and were regular broadcasters. They were successful song writers too and had their own publishing companies – The Yale Music Corporation and Twentieth Century Music. In the 1960s the brothers emigrated to California where they ran the Magic Hotel. Roger died in 1994.

Jimmy Young

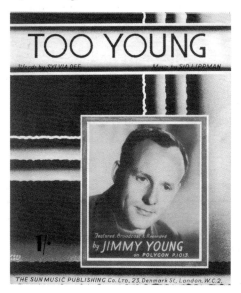

Singer. Born Leslie Ronald Young. Some people have forgotten that Jim, the confidant of politicians and prey to the whimsical wit of TERRY WOGAN, has his roots in Variety. He had quite a track record as a top of the bill balladeer in the mid Fifties via his hit recordings of 'Too Young', 'Unchained Melody' and 'The Man from Laramie'. Indeed he was the first British artiste to have two consecutive number one hits.

Beginning as a pianist, singer and bandleader his radio career started in 1949 with songs at the piano and his first D-jaying was in 1952. He gradually dropped the performing to become the interviewer extraordinaire on television as well as radio. In 1997, the great survivor celebrated forty-five years of employment by the BBC. Nobody does it better.

Joe Young

Sketch comedian. Born Joseph De Yong, London, 1887, began as a Hebrew comedian in a KATE CARNEY show. He was part of a scene called 'My Yiddisher Boy'. He formed a double act YOUNG AND EVANS, and was half of the teams YOUNG AND SIMMS and IDA AND JOE YOUNG (with his wife IDA LEROY). After the First World War he changed his character from a Jewish boy to that of BRUCE BAIRNSFATHER's cartoon creation, 'Old Bill'. His brilliant idea, and most remembered contribution to Variety, was a sketch called, 'Buying a Theatre'. Philip says, 'A most amusing man, off and on stage.'

Lee Young

Song and dance man. Born James Stevenson Young, Glasgow, 1927. He began as a seven-year-old singing in a show in Largs, Scotland. After being turned down for ENSA, as being too young, he came to London and became a regular at the famous 'We Never Closed' Windmill Theatre. He played in revue and Variety with his friend FRANKIE HOWERD and eventually went to Australia where he is now resident.

___ Z ___

Anne Ziegler and Webster Booth

Vocal duettists. Anne, born Irene Frances Eastwood, Liverpool, 1910; Webster, born Lesley Booth, Birmingham, 1902. They were a handsome, beautifully dressed couple (he in immaculate tails and she in NORMAN HARTNELL designed crinolines), the British answer to JEANETTE MACDONALD AND NELSON EDDY. They had separate careers but became household names when they teamed up, on and offstage, in the 1930s. 'Only a Rose' was

their famous signature tune and numerous radio broadcasts and recordings ensured their top of the bill status. When their sort of music went out of favour they emigrated to South Africa and carried on singing. Webster died in 1984.

The Zio Angels

Dance troupe. The act was originally produced by FLORENCE WHITELEY (née ZETINA) in 1930 for a pantomime at the New Theatre, Cardiff. The girls, originally all blondes, were one of the better known dance troupes before and during our period.

The Whiteley family and the Zetinas were well-known names in music hall and the marriage of Florence to Rudolph Whiteley was fortunate. They rapidly established a reputation as a well-dressed, well-drilled group and throughout the Thirties, and the war years, toured all the number ones, and the Continent, in Variety, cabaret, revue and panto. JACK WHITELEY (the son of Florence) for many years a stalwart of the National Theatre, wrote a smashing piece for the BMHS magazine, *The Call Boy*, and that's why I'm able to tell you a bit of the troupe's history.

It was Jack's wife Marjorie who was the driving force behind the act and it was she who devised their two show-stopping routines, 'The Military Tattoo' and 'The Phantom Guard'. As with so many other legendary acts, by the early Sixties there were hardly any theatres left for the girls to play. In 1964, Jack and Marjorie called it a day. They did one of their last summer seasons with me on the pier at Clacton. Their very last show was pantomime at the New Theatre, Cardiff – the place where the act had been formed thirty-four years before.

Claude Zola and Mattie

Comedy acrobat, trapeze artiste and ice skater. Claude was born London, 1900. I knew him very well through his membership of the GOWR and his work on the committee of the EABF. He was a perfect CHARLIE NAUGHTON look-a-like. A member of a famous circus family, he first appeared in the ring at the age of four. He played all the leading Variety theatres in the UK and on the Continent with his brothers THE FOUR ZOLAS. He is best remembered as half of the double act, with his wife, ZOLA AND MATTIE. One week before the outbreak of the Second World War, after playing before Hitler and the rest of his Crazy Gang, they managed to get back home and remained a successful act through to the post-war years. Claude died in 1980.

In one of my first weeks in Variety in 1959, Max Miller, as he always did, told the audience: 'When I'm dead and gone the game's finished.' He was almost right. The Finsbury Park Empire closed on 7 May 1960 and Max died in 1963.